Women Artists in Their Own Words

The idea for this book was originated by
Christian Levett, owner of the Levett Collection
and founder of FAMM, the museum of art
devoted solely to women.

He dedicates the book to his children,
Chap, Charlie, Clemmie, and Bonny.

"Women Artists in Their Own Words"

INTRODUCTION BY
Jennifer Samet

QUOTATIONS COMPILED BY
Eleanor Walker

MERRELL
LONDON · NEW YORK

in association with

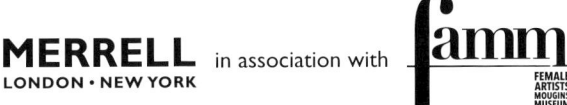

Contents

Flow State
Women Artists in Their Own Words

Jennifer Samet

At moments of deep engagement, the art-making process may involve a state of surrender that allows societal, intellectual, and personal constructs to fall away. In this way, painting can invoke a more expansive way of being, one that is translatable to the viewer across time. In the words spoken or written by women artists compiled within this volume, this theme recurs. The artists describe reaching a state of art-making where identity, roles, preconceptions, and the ego dissolve. This book includes quotations entirely by women artists, from the late nineteenth century to the present day. Historically, becoming an artist as a woman has involved overcoming nearly insurmountable barriers. Women were not granted the access to education, models, and subject matter that men had. Therefore, the opportunity to work in this state of alternate attention—an escape from rigid definitions of women's roles—is especially poignant. The artists discuss how imagery evolves out of the process, as opposed to the intellect, reason, or preconceived ideas. The art speaks without these attachments, and this is palpable across centuries.

In *Jeune fille étendue (Young Girl Lying Down)* (pp. 124–25), Berthe Morisot depicts a young woman reclining on a daybed and gazing toward the wall behind her. The model for the painting was Jeanne Fourmanoir, who also modeled frequently for Pierre-Auguste Renoir. Despite the compressed domestic space of the painting, there is a suggested wallcovering, with hints of a delicate but verdant garden. None of this is articulated in a definitive or naturalistic manner; rather, it is a dream space of imagination and rumination. The cool blues and greens of the wall almost grow off the tones of the brushstrokes that make up the girl's dress. She has conjured another world.

This is a striking metaphor for Morisot's world as a woman painter. She was fortunate enough to grow up in a bourgeois family where she had access to art lessons. However, she chose a course well beyond what was expected of, or considered ideally suited to, a woman in society. In fact, her teacher Joseph Guichard, who took her and her sister Edma to copy Old Master paintings at the Louvre, recognized her talent. He shared this with her parents, warning them that she would not be just an amateur, but rather a serious painter, and that this could be "catastrophic." Morisot continued her studies with Camille Corot, with whom she worked *en plein air*. Working from life, and forgoing the history painting favored by the official Salon, she became allied with the group of artists who were later named the Impressionists. In 1874 she was the only woman to show her work in their independent exhibition—the first in a series of eight exhibitions that would have an indelible effect on art history.

Morisot's technical approach—the openness of her brushwork—was especially radical. In *Jeune fille étendue*, this openness signifies an ability to move symbolically into a larger sphere, one physically inaccessible to women at that time. Morisot works with the enclosed domestic setting, and embraces it as being larger than the cafes, bars, and industrial settings that were favored by her male peers. Morisot stated, "My ambition is limited to the desire to capture something transient."[1] This combination of "ambition" and "limitation" represents Morisot's achievements. She used her limitations to express something larger than life.

Mary Cassatt, an American artist who lived most of her adult life in Paris, also participated in several Impressionist exhibitions, at the invitation of her close friend and collaborator Edgar Degas. Recognizing that the achievements of men dominated art-historical subject matter, she set herself a unique pursuit: to depict femininity, maternal relationships, and the labor of women. *Fillette dans un jardin (Susan Seated in a Garden)* (p. 45) contains a range of different touches within a compact environment. Each area—the flora, the face, the garment, with its translucent scarf, and the young woman's hand—is touched with paint in a slightly different manner. This focus on touch can be read as a symbol of femininity; it suggests caretaking and nurturing, and the web of relationships at the center of a domestic sphere.

While Impressionism sought to capture transient light and sensation, Surrealism, which emerged in Paris in the 1920s, encouraged harnessing the unconscious and rejecting societal norms. This approach to life and art fed the dreamlike, fantastical imagery of the Surrealists, with its unique combination of materials and techniques, and was particularly radical for women, who, more than men, were expected to be tethered to their roles and identities. Leonora Carrington suggested as much when she stated, "I didn't have time to be anyone's muse. I was too busy rebelling against my family and learning to be an artist."[2]

Carrington's painting *Mid-Day of the Canary (The Pink Room)* (p. 43) is populated by feathery, flattened figures, both birdlike and fishlike, whose heads meet at a skylit oculus. They wear high-necked, gauzy buttoned garments. Carrington painted it as a commissioned wedding gift, and it suggests a ritual ceremony—perhaps a wedding. The figure on the left might be a bride. A hybrid creature with a spotted head, dressed in a cloak, holds a doll-sized pet on a leash with one hand, while his other hand lifts the train of the woman's dress. The central figure might be the officiant. He has rounded eyes, similar to those of her former lover Max Ernst in an earlier portrait by Carrington. At the right are two figures who could be the groom and his attendant. On the ground, small but vibrantly colored creatures reach upward or recline. The scene is contained within a simple geometric architecture that feels confined apart from the oculus, and is painted with greenish grays and pinkish browns. The figures are joined to one another at their elongated scaly crowns. While the skylight suggests a special setting for this ritual, it also signals a means of escape, under which the figures' heads are compressed. The leopard-like creature looks male, and he acts like a puppeteer. The painting may be interpreted as celebratory, but it also contends with control and a desire for escape—a theme in Carrington's life.

Born into a wealthy Roman Catholic family, Carrington was sent to boarding school and was expected to be a debutante. She felt she did not belong, and found refuge in art, studying at the academy founded by Amédée Ozenfant in London. She met the Surrealist Max Ernst in London in 1937 and lived with him in southern France after he divorced his wife. By this time, her family had disowned her. At the outbreak of World War II, Ernst, who was German, was placed in an internment camp, and Carrington fled to Spain, where she suffered an emotional breakdown and was committed to a psychiatric hospital. It was a deeply traumatic experience. Carrington was eventually able to travel to Mexico. For much of the rest of her life, she remained in Mexico City, where she found a vibrant artistic community.

The Surrealists championed the power of the unconscious mind as a means of allowing images to appear without willful direction. The automatism prized by the Surrealists is closely connected to the state of flow that many artists describe in this volume. Dorothea Tanning, born in Illinois, explained that the dreams and Midwestern landscape of her childhood found their way into her paintings spontaneously: "I watched images appear on the canvas, images I had never seen."[3]

Tanning studied at Knox College in her hometown of Galesburg, before briefly enrolling in the Chicago Academy of Art. Her real education came from the museums: the Art Institute of Chicago and the formative exhibition *Fantastic Art, Dada, Surrealism* in 1936–37 at the Museum of Modern Art, New York. She traveled to Paris in 1939, hoping to meet Ernst, Picasso, Yves Tanguy, and Chaïm Soutine, only to realize that most artists were in exile at the brink of the war. She returned quickly to New York and met Ernst in 1942, when he visited her studio to select a work for an exhibition at Peggy Guggenheim's Art of This Century gallery. At this time, Ernst was married to Guggenheim. After their divorce, Tanning and Ernst became a couple; they married in 1946, living first in Sedona, Arizona, and then dividing their time between Paris and the Loire Valley.

Tanning's work evolved from tightly rendered dreamscapes in the 1940s and early '50s into expanses of abstracted figures. The large-scale painting *Éperdument* (pp. 178–79; the French term is roughly translatable as "desperation") falls into this stylistic category. Tanning recalled, "Gradually, in looking at how many ways paint can flow onto canvas, I began to long for letting it have more freedom."[4] Although abstracted by its state of movement, *Éperdument* suggests female erotic pleasure. More broadly, it is also about a state of being consumed by the act of art-making, of allowing images to emerge through the process of opening oneself.

Surrealism led to the emergence of a new artistic movement centered in New York City: Abstract Expressionism. The Abstract Expressionists connected to the valuing of automatism—to the notion that art should come from the unconscious, the embrace of spontaneity, and experimental techniques and processes. Lee Krasner acknowledged this approach when she stated, "I never violate an inner rhythm. I loathe to force anything ... I know it is essential for me. I listen to it and I stay with it. I have always been this way ... I have regards for the inner voice."[5]

Krasner was the daughter of Orthodox Jewish refugees from Odessa, Ukraine, and grew up in a working-class family in Brooklyn, New York. She was able to enroll in the National Academy of Design, though she was forced to withdraw and work as a waitress when the Great Depression hit. In 1934 she found employment at the Public Works of Art Project, followed by the mural division of the Works Progress Administration. While working for the WPA, she studied under Hans Hofmann, who ignited her interest in and exposure to School of Paris painting. Krasner would become a link to this history and to a new generation of painting, sharing her knowledge and expertise with her contemporaries, among them Jackson Pollock, whom she met in 1941 and married in 1945.

Prophecy (p. 105) exemplifies the combination of lyricism and fearless deconstruction that characterizes much of Krasner's work, with forms that are both phallic and vulval, looping and monstrous, outlined in black and pushing against vertical bounds. A sideways head with a bright-red gash struggles to find space in every direction. A scratched-in eye at upper right hovers against the black ground. Enlarged legs and feet stamp at the bottom. It was painted the year of Pollock's violent death in a car crash, and it marked a distinct juncture in Krasner's stylistic evolution. She had shared with Pollock that the painting "disturbed [her] enormously," and he encouraged her not

to think about it, but just continue by making another painting.[6] Then he died, and she returned from a trip to Europe. She was forced to face the painting yet again. The title was suggested by the painter and collector Alfonso Ossorio, and Krasner later acknowledged that the work had "a prophetic quality" in its violent, sexual imagery, and that it "becomes an element of the unconscious."[7] The intensity, raw power, and clarity of this important American painting resulted from her faith in the art-making process.

Joan Mitchell (pp. 120–21), one of the most significant Abstract Expressionist painters, also recognized the flow state of art-making, where identity dissolves. She stated, "Painting is a way of forgetting oneself ... I am not there any more. It is a state of non-self-consciousness. It does not happen often ... It is lovely."[8] Mitchell's feisty personality and scathing interactions have often dominated the art-historical literature, so her description of an escape from identity is particularly profound.

Mitchell carved a unique path among her peers. Coming from a wealthy and culturally erudite family in Chicago, she studied at the Art Institute of Chicago. But unlike her contemporaries, she looked toward French Impressionism as inspiration, and this led her to Paris. In those early years, she wrote, "[I] just arrived at a real knowledge of where I don't belong, which is everywhere."[9] By 1959 Mitchell was living virtually full-time in Paris, and almost a decade later she moved to the French countryside, following in the footsteps of Van Gogh, Matisse, Cézanne, and Monet. She bought a property in Vétheuil, near Giverny, from where she could see, from high above, the land that had once belonged to Monet.

A state of non-thinking was articulated as beneficial to the art-making process by Pat Passlof and Elaine de Kooning. Passlof (pp. 134–35) said, "I tell students, 'If you can think it, don't bother doing it. Think with a brush—the finger of your brain.'"[10] De Kooning compared this flow state to dancing: "When I start painting, I don't know what's going to happen. I begin by resisting what I think I already know ... When you're dancing, you don't stop to think: now, I'll take this step, now that. You allow it to flow."[11] Both artists were describing the primacy of the direct, intuitive interaction between the painter and the canvas. This interaction was Passlof's guiding force. She prioritized the interchange that happened as she faced the painting, that call and response.

Elaine de Kooning was a founding member in 1949 of The (Artists') Club, a gathering of New York artists who began to meet weekly in a loft on Eighth Street to discuss their work and ideas. Though de Kooning's early work was rooted in the Abstract Expressionist vocabulary, she eventually became known for her portraits, particularly of men. Walter Auerbach is the subject of an acute portrait of 1954 (p. 53). A set designer and theater director with communist ties in Germany, Auerbach was a refugee in the United States during the war. His wife, Ellen Auerbach, was an avant-garde photographer who had specialized in advertising imagery during the Weimar Republic. De Kooning's painting *Walter (Auerbach)* is characterized by the energetic calligraphic and linear mark-making that defines the seated posture of the sitter. However, the softness of his facial features expresses Auerbach's perceptive state of awareness.

Portraiture also defined the work of Alice Neel (pp. 128–29), whose subject matter was the people around her. Her early work was autobiographical, and contended with the tragedies of life as a woman artist without adequate support: the loss of her first two children, relationships with abusive men, and mental-health struggles. As Neel established her life in New York City, she was supported by the Works Progress Administration. Under the WPA, she painted New York street scenes of the poor and disenfranchised, as well as her family, people in her neighborhood, and visitors to her apartment. Herself dedicated to social causes, Neel represented activists demonstrating against fascism and racism, leaders from a range of political organizations, and writers and artists of the New York counterculture in the 1960s and '70s. Her portraits paint a picture of the zeitgeist and the cultural shifts that rocked US society from the 1940s through the '80s.

An empathic relationship to her sitters is palpable in Neel's work. The material tactility of each brushstroke suggests a direct and unembellished understanding of the person. Neel got to the truth of her sitters' relationship with society not by planning or posing, but by creating an environment in which she and the subject could tune into a deeper reality. As she said, "I do not pose my sitters ... I do not deliberate and then concoct ... Before painting, when I talk to the person, they unconsciously assume their most characteristic pose, which in a way involves all their character and social standing— what the world has done to them and their retaliation."[12]

Alma Thomas, an African American painter born in Georgia, was also a close observer of a changing society and of the racial tensions of her time. The Atlanta Race Riot of 1906, which left dozens of

African Americans dead, broke out just a year before her family left for Washington, DC. Thomas would depict the 1963 March on Washington for Jobs and Freedom, the largest civil rights demonstration at the time. However, most of her paintings focused on nature, music, beauty, and the cosmos. *Etude in Brown (Saint Cecilia at the Organ)* (p. 183) also dates from this earlier period of the artist's career. The figure of Saint Cecilia, in the foreground, occupies a small part of the composition. The music's resonance is transformed into rhythms of orange, brown, and white paint. Thomas stated, "Through color, I have sought to concentrate on beauty and happiness, rather than on man's inhumanity to man."[13] As her work developed in the 1970s and '80s, she began to use smaller bricks and dashes of rich, saturated color. Thomas employed painting as a kind of meditation in which music, light, and color visualize a brighter future.

Howardena Pindell is a Black artist and activist whose abstractions are charged with a search for autonomy. At the time she turned to this style of art, abstraction by Black artists was particularly marginalized; African Americans were expected to make work overtly about experience and social history. *Untitled*, 1971 (pp. 140–41), is an ethereal abstraction composed of thousands of tiny marks, made by spray-painting in layers through a hole-punched stencil. It has an earthy palette of deep reds, dusky blues, and greens. Pindell was the first Black woman to occupy a curatorial position at the Museum of Modern Art, New York, and this painting exemplifies her interest in Pointillism and Georges Seurat. However, Pindell's meaning and process also refer to Blackness and feminism. She ties her use of the circular form to a childhood memory

of being served root beer in a mug with a red circle at the bottom, signifying that it was to be used only by people of color. Her retention of the hole-punched chads produced by creating stencils, which she would soon integrate into mixed-media works, signals her application of craft and remnants to modernist painting.

An activist writer and founder of collectives addressing structural racism and misogyny in the art world, Pindell has acknowledged that her paintings contain a complete spectrum of feeling, including anger at societal wrongdoing. She has also expressed a belief that the act of making art can release and encompass an internal state, one that becomes embedded in the final work: "That's what painting is about, a fabric of sensations, emotions and feelings are all there in a tapestry. That's why I'm not a hard-edge painter. There is a tapestry of emotions, and people understand that your feelings come through the hand. Every time I touch the brush, I write my signature, and I am in a certain mood so it's different."[14]

Jenny Saville, the contemporary British artist known for her large-scale paintings of nude women, has noted that the experience of motherhood opened the door for a new freedom in her work. Saville's *Generation* (p. 156) explores the simultaneity inherent in the experience of motherhood. Painted with pencil, charcoal, and oil in grisaille (other than a pale-pink rectangle culminating in reddish-pink drips), it is a self-portrait of the artist pregnant with her daughter and holding her son. Both bodies are painted and drawn in layers that show their movements: twisting and turning toward and away from each other. The bodies are entangled, and the crisscrossing strokes under the mother's breasts also suggest an umbilical cord.

Saville was born in Cambridge and attended the Glasgow School of Art, where the focus was on a sustained studio practice of working from the model. She spent a term at the University of Cincinnati, where she was exposed to feminist studies. Seeing larger bodies in Midwestern shopping malls, she was inspired to make obese women the subject of her graduate exhibition. This work led to her early renown. Throughout her career, Saville has continued to explore the flesh, the body, and societal constructs of imperfection. She debated whether to show motherhood in her painting, concerned that revealing that aspect of herself would make her seem a less serious artist. However, as in the case of Morisot and Cassatt, it proved fertile ground, allowing a renewed exploration of movement and understanding of flesh.

The artists' own words reveal the complications inherent in how we perceive the relationship between identity and artwork. The challenges of occupying multiple roles—of artist, lover, wife, mother, feminist, activist—are embedded in the works illustrated in this volume, even abstract ones. Such multiplicity gives the work its potency and also flips the lens on centuries of art history. And yet the process of art-making can also represent a freedom from societal constructs of self. It can mean temporary autonomy from the intellect, the ego, and personhood. And in this state of intuitive flow, deeper meanings emerge, translatable to the viewer through the artist's unique painterly means.

Notes

1 Berthe Morisot, *Carnet noir*, 1890–?, translated in *Berthe Morisot: Impressionist*, exhib. cat., National Gallery of Art, Washington, DC, September 6–November 29, 1987; Kimbell Art Museum, Fort Worth, TX, December 12, 1987–February 21, 1988; Mount Holyoke College Art Museum, South Hadley, MA, March 14–May 9, 1988, p. 15.

2 Carrington quoted in Katy Hessel, *The Story of Art Without Men*, Hutchinson Heinemann, 2022, p. 171.

3 Tanning quoted in Alexander Watt, "Paris Commentary," *The Studio*, vol. 158, no. 798, October 1959, p. 92.

4 Dorothea Tanning, *Between Lives: An Artist and Her World*, W.W. Norton, 2001, p. 213.

5 Krasner, Gaby Rogers Interview, 1977, Jackson Pollock and Lee Krasner Papers, *c.* 1914–84, bulk 1942–84, Archives of American Art, Smithsonian Institution, Washington, DC.

6 Krasner interviewed in Richard Howard, "A Conversation with Lee Krasner," in *Lee Krasner: Paintings 1959–1962*, exhib. cat., Pace Gallery, New York, February 3–March 10, 1979, n.p.

7 "Prophetic quality": Krasner, oral history interview by Dorothy Seckler, December 14, 1967, Archives of American Art, Smithsonian Institution, Washington, DC. "Element of the unconscious": Krasner interviewed in Howard, "Conversation with Lee Krasner."

8 Mitchell quoted in Yves Michaud, "Conversations with Joan Mitchell, January 12, 1986," in *Joan Mitchell: New Paintings*, exhib. cat., Xavier Fourcade, New York, April 3–May 10, 1986, n.p.

9 Mitchell to Barney Rosset, October 1948, quoted in Tausif Noor, "The Roots of Joan Mitchell's Greatness," *New York Times*, September 2, 2021, https://www.nytimes.com/2021/09/02/arts/design/joan-mitchell-sfmoma.html.

10 Passlof quoted in *Pat Passlof: The Brush Is the Finger of the Brain—Paintings 1949–2011*, exhib. cat. by Karen Wilkin, The Milton Resnick and Pat Passlof Foundation, New York, October 11, 2019–April 11, 2020, p. 14.

11 Elaine de Kooning, *The Spirit of Abstract Expressionism: Selected Writings*, George Braziller, 1994, p. 30.

12 Neel quoted in Patricia Hills, *Alice Neel*, Harry N. Abrams, 1983, p. 141.

13 Thomas, 1970 statement, quoted in *Alma Thomas*, exhib. cat., ed. Ian Berry and Lauren Hayes, The Frances Young Tang Teaching Museum and Art Gallery at Skidmore College, Saratoga Springs, NY, February 6–June 5, 2016; The Studio Museum in Harlem, New York, July 14–October 30, 2016, p. 18.

14 Pindell interviewed in Hans Ulrich Obrist, "Why I'm Not a Hard-Edge Painter: A Conversation with Howardena Pindell," in *Howardena Pindell: Rope/Fire/Water*, exhib. cat., ed. Adeze Wilford, The Shed, New York, October 16, 2020–April 11, 2021, p. 26.

"Women Artists in Their Own Words"

Mary Abbott

(1921–2019)

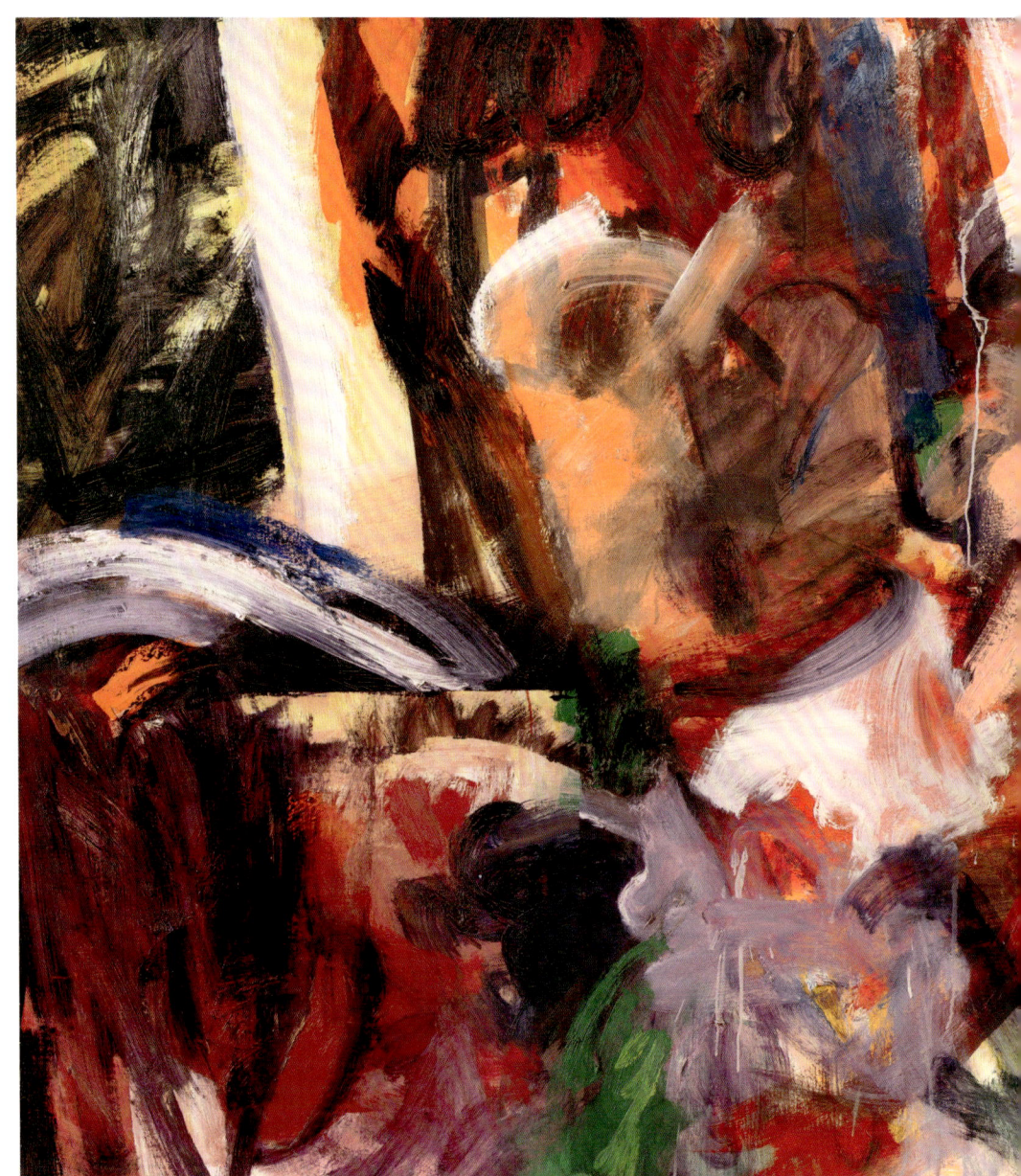

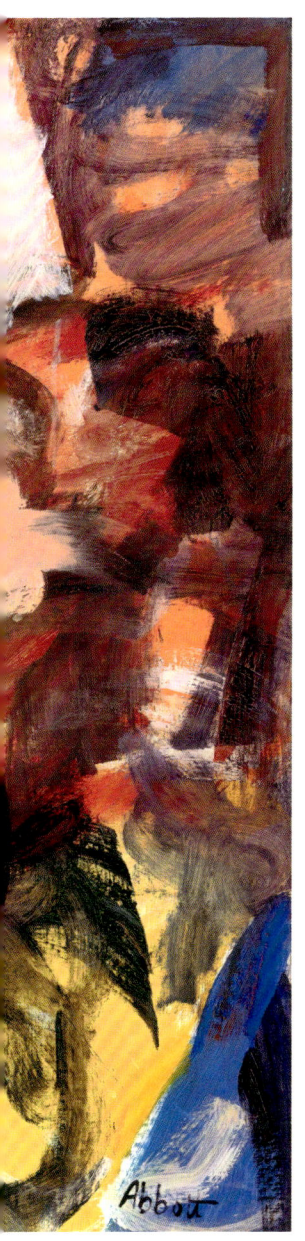

It just hit me ... trying to do things representationally didn't work for me. [With abstraction] I could talk in a different way.[1]

I like the process of painting. The intensity of living nature through myself—using the medium, paint, color and line defining the poetry of living space; that is my aim, life and work.[2]

On claiming that yellow is her favorite color:

Because yellow is a simple color. Green is more complex—there's very little green in nature; you think you see it, but you don't, it's variations of light. Purple is just as complex—composed of many colors. Difficult colors, both of them. To mix is difficult.[3]

Purple Crossover
1959
Oil on canvas
52 × 62 in.
(132.1 × 157.5 cm)
CL824

15

Stacey Gillian Abe
(b. 1990)

Whispers of Sorghum is a continued exploration of emotion through shared memories and how these emotions are transported through generations in my lineage. This work alludes to absorbing and transforming the old ways through memory ... My work is also informed by identity, history, femininity, and representations of the black body in space.

In the summer, the wind passed across the sorghum fields just as they were about to be harvested. Every morning I would get up just before dawn and have breakfast behind my grandmother's kitchen, overlooking the sorghum fields ... In that field were the sorghum's faint whistles and twirls. A stunning view during the day, but [it] terrified me greatly at night.[1]

My body is very much present in the work, but is not limited to a purely physical presence; instead I'd say that the indigo women are extensions of my being. The figures are fragments of memories or materialisations of emotions that I want to retain by fixing them in the work. They are also figments of my past, present and future selves, through which I channel the lineage of my ancestors whom I never got to meet. So the indigo figures could be read as my ancestors represented in these bodies, they could be fragments from our present, they could be versions of my future self. Alongside memory, time is an important concept in my work and this non-linear approach gives me the opportunity to revisit the past, or the future, through these subjects.[2]

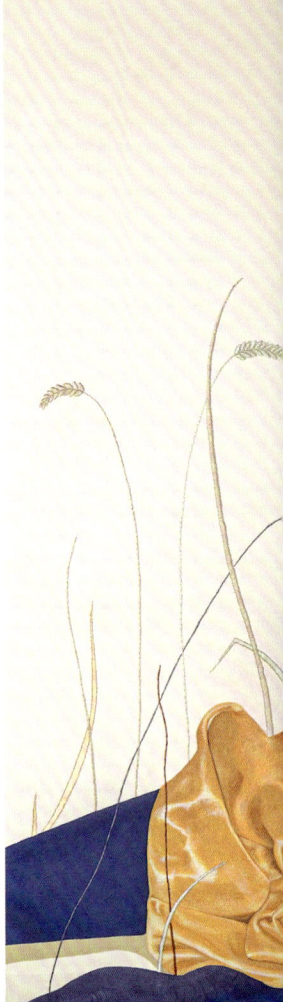

Whispers of Sorghum II
2023
Acrylic and
hand-embroidered
details on canvas
59 × 78¾ in. (149.9 × 200 cm)

CL1351

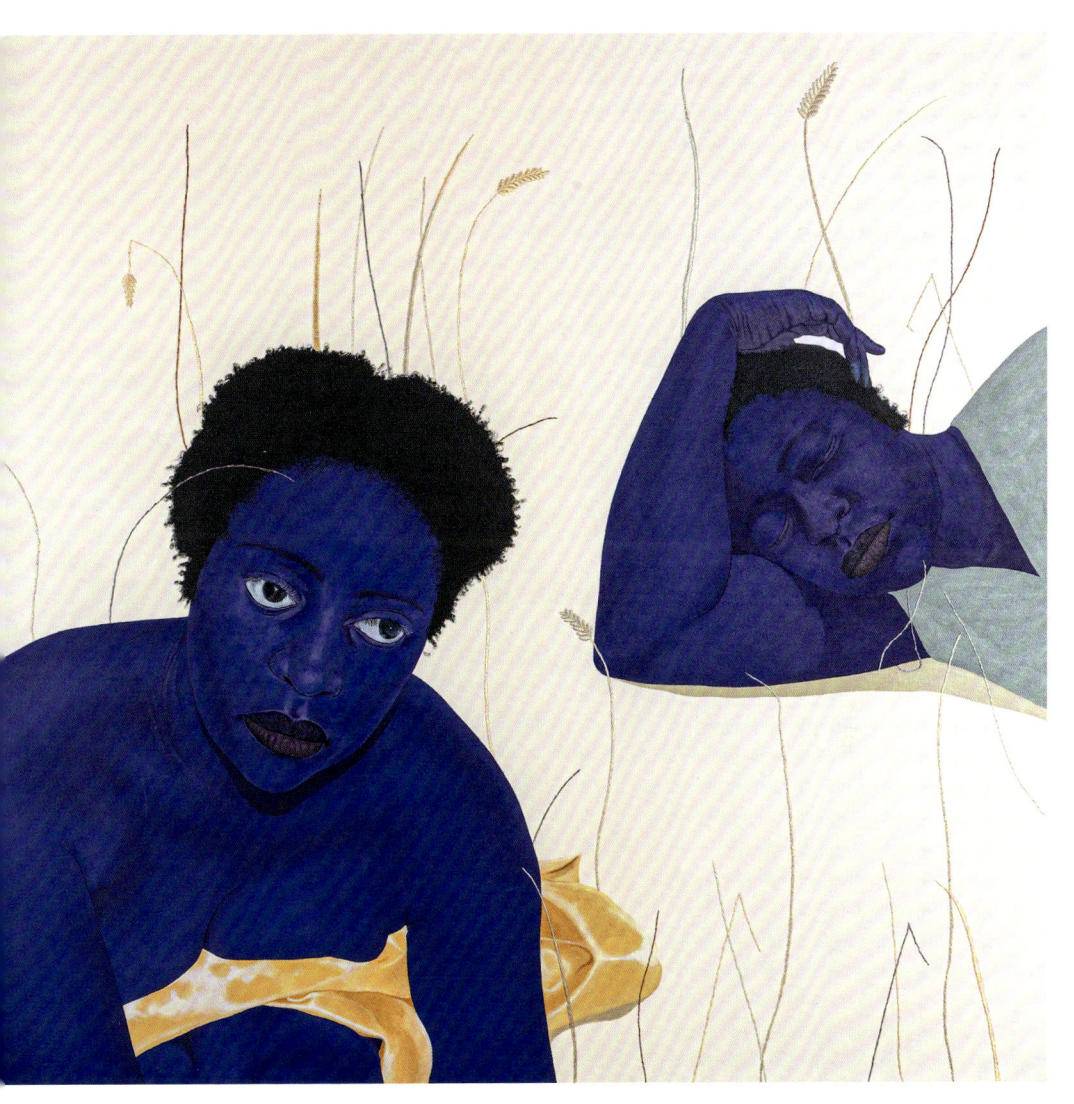

Marina Abramović
(b. 1946)

I made this work in 2008 during a very difficult and
emotional moment in my life. I felt lonely and had an
intense awareness of my own mortality. I found a skeleton
that was my size and decided to carry it into the black void.[1]

Art must have many layers. Art is not just about another
beautiful painting that matches your dining room floor.
Art has to be disturbing, art has to ask a question, art has
to predict the future. It has to do all these kinds of things.
An art concept has to have so many layers so that every part
of society can take what it needs.[2]

My whole purpose in life is to communicate what I'm doing.
I see myself as a modern nomad and a soldier at the same
time. Being mainstream won't change me because once
I have something to perform, a task, then I'm a soldier.
And I've always been a soldier.[3]

*Carrying the
Skeleton*
2008
Color chromogenic print
80 × 71 in.
(203.2 × 180.3 cm)
No. 5 from an edition of
9 plus 2 artist's proofs
CL1229

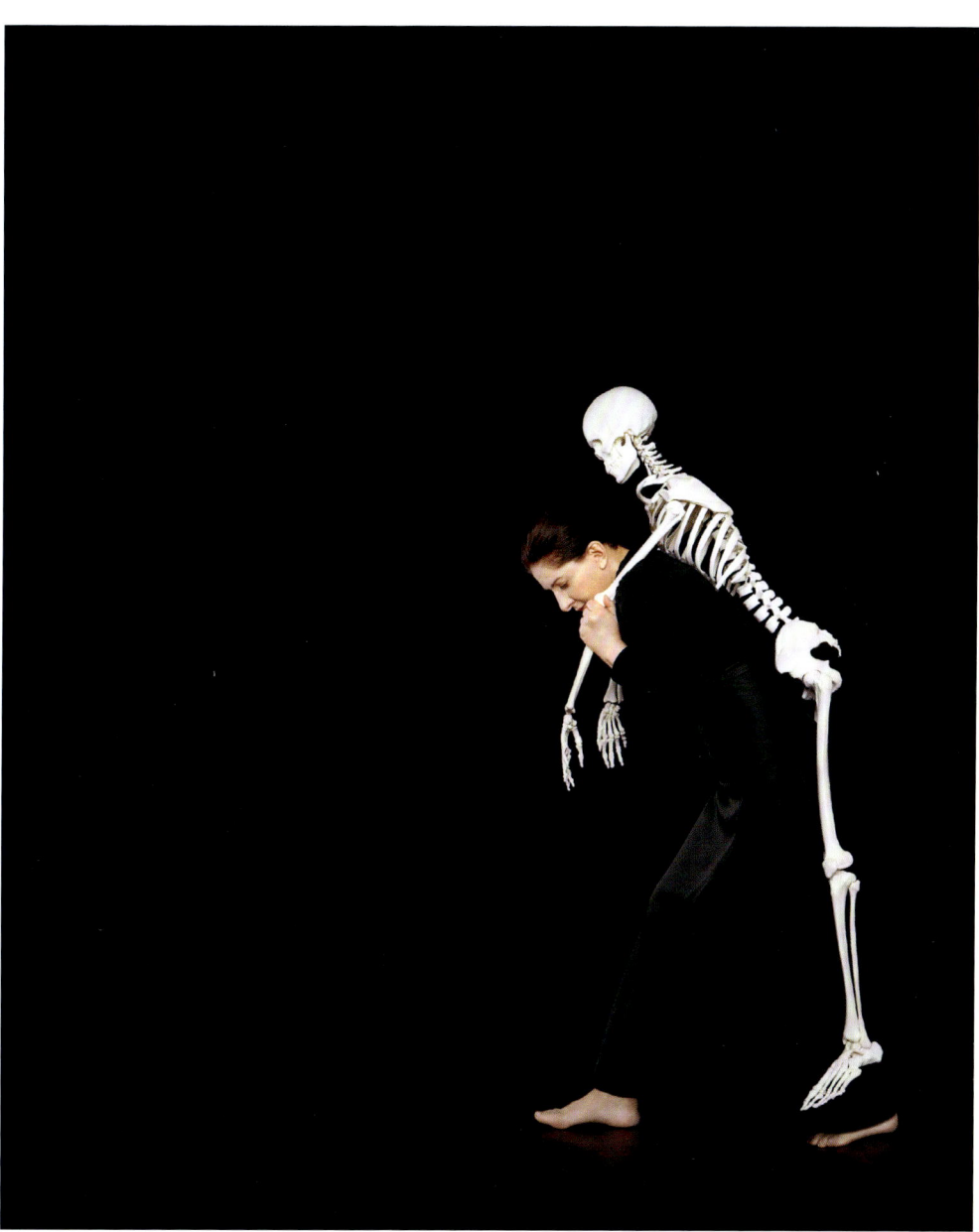

Carla Accardi
(1924–2014)

A painting must tell you what it wants to tell you in a very short time and it must tell you with a sensation.[1]

For me, art and life run parallel to each other. On the one hand, I mythologized art, holding it in very high regard, but at the same time, I had a tendency to demystify it. I wanted to understand what lay behind it. But above all, I wanted the public to not feel stuck in front of a work, an attitude which I found to be too pervasive. I wanted the audience to be shaken, to appreciate art, to discover that behind it, lies life. And to show them that both can be united, in the same way that others have done in the past. But first and foremost, I wanted to be a contemporary artist, I wanted to find out what "contemporary" meant.[2]

Nothing satisfies me. Going further is an inherent, physiological need. I seek all the time and never let myself get bogged down by formulas. Returns and reiterations help me to go forward. Every painting is conceived in relation and contrast to the one before ... I try to go as deep as possible and not to remain on the surface. I feel the whole as inner content.[3]

Verderosafluoro
1964
Casein on canvas
51⅛ × 36¼ in.
(129.9 × 92.1 cm)

CL1314

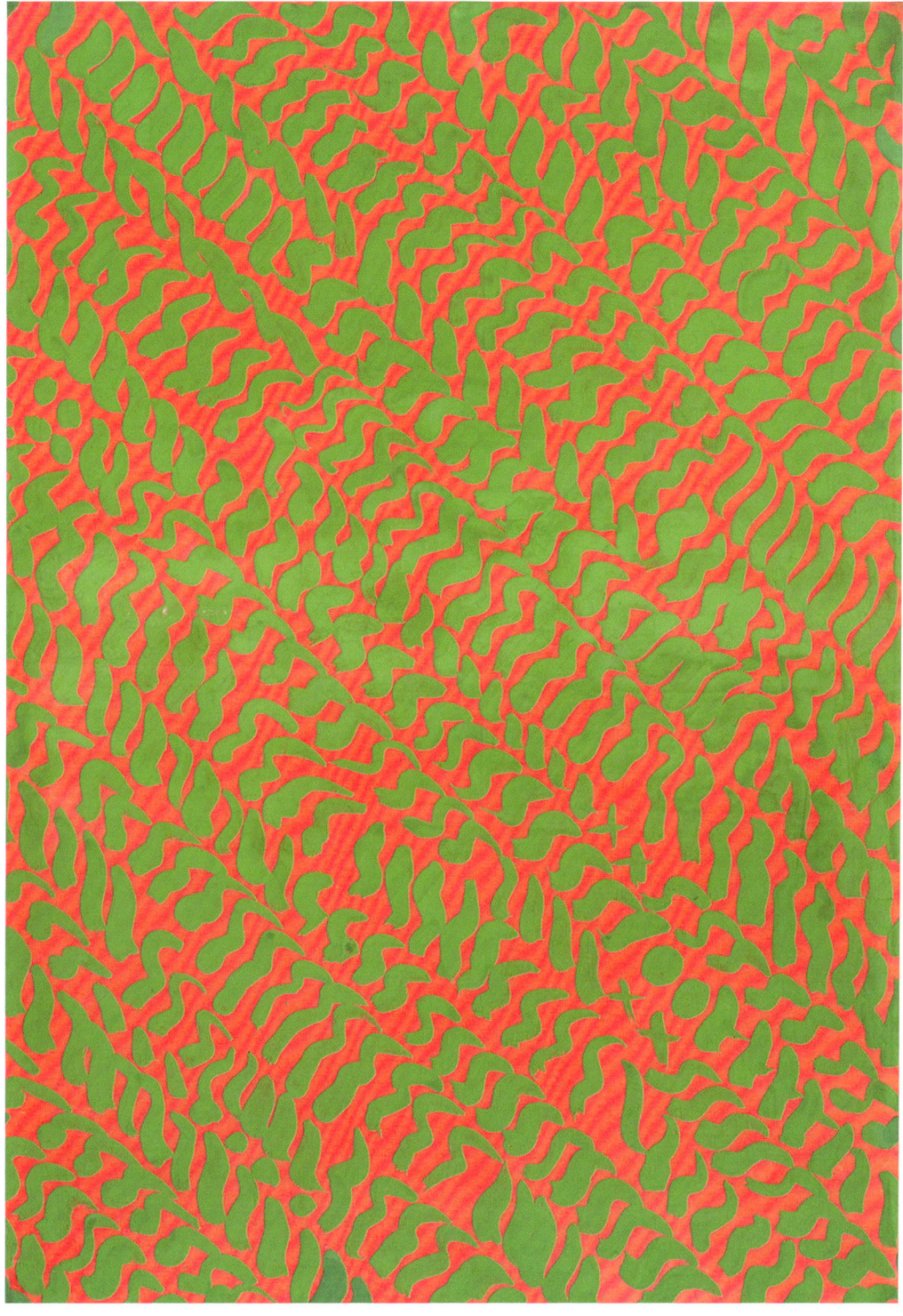

Evelyne Axell
(1935–1972)

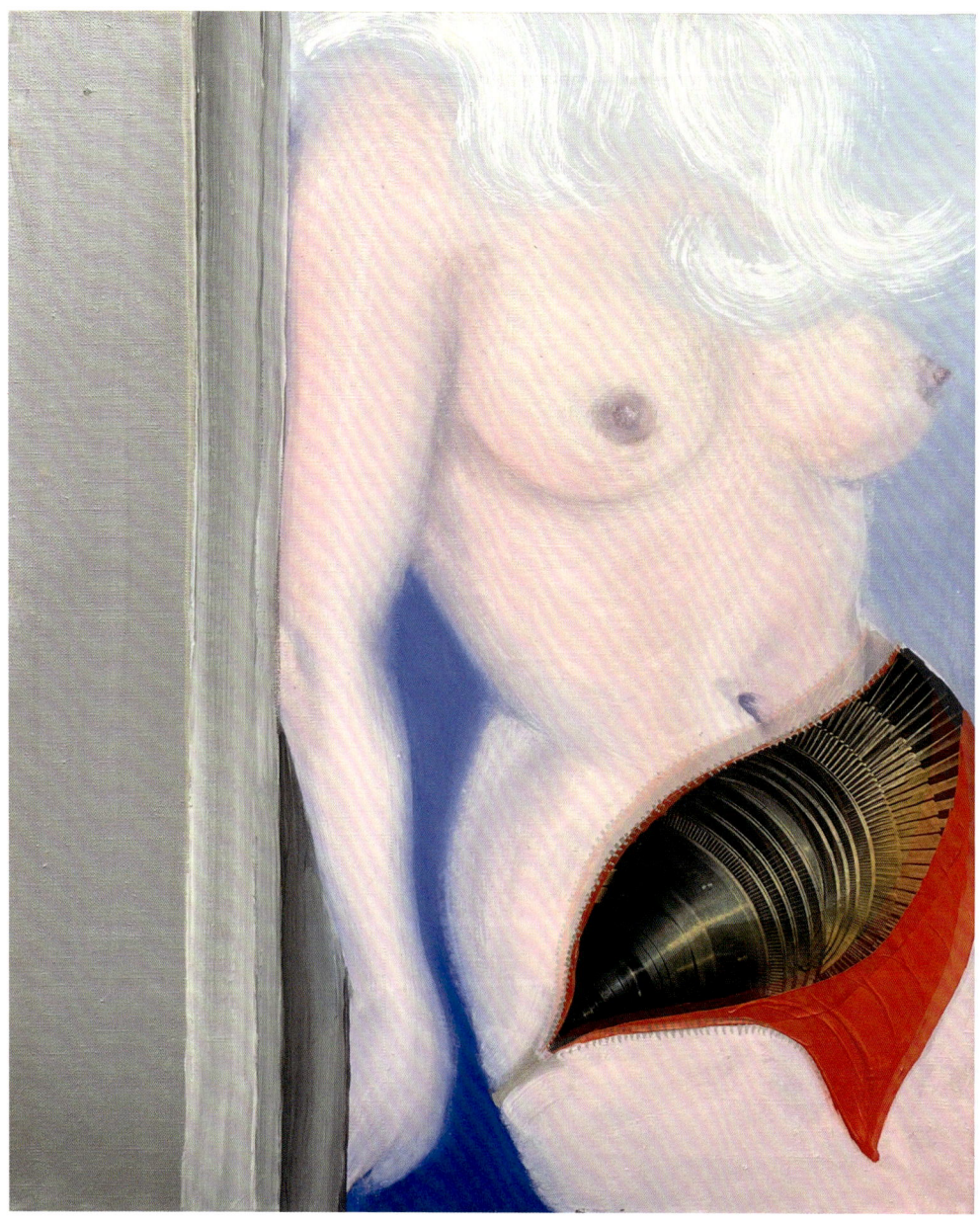

La Machine érotique ou Conception du Mec Art
1964
Oil and printed-paper collage on canvas
23½ × 19⅝ in.
(59.7 × 49.9 cm)

CL1260

My subject is clear: nudity and femininity experiment in the utopia of a bio-botanical freedom, that means a freedom without frustration or gradual submission, and that tolerates only the limits that it sets itself.[1]

The most extraordinary beings I ever met were almost all women, I find women most exquisite. They are everything at once: voluptuousness, luxury, frivolity, tenderness, courage, greed, and total selflessness. That is to say, the synthesis of the weaknesses and strengths of mankind.[2]

Gillian Ayres
(1930–2018)

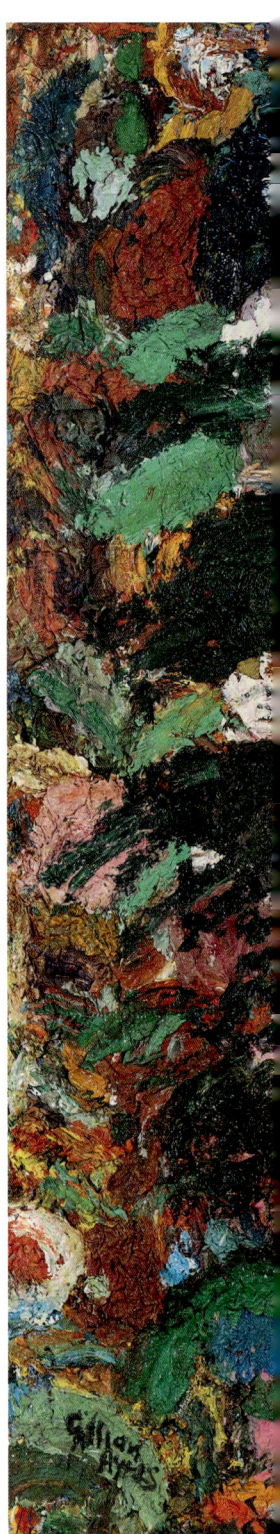

To me, art—colour in art—is wonderfully indulging.
I don't see why you shouldn't be filling yourself up, making
yourself happy. Enjoying yourself. Feasting on beauty.
I want an art that's going to make me feel heady, in a high-
flown way. I love the idea of that. I'd use the word spiritual.
I'm not frightened of all that.[1]

All the painting I've liked has always been colour painting.
I've found that I respond to colour more than anything. Do
you know that every artist has their own colour? If I name
artists, I start spinning out their colour in my mind. If I
think of Matisse, I'm going to think of red or emerald green.
I'm going to think of those pinks and lemon yellows. But if
you said Kandinsky, I'm going to think of more beetroot red
and yellows. And if you said Pollock, I'd say black and white.
Black and white can certainly be colour too.[2]

When you're a born artist, it's almost like you're trying to
breathe. You can't do anything else.[3]

I do remember a woman saying if you are female and you
want to get on, you'd better teach needlework or graphic
design or something. You certainly won't get a job teaching
painting. And I can remember women saying that they
wanted to give up their lives for their boyfriend, who was
a great artist. I was always very ratty if there was any of that
sort of thing.[4]

Scarba
1979–82
Oil on canvas
47¼ × 44⅛ in.
(120 × 112.1 cm)
CL1057

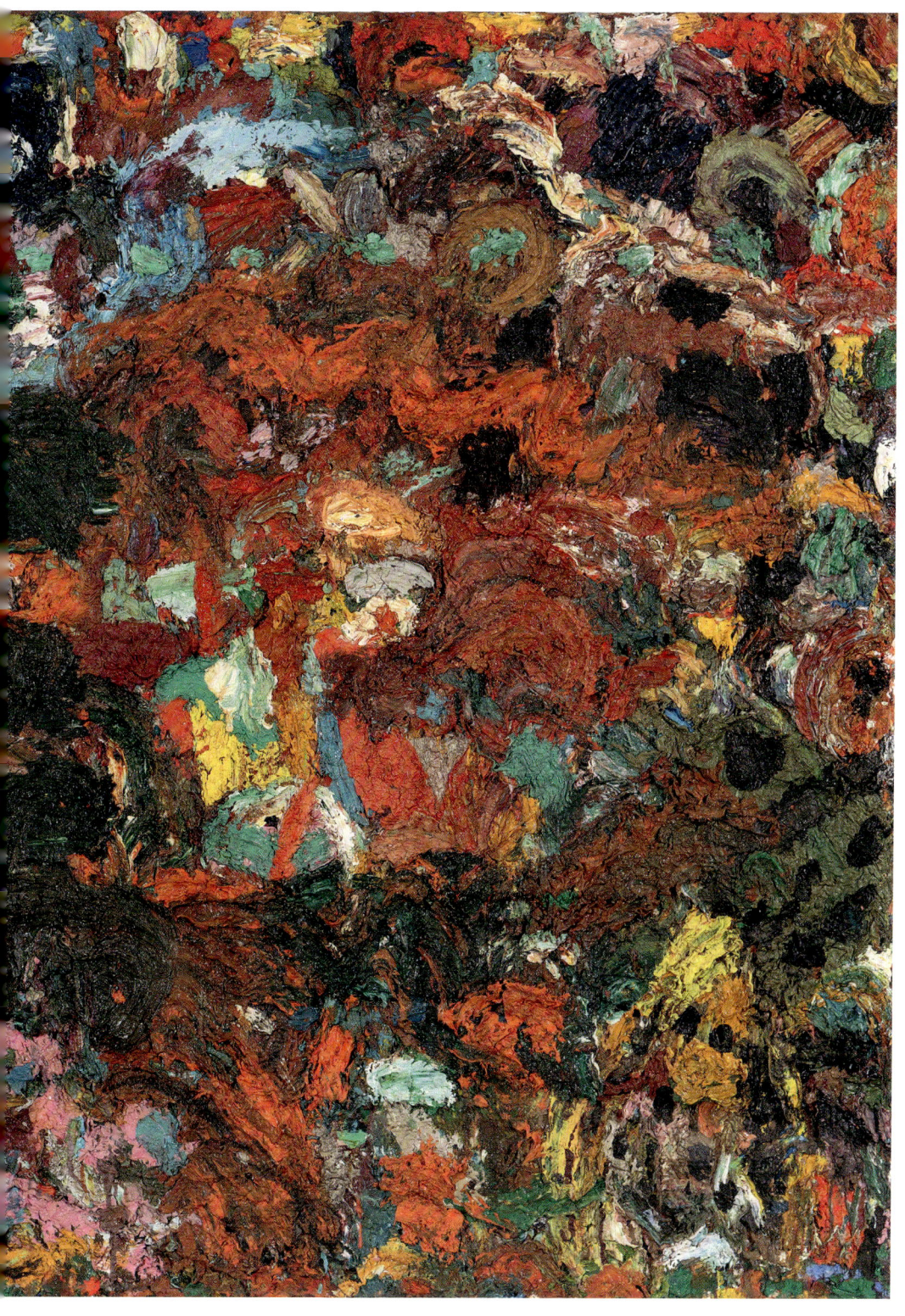

Anna-Eva Bergman
(1909–1987)

I paint my worldview. I have the curious impression that when I write something, it is like I am taking dictation, so that I often write things I don't understand, often not for a long time, months, years. Ready-made sentences come to me in this way and don't leave me until they have been written—and deciphered. The same is true, to a greater degree, in painting. What I am painting now is far beyond my understanding. It is as if I am not the one painting; I just have to obey. It's hard to define. I know that it is right, and I also guess why it is right—and this obedience to natural laws is quite convincing, and yet I cannot say where it comes from. I only know it—and I obey as best I can. It is a duty that I cannot escape![1]

Although my painting is obviously constructed, I work intuitively. For example, over the years landscapes have crept into my abstract compositions without my wanting them to ... I think this has to do with homesickness. It is Finnmark and the north of Northern Norway that I dream of. The light there makes me ecstatic. It may seem that there are layers of air between the light rays, and these layers of air form a perspective of their own. It is a mystery. It's been at least ten years since I've been to Norway, I work mostly from my memories.[2]

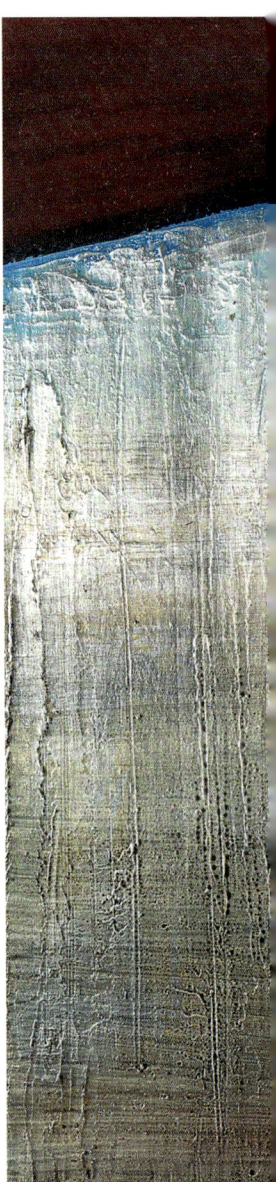

Mur de glace en brume (no. 12-1971)
c. 1971
Acrylic, modeling paste, and metal foil on Isorel wooden panel
21¼ × 25⅝ in.
(54 × 65.1 cm)

CL1429

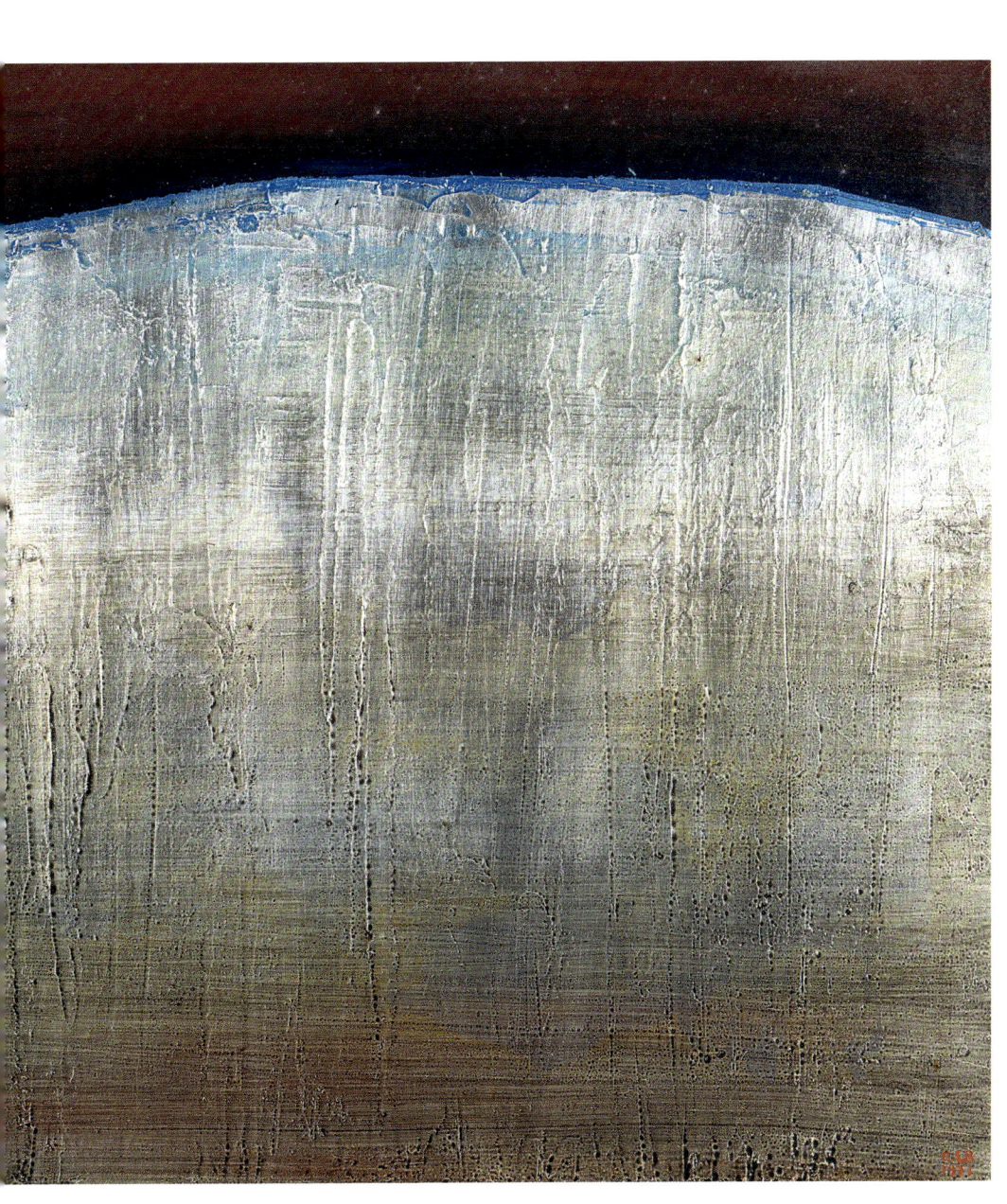

Bernice Bing
(1936–1998)

[In 1967] I investigated [the retreat center] Esalen and it just seemed like a new world there. They were developing a whole new concept of parapsychology, looking into altered states ... it was quite intense and all very new ... This was the period when I painted *Big Sur*. Earlier on, I had done some small works in watercolor and on cardboard but this particular painting is the only one I completed at Esalen. Everything is horizontal with the ocean, and then there's this vertical rock. Basically it was about the intensity of breaking through the rock to the core of the inner self. It has the intensity of the red sky with a mythical creature, a sort of demonic unconsciousness, breaking through. It's a pretty intense painting.[1]

Art has really been the way I have been able to understand both cultures [Chinese and American], and to undo the wrongdoing of both cultures.[2]

For me, all nature is pure, and purely abstracted; the spiritual union links both the seen and the unseen forms of nature. Freedom, for example, is seeing trees as pure energy, light, and mass made up of linear particles.[3]

Big Sur
1967
Acrylic on canvas
$32^1/_8 \times 26^7/_8$ in.
(81.6 × 68.3 cm)

CL907

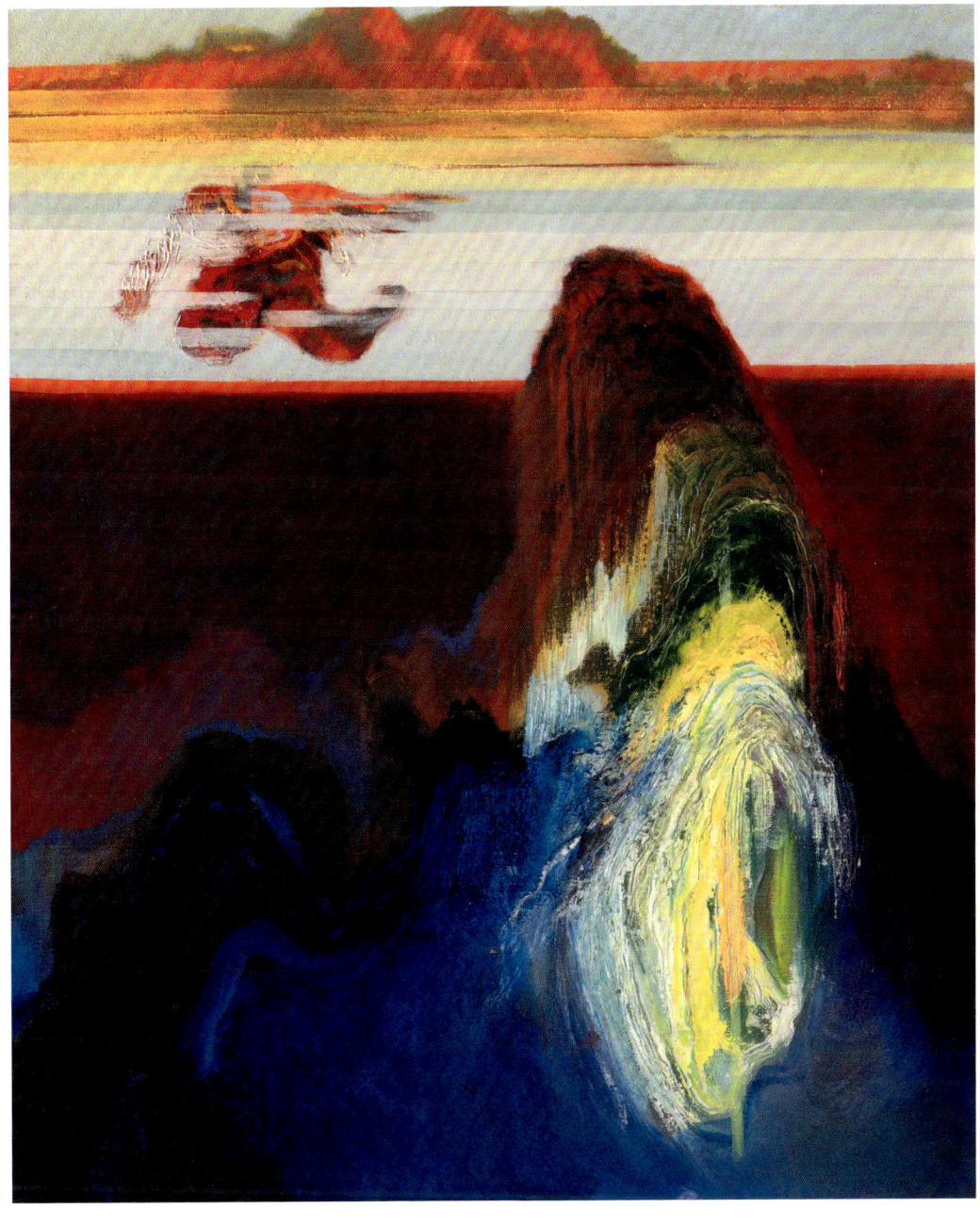

Han Bing
(b. 1986)

As the title of the painting indicates, sometimes I find a resemblance between the process of painting and the process of cooking, where, as I work, I allow some things to sink to the bottom and settle, and others to float up to the surface. In a perpetual stew, over time, some elements no longer hold their original shape but function as bases or exhale in the form of a faint smoke, while other elements just jump in and sense the heat. There is a juxtaposition between the raw and the well-cooked, naturally layered in front of me.[1]

I take something that is meant to be ignored or quickly forgotten and turn it into something that makes me wonder and linger. That is my way of combating the feeling of being overwhelmed by all the information that is thrown at us on a daily basis.[2]

Perpetual Stew
2024
Acrylic and oil on linen
80 × 68 in.
(203.2 × 172.7 cm)
CL1447

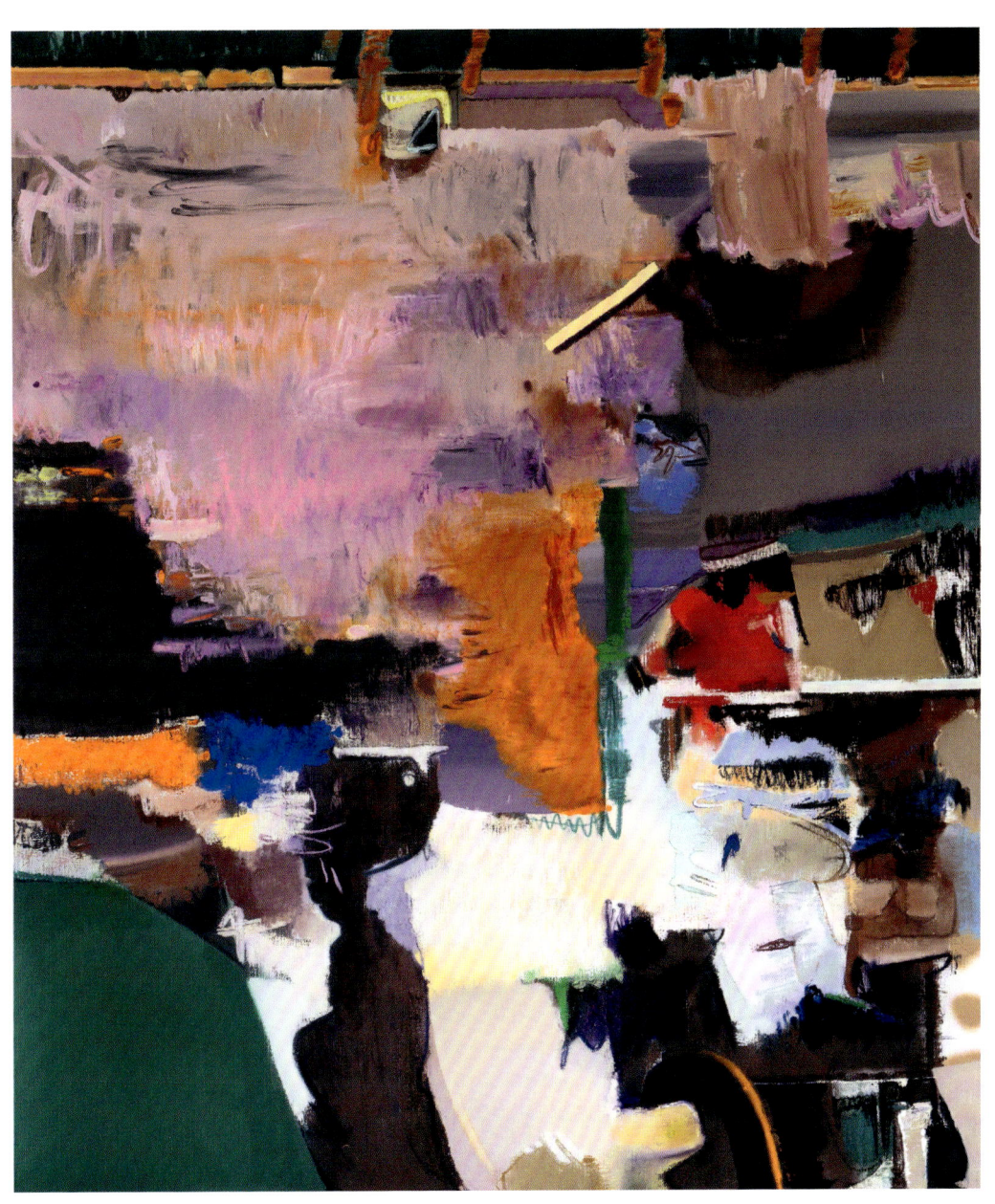

Louise Bonnet
(b. 1970)

Figure with Satin Drapery takes inspiration from 17th-century Dutch still-life *vanitas* paintings. The depicted figure is a representation of the lives that precede and follow our own. The figure's body is exposed like an expensive and valuable object that has mutated in the process of renewing itself through its many iterations. The pieces of wood are placeholders for the body to slip into position, similar to "marks" that actors use to record their positions between takes or models' use of supports when spending long periods of time in a pose.[1]

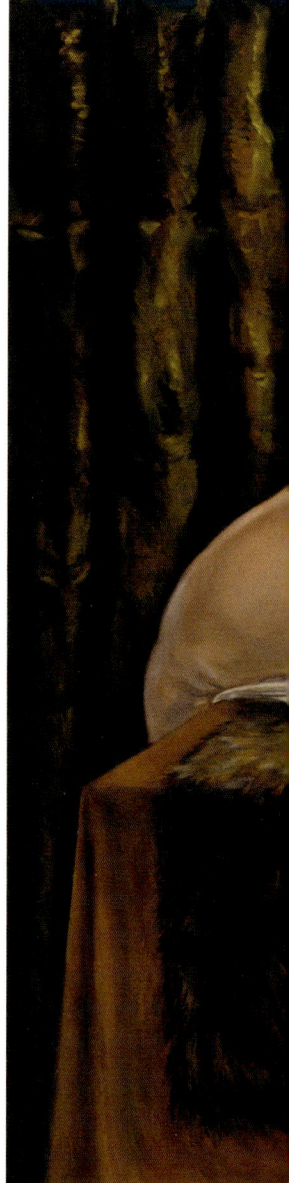

Figure with Satin Drapery

2023
Oil on linen
60 × 72 in. (152.4 × 182.9 cm)

CL1327

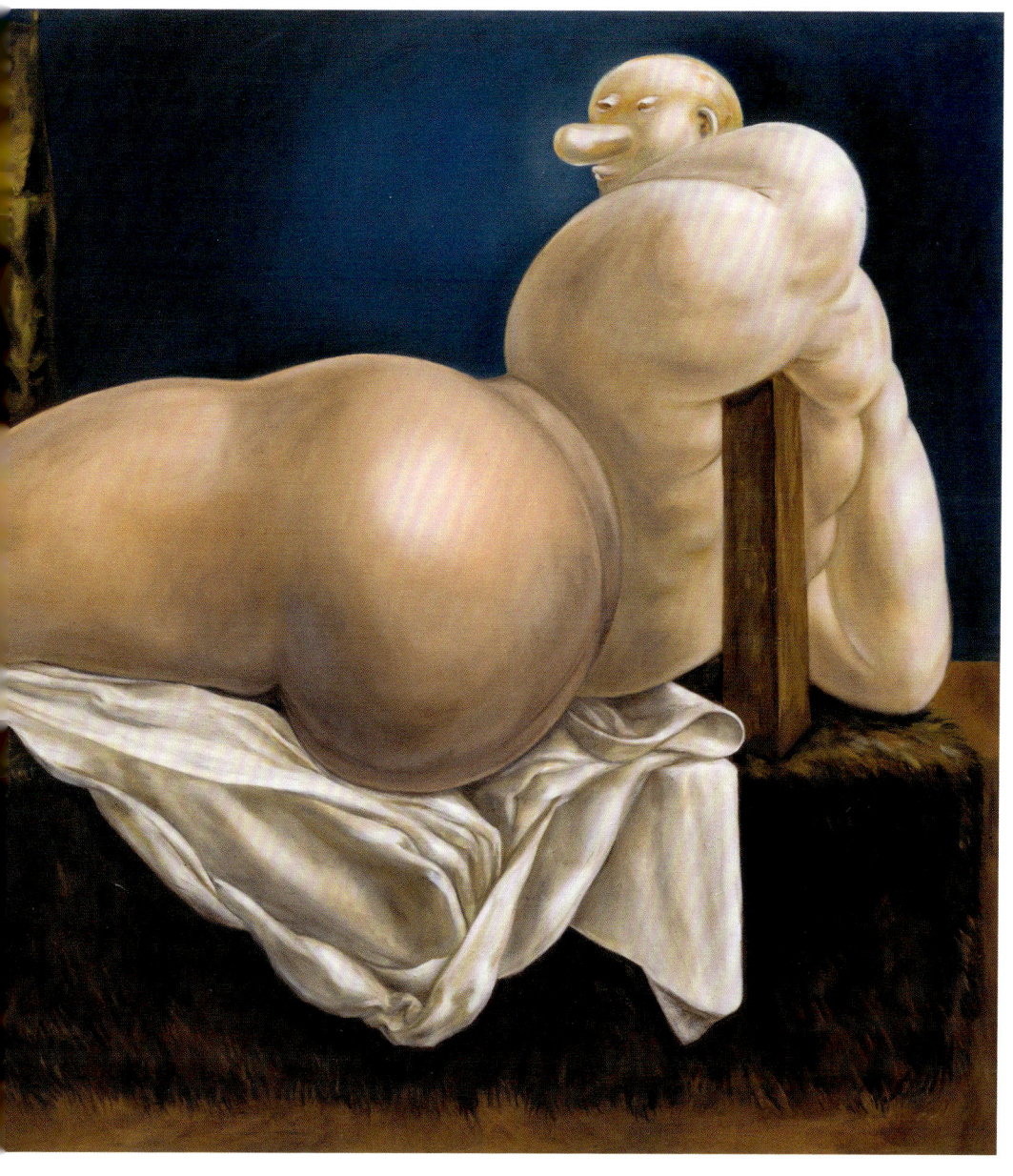

Louise Bourgeois
(1911–2010)

I organize a sculpture the way we organize a treatment for the sick. You'd better know what you're doing. You have to have a strategy to get the wanted results. My sculptures are infallible equations. Equations have to be tested. Does the tension go down, is the compulsion eliminated, is the pain gone? Either it works or it doesn't work.[1]

The phallus is the subject of my tenderness. After all, I lived with four men ... I was the protector. Though I feel protective of the phallus, it does not mean I am not afraid of it.[2]

Perhaps it is necessary for the artist to talk of the why of his work. It is also true that if the work does not speak for itself nothing I can say will be an excuse for its silence; if the work functions as a bridge between artist and spectator it has fulfilled its function. I believe that basically the motivation of many of us is very much the same—individual differences are made, insofar as they are essential, through the character of the work as it finally emerges. The what and the how are more important than the why.[3]

Nature Study
Conceived 1984–96,
cast 2007
Gold porcelain
28¼ × 16¼ × 12 in.
(71.8 × 41.3 × 30.5 cm)
Artist's proof no. 2 from
an edition of 2 plus
2 artist's proofs

CL.697

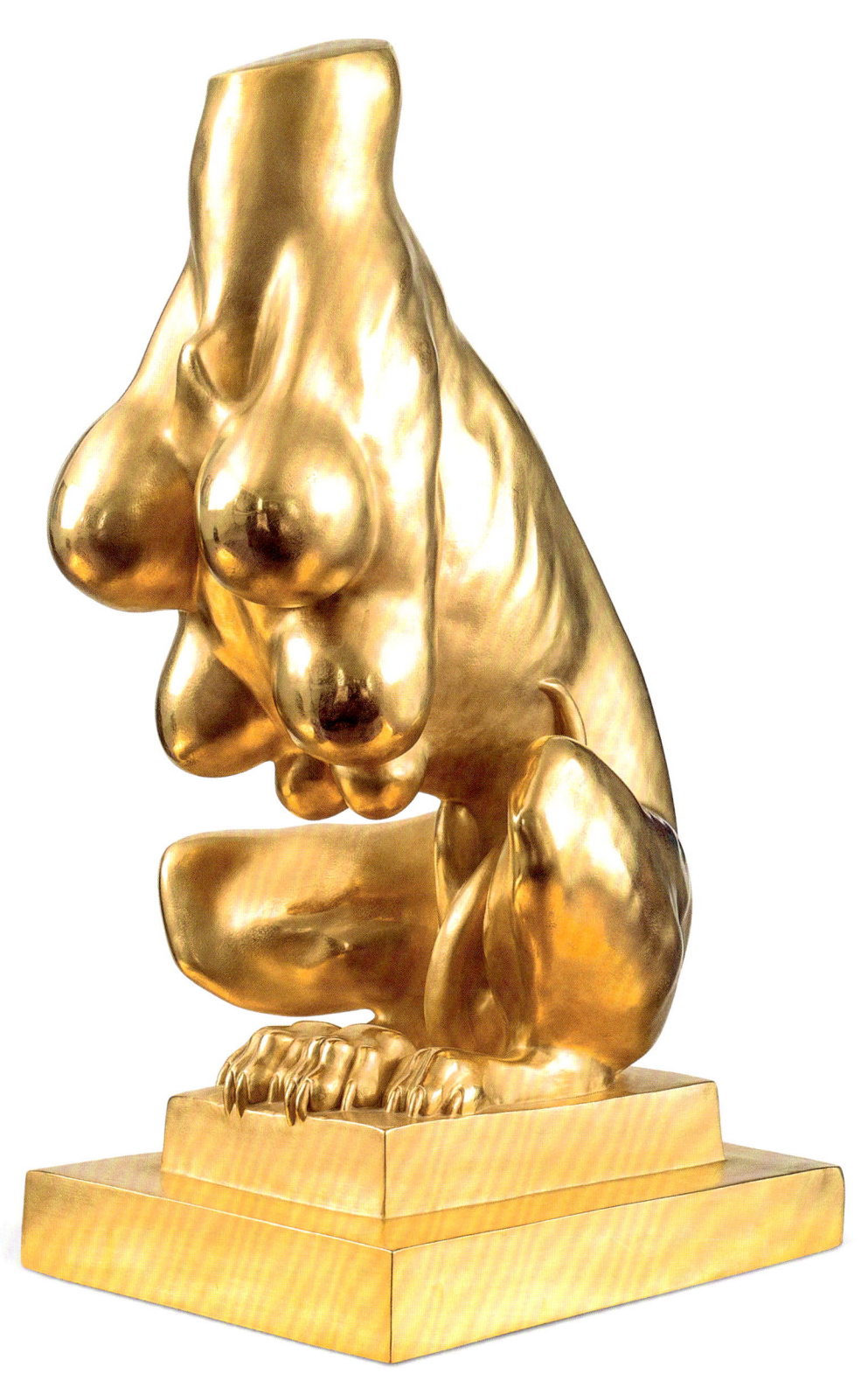

Carol Bove

(b. 1971)

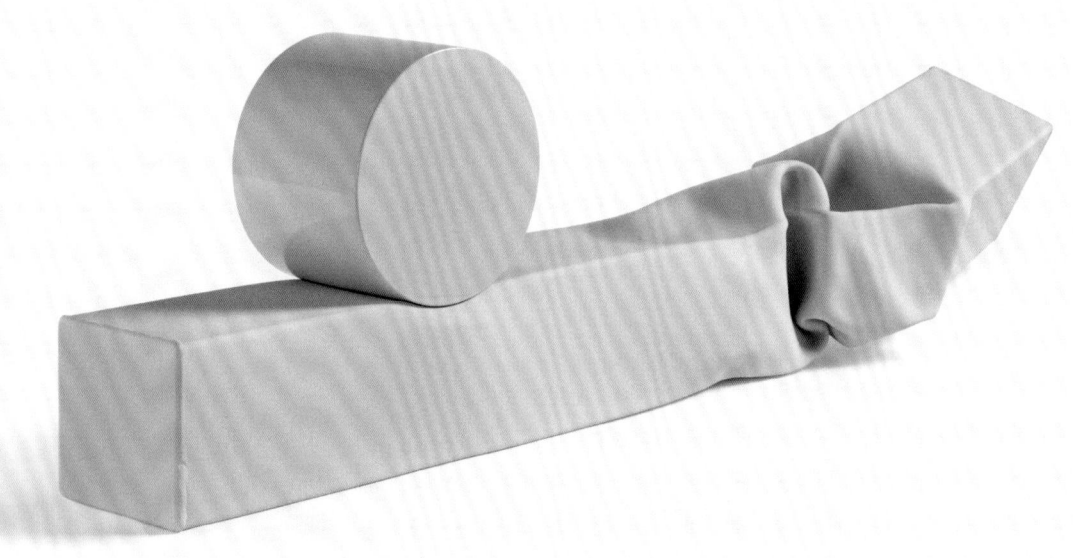

Sensual Math
2023
Stainless steel and
urethane paint
14 × 56 × 15 in.
(35.6 × 142.2 × 38.1 cm)

CL1310

The form always comes out of the material. It's not theoretical. There's not an abstract ideal that the work is trying to accomplish. The idea is emerging at the same time as the form, and the form is led by the material.[1]

Almost everything I make has multiple parts and can be disassembled. Parts are never glued together. This is important to me—it gives the sculptures energy. When they are packed up in a crate I think of them as being off-duty, relaxed. When they are assembled or configured in an exhibition setting they are performing.[2]

As a viewer you can have your conscious attention held by stylistic riddles, trying to identify stylistic references, while your unconscious mind has a different kind of relationship to the artwork. A psychotherapist I used to see always illustrated the artistic process with the magician tarot card: the magician is manipulating objects on a table, but he is looking somewhere else; the object of his attention is not his intention. There's a similar mechanism at work in viewing art.[3]

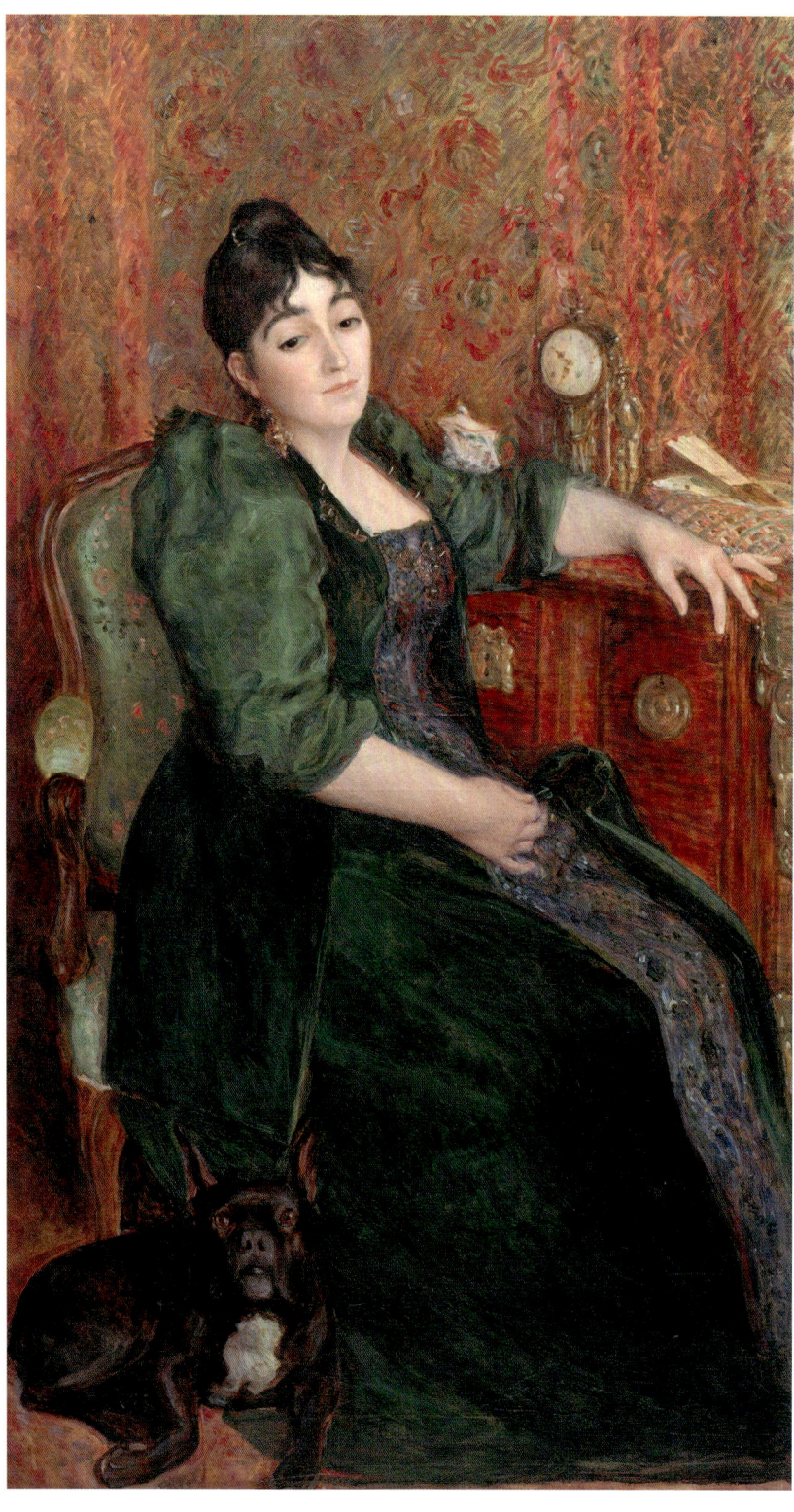

Marie Bracquemond
(1840–1916)

There is in me a strong determination to overcome all obstacles. I wish to work at painting, not to paint some flowers, but to express those feelings that art inspires in me.[1]

Autoportrait de l'artiste dans un fauteuil en compagnie de Bob, son bouledogue français

1892
Oil on canvas
51⅛ × 28¾ in.
(129.9 × 73 cm)

Cecily Brown
(b. 1969)

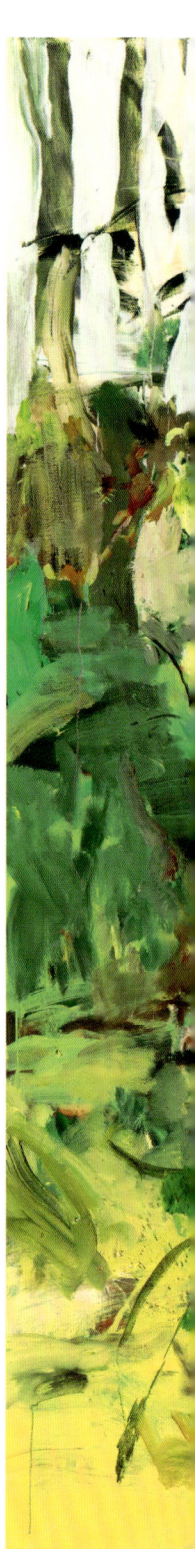

I use drawing a lot. I draw pretty much every day. I almost always draw from photographs, from other people's art. It's really a way of getting information but also understanding what they were doing. I find I only really understand a painting once I've copied it.[1]

The woman looking in a mirror is a subject I've returned to so many times over and over again. It's the world reflected back at you, but you also feel like you're seeing into another world. It is that sense of looking into another world that's so fascinating about art in the first place.[2]

Once you have drawn something ... four or five times they become part of your lexicon. It's as if you internalise the paintings or the images you copy and when you need a figure you can use it as your own. It's not exactly like sampling in music, but similar. Once you have got the cast of characters, they can perform different roles in different paintings.[3]

I often think looking at art is the ultimate escapism. You're in this total and complete world.[4]

Couple
2003–2004
Oil on linen
90 × 80 in.
(228.6 × 203.2 cm)

CL105

40

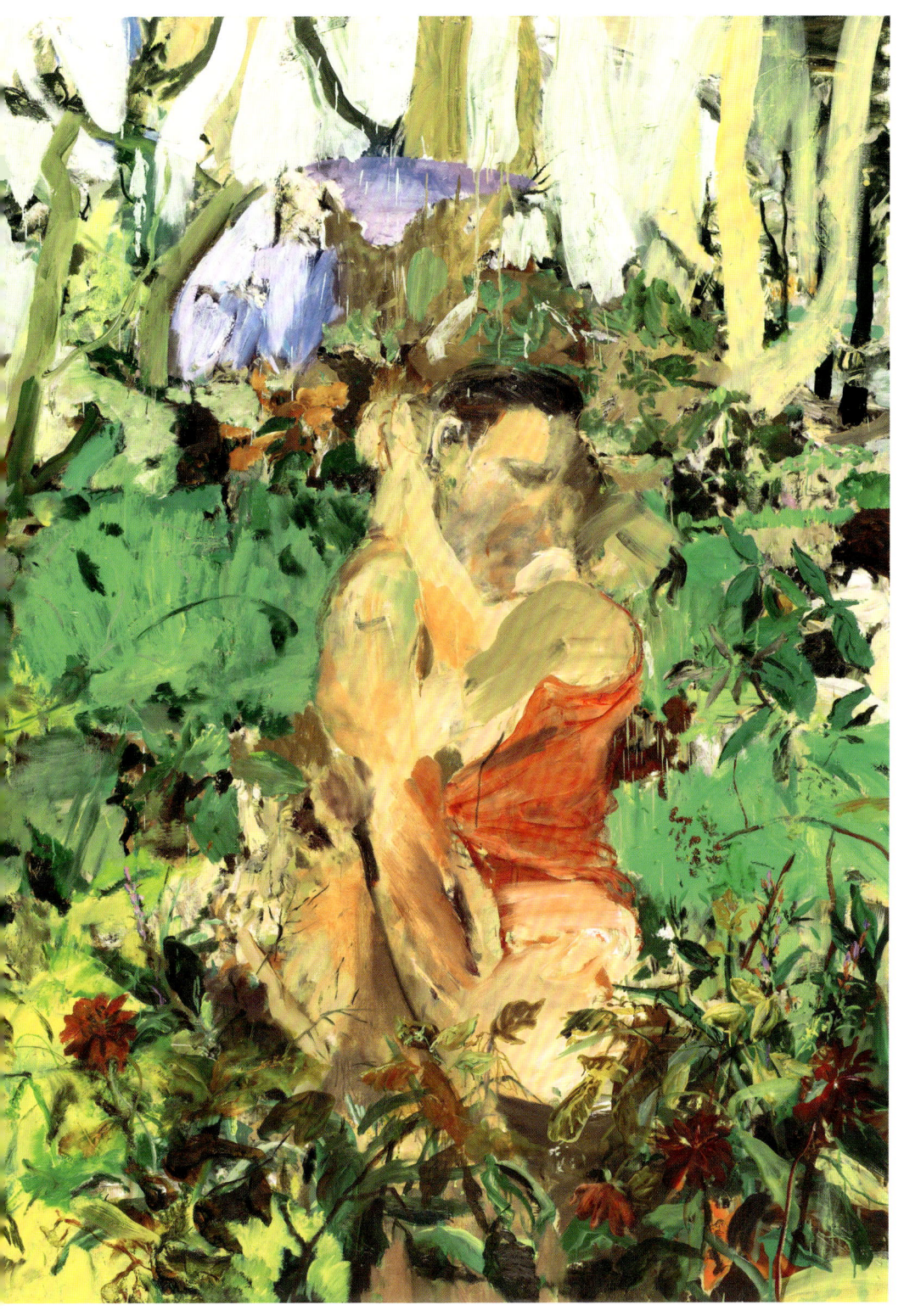

Leonora Carrington
(1917–2011)

Until the artist has become once more a magician, that is, ruling over the magical art, that begins with himself, we may only say that destinies in art are as obscure and dangerous as weapons in the hands of modern politicians and heads of state.[1]

Writing and painting are alike in that both arts—music as well—come out of fingers and into some receptive artifact. The result, of course, is read, heard or seen through the receptive organs of those who receive the art and are supposed to "Be" what all these different persons perceive differently. Therefore it seems that any introduction to art is fairly senseless since anybody can think or experience according to who he is. Very likely the introduction will not be read anyhow.

Once a dog barked at a mask I made; that was the most honorable comment I ever received.[2]

Asked by Whitney Chadwick for her thoughts on the Surrealist muse:

I thought it was bullshit. I didn't have time to be anyone's muse. I was too busy rebelling against my family and learning to be an artist.[3]

Mid-Day of the Canary (The Pink Room)
1967
Oil on canvas
32 × 23⅝ in.
(81.3 × 60 cm)

CL1245

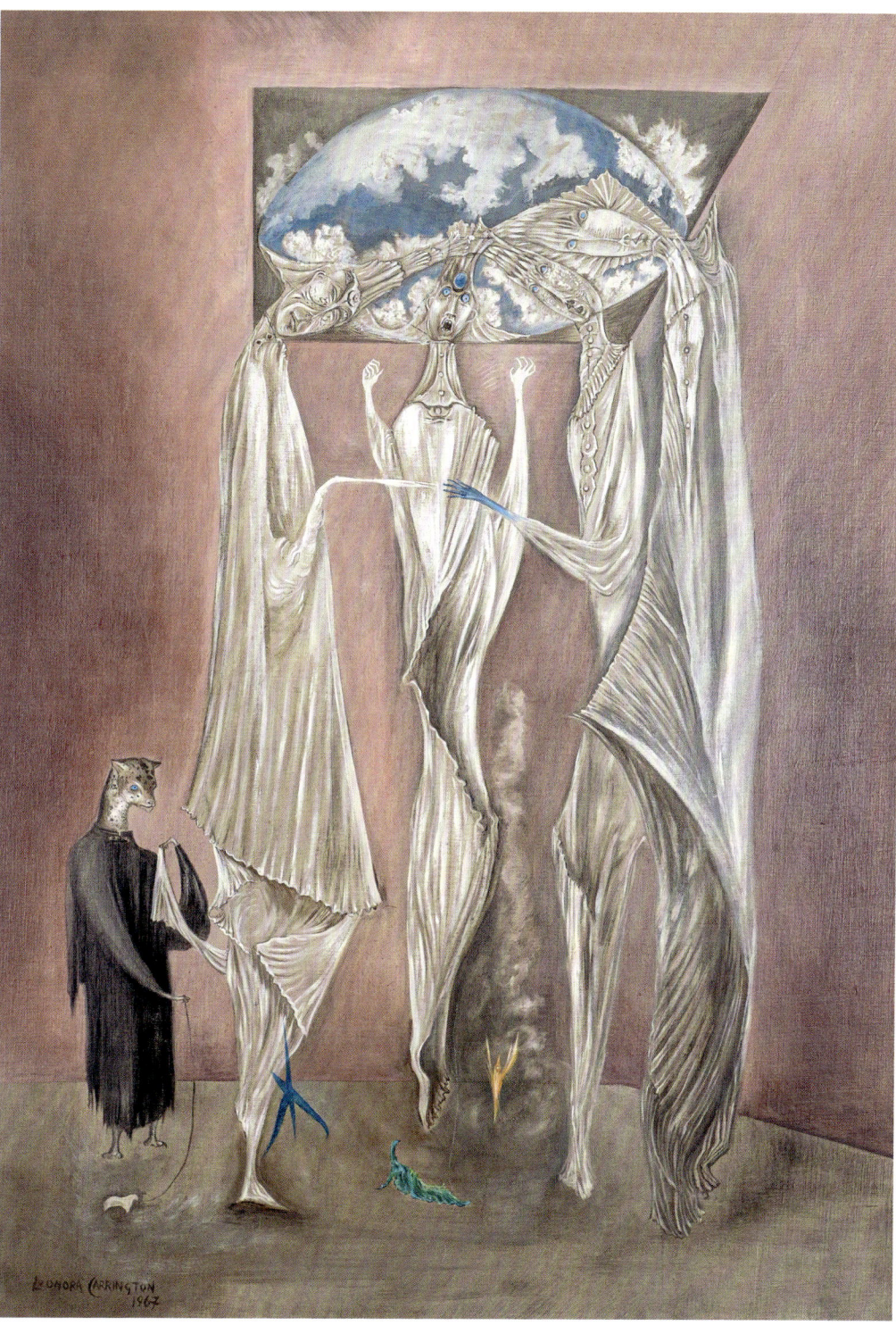

Mary Cassatt
(1844–1926)

On her commission to paint the mural Modern Woman *for the Woman's Building at the 1893 World's Columbian Exposition in Chicago:*

Men, I have no doubt, are painted in all their vigor on the walls of the other buildings; to us the sweetness of childhood, the charm of womanhood, if I have not conveyed some sense of that charm, in one word, if I have not been absolutely feminine, then I have failed.[1]

Fillette dans un jardin (Susan Seated in a Garden)

c. 1882–83
Oil on canvas
$25\frac{5}{8} \times 20$ in.
(65.1 × 50.8 cm)

CL1335

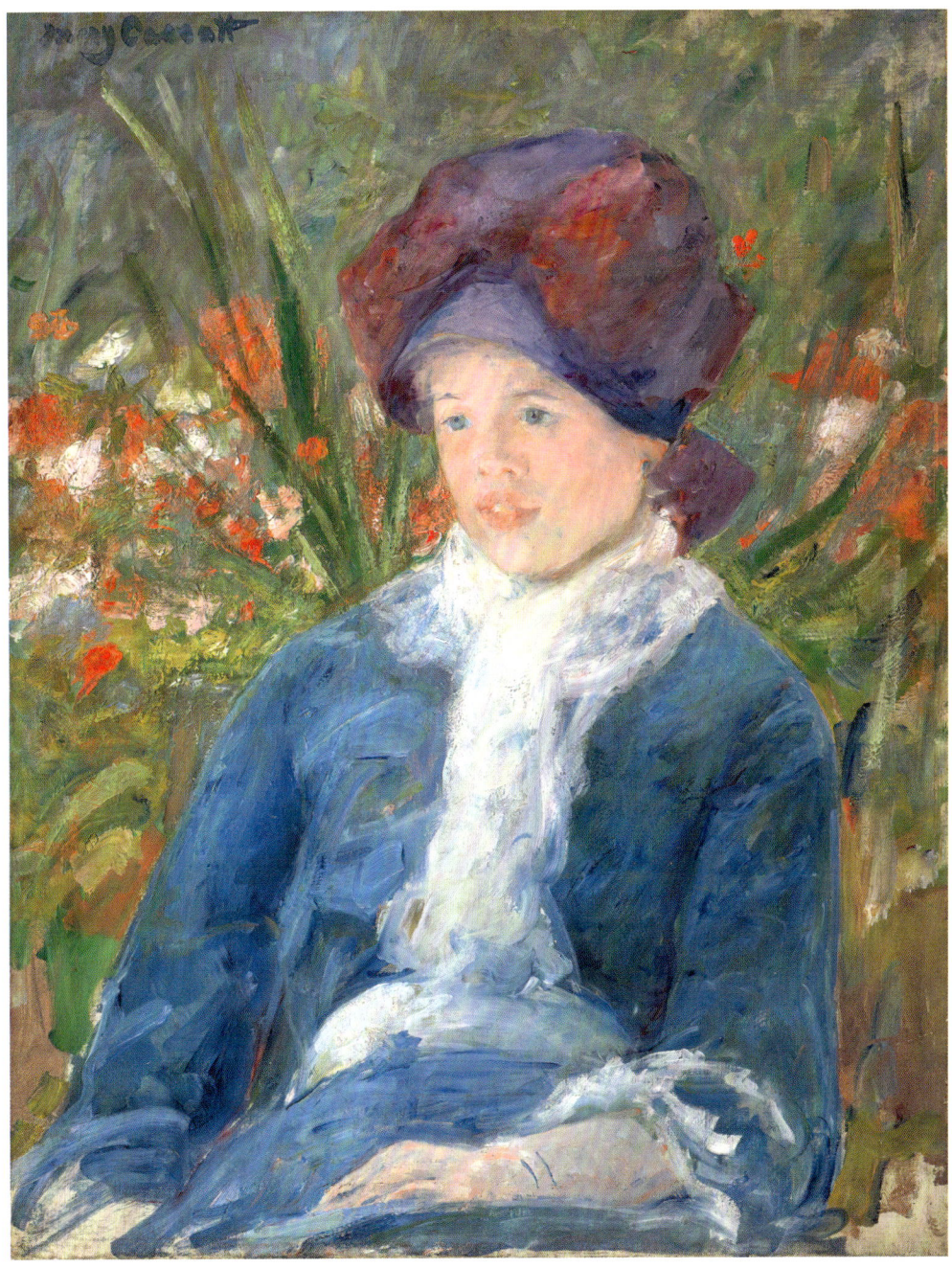

Joana Choumali
(b. 1974)

My use of embroidery was in response to an instinctive need to touch and physically intervene on my photographs ... The fact that I was able to allow myself to embroider on my images in an instinctive way really marked a turning point in my way of understanding and processing life through my art. My inner universe merges with the exterior; the photo I shot. This meditative approach allows me to discover another way of experiencing certain events in my life.[1]

My art comes from this perception of the environment and the tacit connection I feel between the people I photograph and myself, as well as the relation to space, to the landscape, the ambient energy of a place. The non-verbal dialogue that can take place with the other and with an environment. I use my imagination. I focus on the meeting point between my emotions and how other people's emotions contribute to this captured moment.[2]

Inner Chatter of the Mind
2018
Embroidery, collage, and digital photo printing on canvas
21⅝ × 21⅝ in.
(54.9 × 54.9 cm)
CL999

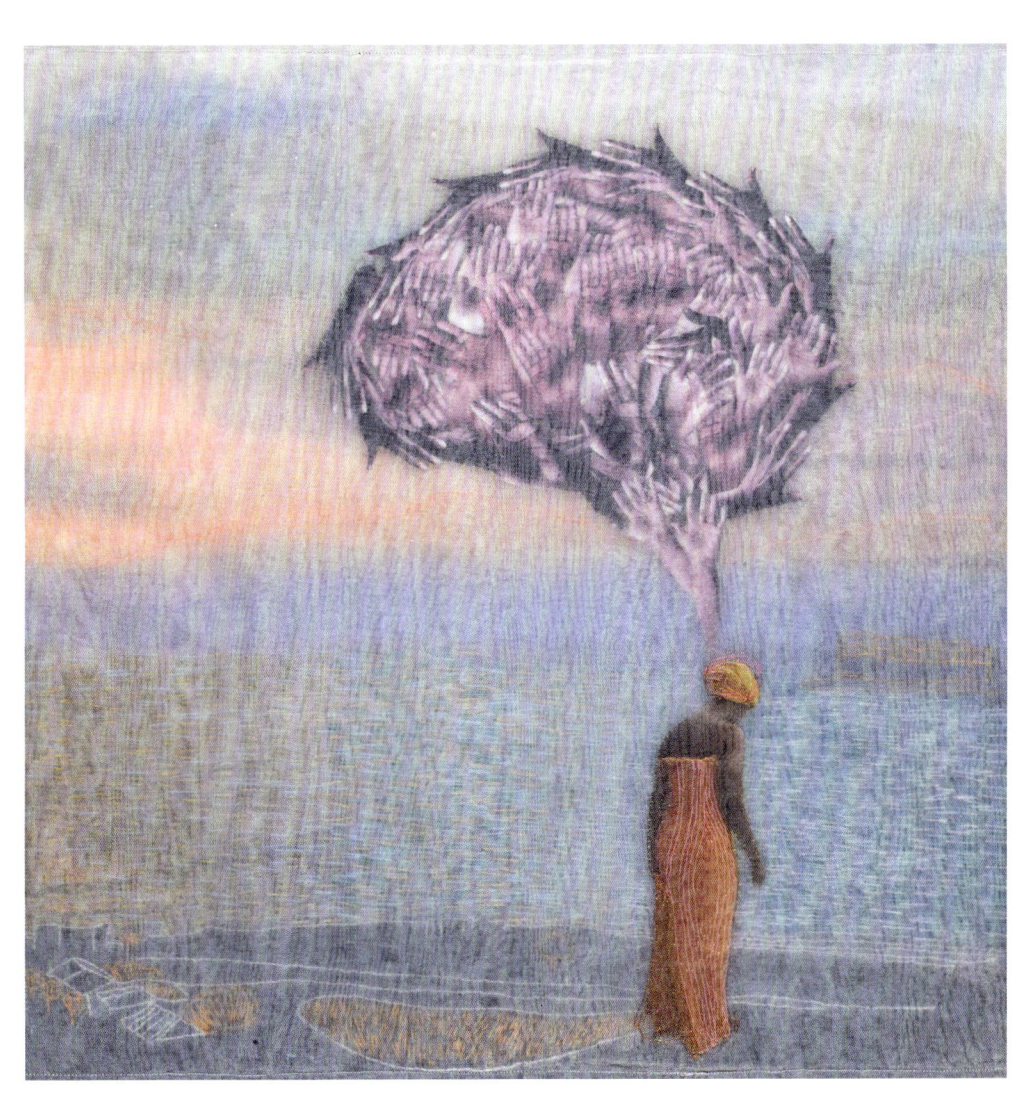

Elizabeth Colomba
(b. 1976)

The Wheel of Fortune in tarot is about change. It embodies the playful and cosmic character of fate, abundance, chance and fortune in all its forms. But what appears as a traditional 19th-century society portrait suddenly calls us to look again. The figure's blackness both radically challenges history and rewrites it. A young black girl of nobility surrounded by wealth, she's both past and future. She is the embodiment of change, her own agent, as inspiration and in her own voice.

This painting operates on two levels. On one hand, it is a rendition of a tarot card showing all forms of abundance. There is a cornucopia of food and fruit, the cherry tree outside, the emblem of bounty and life. The wallpaper is de Gournay, the harpsichord represents the luxury of the arts.

On the other hand, the painting rewrites the way we read luxury. While this girl is classically posed, holding a traditional Victorian hoop toy, I wanted to showcase wealth as defined by both Western and Caribbean symbols. For example, her dress is the Victorian style but is of Caribbean cloth using three different materials. Whilst there is a feast on the table, it does not include traditionally Western pheasants and hare. Instead, I chose fruits from the Caribbean: mangoes, papayas, bananas, pineapples, etc. And if you look to the Louis XVI chairs, one has an open passion fruit, while the other holds a scorpion. One celebrates resources from the islands; the other, cosmic symbolism.

Showing her with her toy, I wanted to capture playfulness in divination. Like in life, while we can guide a hoop, its true root ultimately rests in the hands of physics and fate. Under her steady and focused gaze, we, the viewers, lie in wait to see where the wheel will spin.[1]

The Wheel of Fortune

2023
Oil on canvas
60 × 48 in.
(152.4 × 121.9 cm)

CL1184

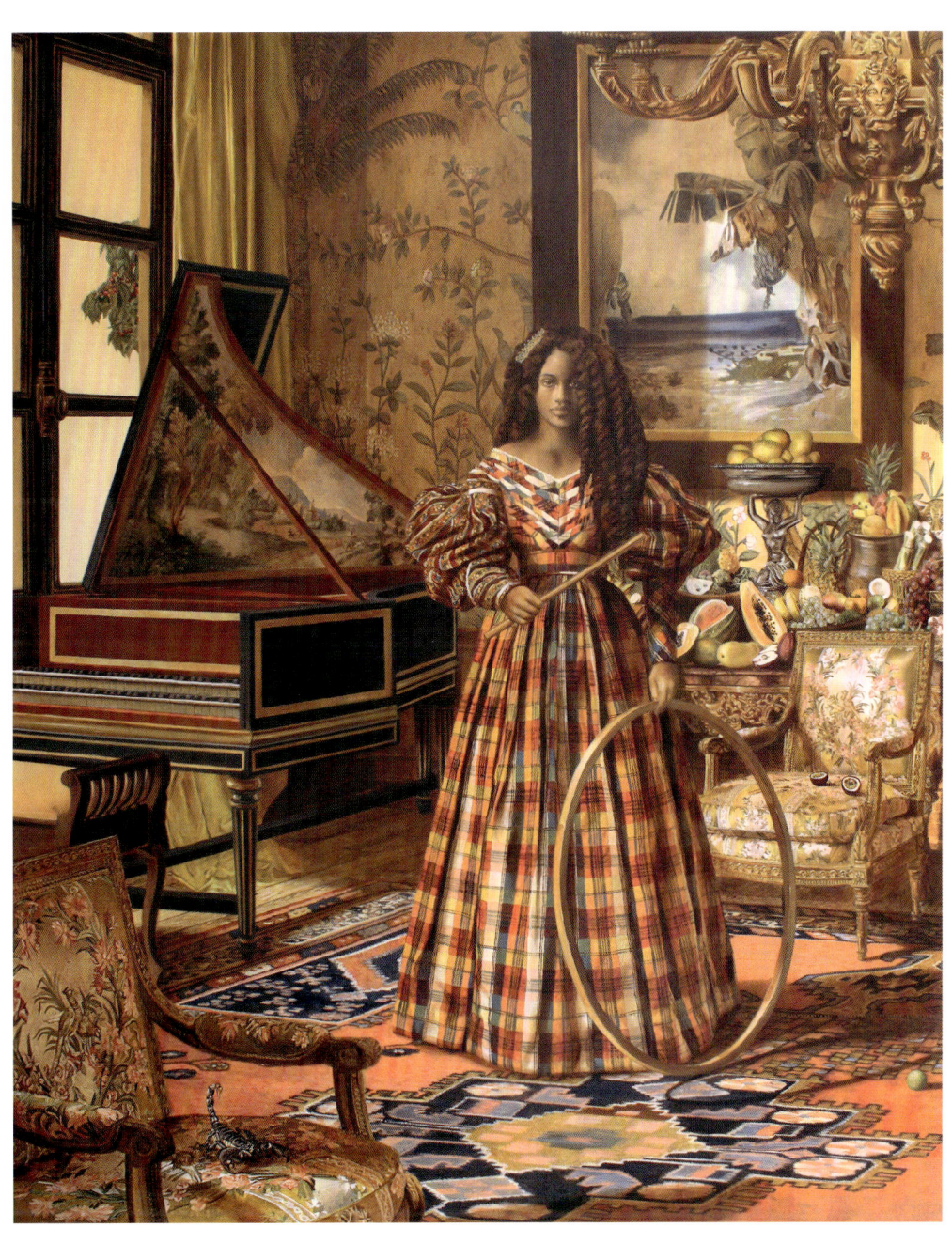

Dadamaino
(1930–2004)

I made a series of drawings with white and black squares that became circular. They had the effect of an optical illusion. So I continued with this plan. I tried using aluminum, wire, always to give this sense of transparency. It was the idea of movement that attracted me, but without the use of motors.[1]

I let my hand flow freely. Thus the ensemble appears denser or more sparse at times, but I do not seek these diversifications, which come spontaneously and are possible in spite of myself. For the moment, I call these signs "The alphabet of the mind" because I believe that they are the codes of a personal language.[2]

Oggetto ottico-dinamico
1962–71
Milled aluminum plates on nylon threads on wooden structure
41¾ × 41¾ in.
(106.1 × 106.1 cm)

CL946

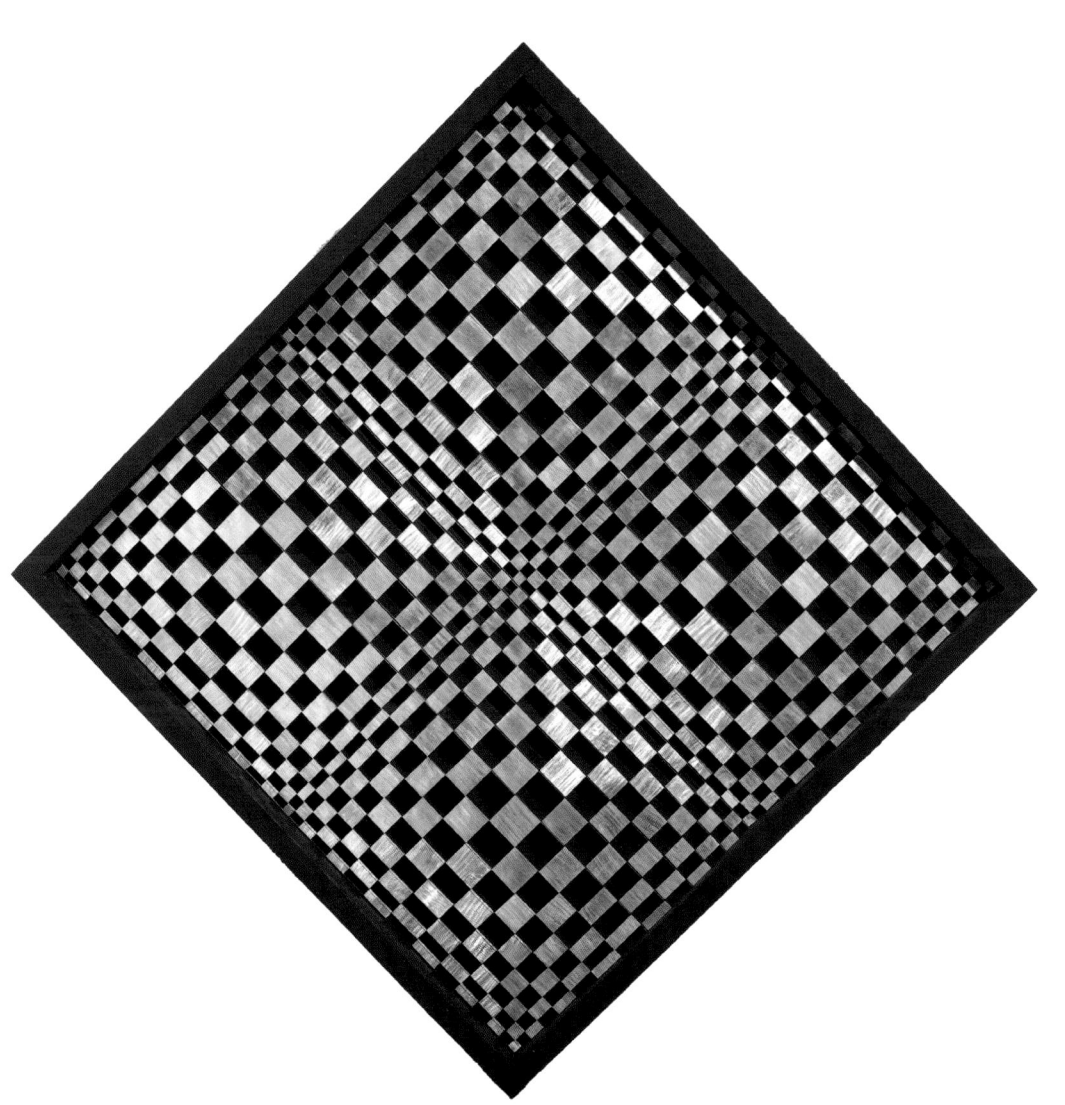

Elaine de Kooning
(1918–1989)

[My husband] Bill always thought that portraits were pictures that *girls* made. So, I made portraits. I had that area free. I had to do it myself; I didn't have to make decisions. I knew I was going to make a portrait and it didn't much matter of whom; once you are set to make a portrait, you're free to make a painting.[1]

I was always interested in portraiture. If you see someone three blocks away, you recognize them immediately. You do not see the face, but you recognize them … a glimpse, the proportions, the kind of rhythm. You don't need to see features, a kind of redundancy.[2]

[In the past] women painted women: Vigée-LeBrun, Mary Cassatt, and so forth. And I thought, men always painted the opposite sex, and I wanted to paint men as sex objects.[3]

I was very interested in the male attire, the fact that men's clothes divide them in half. You know, the parting of the jacket, and the trousers, and so on. I was interested in the way men sat in about five different poses. There are men who fold themselves up, press their arms, cross their legs, and there are men who sit up only with their arms at their sides, and their legs akimbo. I just reduced it to these formal elements, and since they were the center of the space, I just had that image of the gyroscope in mind. I talked about it in 1960 to [existential psychologist] Rollo May, who later coined the term "gyroscope men."[4]

Walter (Auerbach)
1954
Oil on canvas
66 × 50 in. (167.6 × 127 cm)
CL974

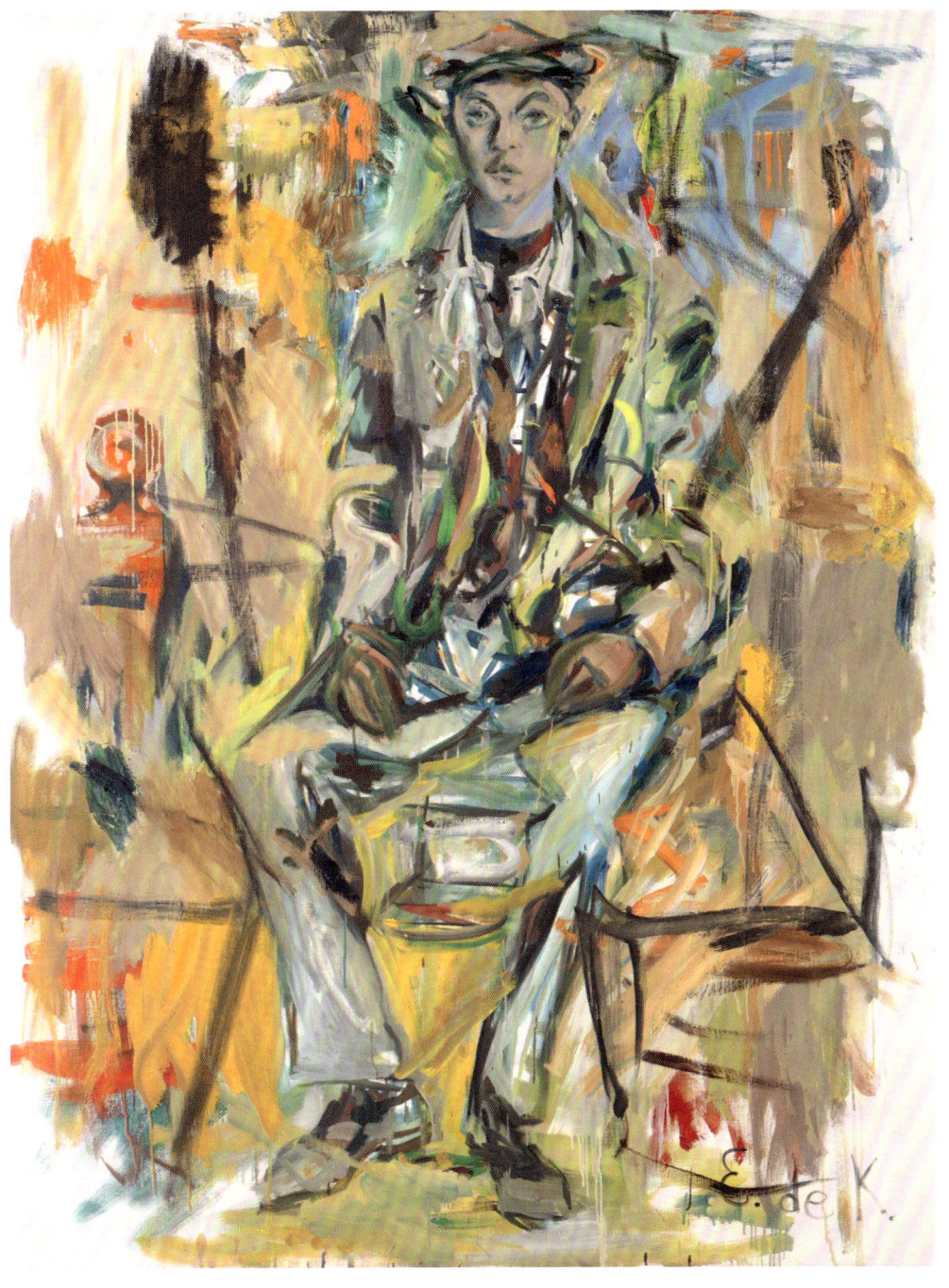

Dorothy Dehner
(1901–1994)

The past, the present, my visions, my memories, everything I know and see, and what is true to my spirit are in my work. My sculpture is a struggle to capture these things. It establishes a dialogue. It is saying in images what I cannot say in words. It contains contradictions. It is close to me and it is remote. It speaks to me and it is dumb. It can reveal myself to me and it can be closed. It is concerned with my deepest feelings, and it considers the minutiae. It speaks of what I know and see; what is actually there as well as the unseen realities. Out of these ingredients new images are made, and the cycle begins again. Each work gives birth to the next. In the end no matter what it is, it is what I have to do.[1]

We are creating an image, a visual language out of the spirit of our time. This of course has not been a conscious goal, but it is an inevitable one. This same thing has happened all over the world at different times, that some writers or artists in some geographical location found the words or the plastic expression that best identifies for posterity the presiding spirit of a given age. In our world of unprecedented and supreme scientific progress, a world that has produced atomic fission, a world that had produced the mechanistic civilization in which we live, a world of great and unreconcilable [*sic*] extremes, we are bound to create an art that anticipates this as well as reacts to it.[2]

Jacob's Ladder No. 2
1957
Bronze
30⅞ × 8¾ × 7¼ in.
(78.4 × 22.2 × 18.4 cm)
MMoCA233MA

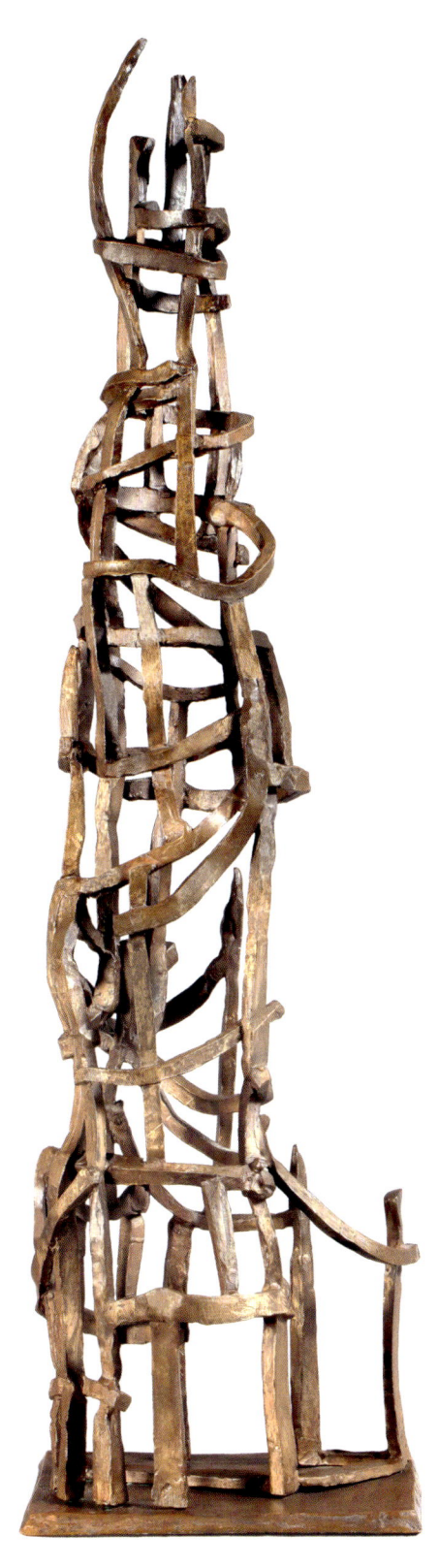

Sonia Delaunay
(1885–1979)

If there are geometric forms, it is because these simple
and manageable elements have appeared suitable for the
distribution of colors whose relations constitute the real
object of our search, but these geometric forms do not
characterize our art. The distribution of colors can be
effected as well with complex forms, such as flowers, etc. ...
only the handling of these would be a little more delicate.[1]

About 1911 I had the idea of making for my son, who had just
been born, a blanket composed of bits of fabric like those
I had seen in the houses of Russian peasants. When it was
finished, the arrangement of the pieces of material seemed
to me to evoke cubist conceptions and we then tried to
apply the same process to other objects and to paintings.[2]

Ville de Paris
c. 1970
Aubusson wool tapestry
68½ × 55⅞ in.
(174 × 141.9 cm)
CL1401

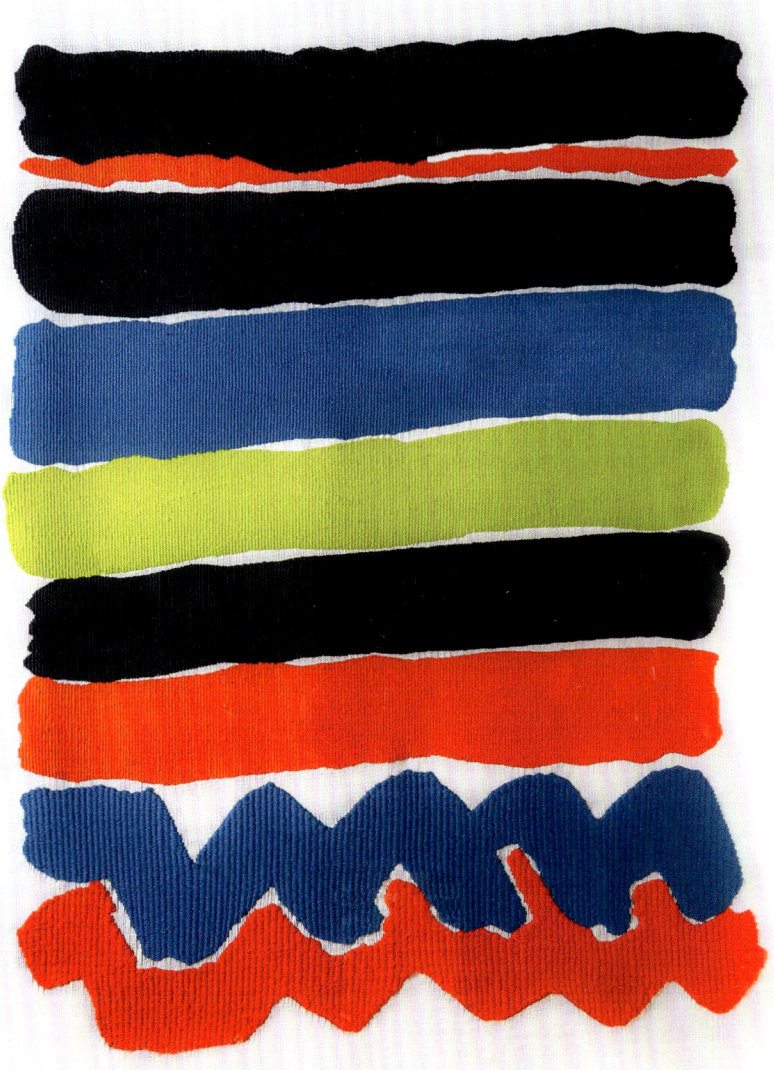

Marlene Dumas
(b. 1953)

I never wanted to paint symbols. I also never wanted a painting to be a symbol. Jean-Paul Sartre said it was out of cowardice that we fell into the symbolic. I've said, I paint because I am afraid to be dead while still alive.[1]

When I was at art school I wanted painting to have a stronger connection to reality, to be more like "real life." I wanted to be a photographer because I thought it was closer to real life. People who made paintings or fantasy images where figures floated in the air were removed from reality, I thought. Performance artists seemed closer to the real thing. Why make an enormous painting in order to tell you that I love you when I can simply write you a letter? But I really love to make images with my hands, so to resolve this contradiction, I started to make use of all the things that bothered me about painting. I realised that I don't want to make a human being. I'm not God. I'm making something else. When I started to embrace the ambiguity of the image, and accepted the realisation that the image can only come to life through the viewer looking at it, and that it takes on meaning through the process of looking, I began to accept painting for what it was.[2]

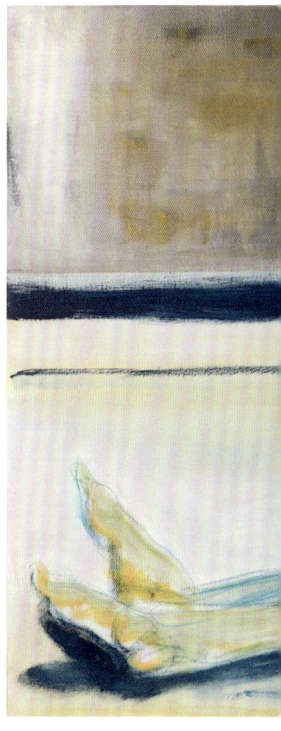

*Cultural Exchange
(Mummie wants to
go home)*
2008–2009
Oil on canvas
39⅜ × 78¾ in.
(100 × 200 cm)
CL109

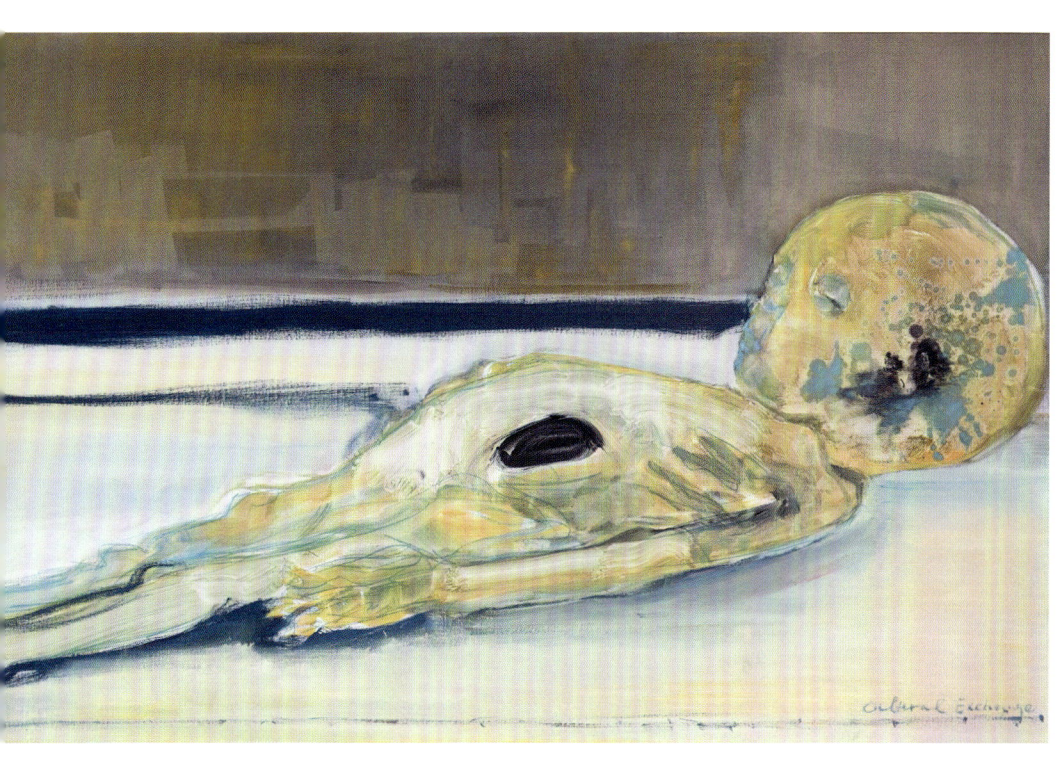

Amaranth Ehrenhalt
(1928–2021)

I do just that in my work: jump in and move around. I try to get into some very deep emotional state and then not really think on an intellectual or analytical level. If I think too much, it's less effective than if I just start *doing* and put a blob on canvas. Once I put that blob on canvas … it's almost like the painting is directing me in what to do.[1]

There were shows of American artists, and I participated in many of them. I showed with Sam Francis, met Beauford Delaney. I met Giacometti and Yves Klein. I also met Natalia Goncharova, she was wonderful, and I took an American collector to buy her work. I knew Joan Mitchell, who was financially independent and for that reason she could stand her ground amongst the male artists … In the 50s and 60s, there were only two categories a woman could belong to: she either had to be the wife or girlfriend of one of the major male artists, or she had to be independent like Joan Mitchell. It was very challenging when I wanted art dealers to see my work, because there was so much at stake. During another show I met Alix de Rothschild, who was a big art collector. At some point, she came to visit but kept her coat on, because my place was so cold. She asked, "How do you heat?" And I said, "I don't." The children were wearing snow suits in the living room.[2]

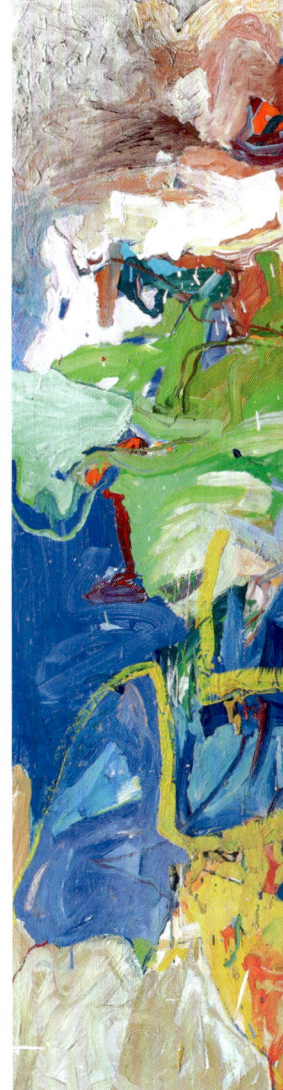

Jump In and Move Around

1962
Oil on canvas
59 × 77 in.
(149.9 × 195.6 cm)
CL840

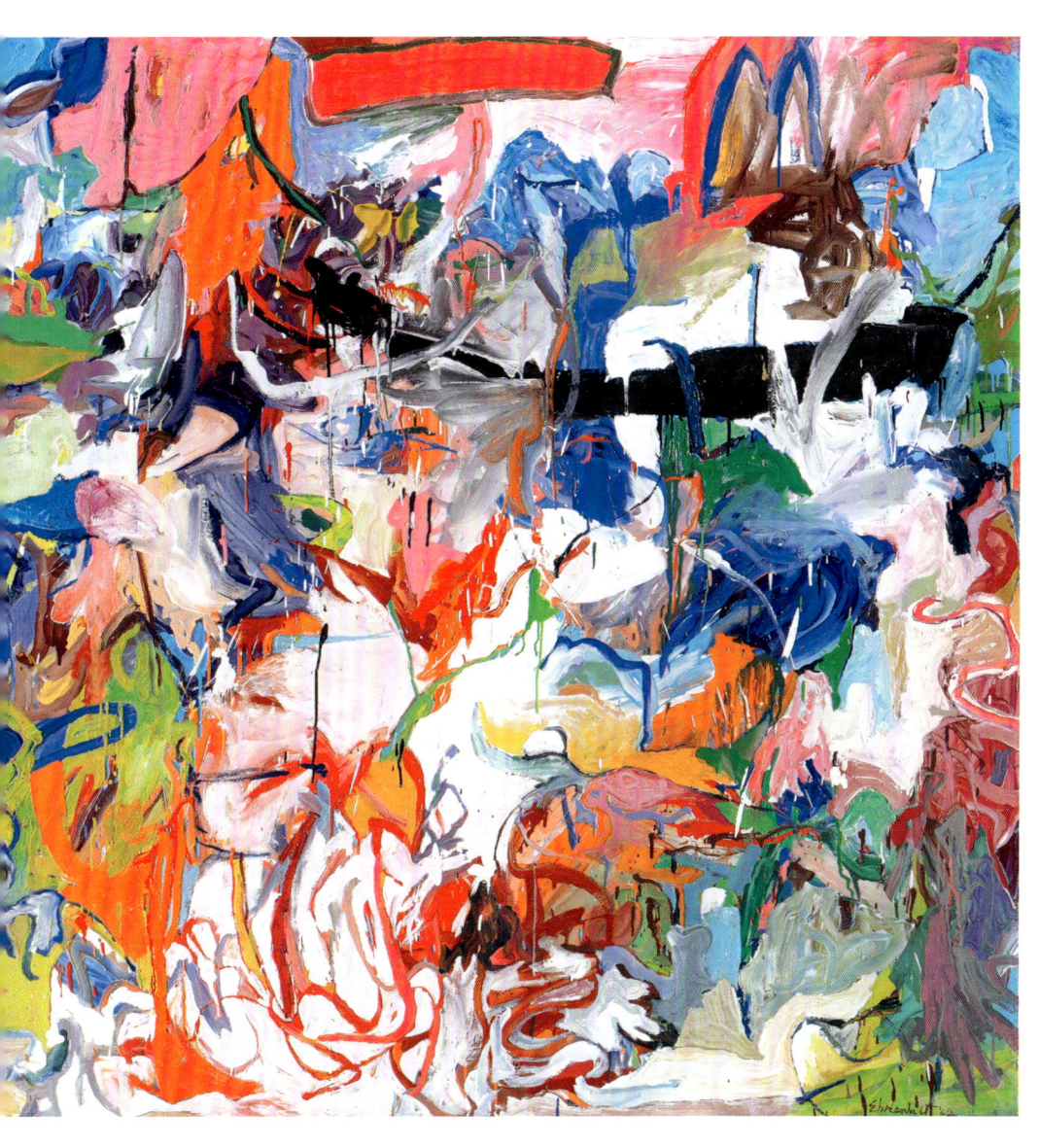

Aube Elléouët
(b. 1935)

It's obvious that I was fed on Surrealism from the very start. It was natural. It was my environment; I didn't know any other.[1]

Le Jugement de Salomon

1979
Collage on paper
17¾ × 13⅜ in.
(45.1 × 34 cm)

CL1329

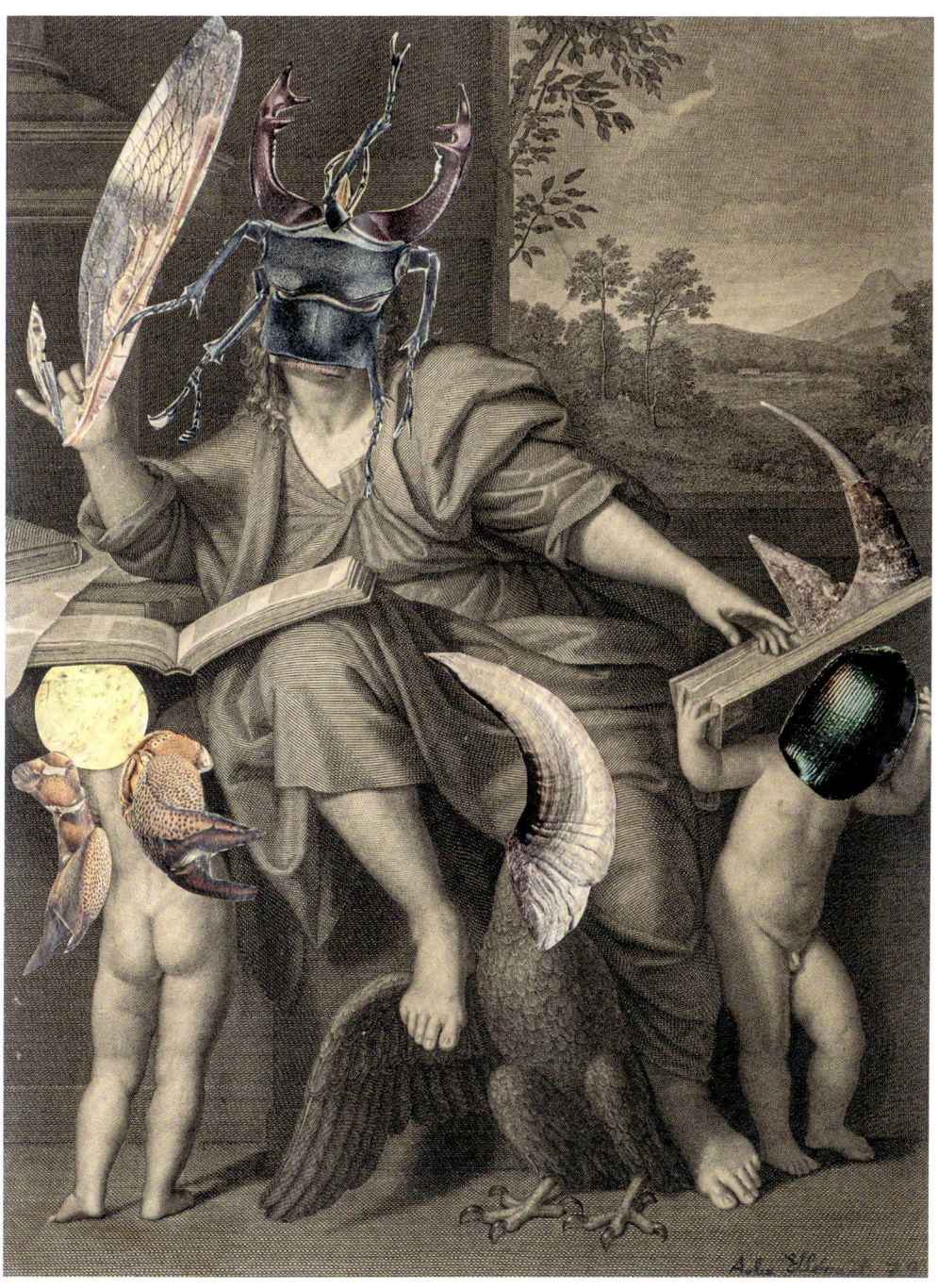

Dame Tracey Emin
(b. 1963)

Most people would have a nervous breakdown if they didn't have their phone for a day; I would have a total breakdown if there was no culture, no art. I couldn't live without art, it would be impossible. People don't even realise the value of art, they take it for granted.[1]

True art is very powerful; the greatest paintings have souls. They breathe and stare at us; we are looking through the artist's eyes.[2]

I am the custodian, the curator of the images that live in my mind. Every image has first entered my mind, travelled through my heart, my blood—arriving at the end of my hand. Everything has come through me.[3]

Hurricane
2007
Oil on canvas
72 × 72 in.
(182.9 × 182.9 cm)
CL220

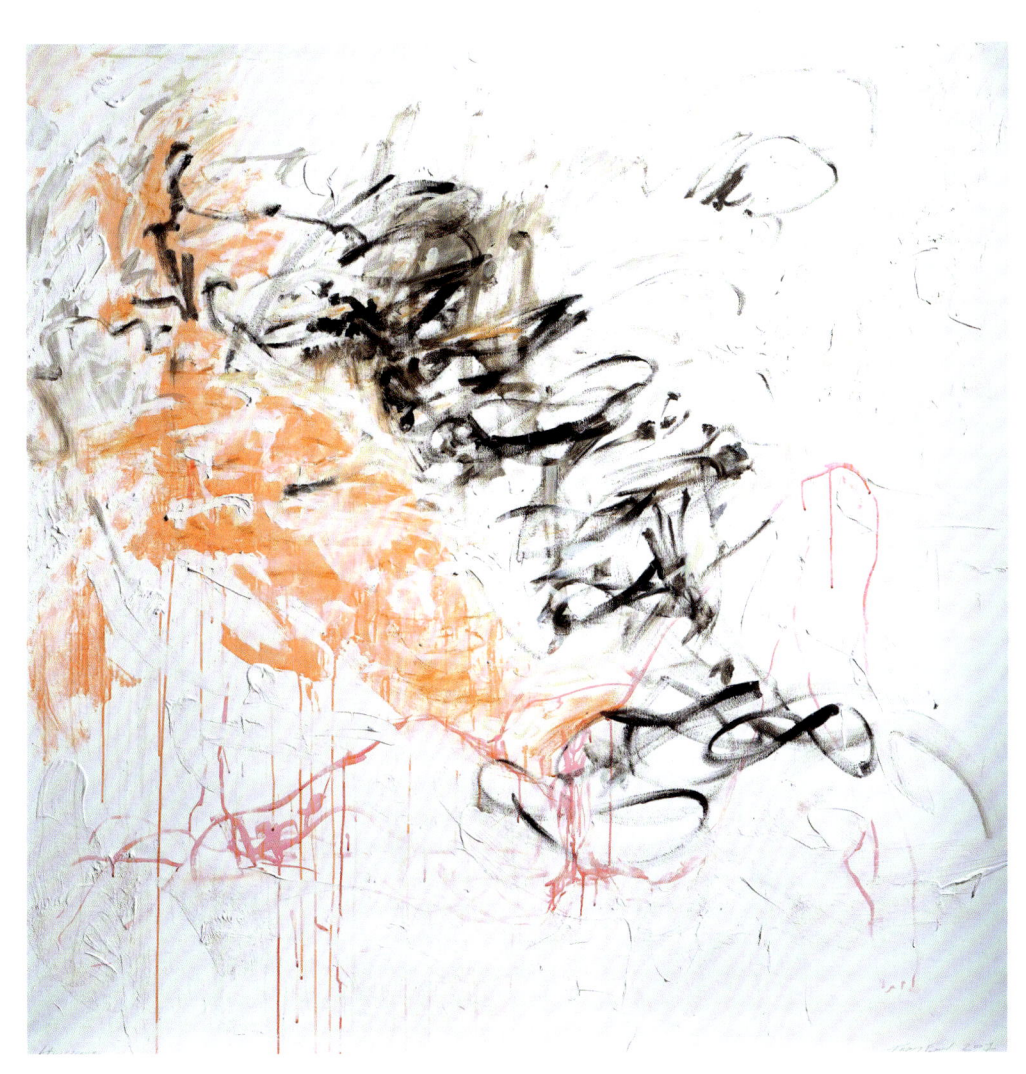

Jadé Fadojutimi
(b. 1993)

[My works] question the existence of feelings and reactions to daily experiences. They question our perceptions and perspectives whilst manifesting struggles. They recognise a lack of self caused by automatically thinking that my identity is already defined, and also a frustration that paint can accept these characteristics better than myself.[1]

I am leaning my eye upon different areas of the painting, and then I follow a line and meet something else. And before it I am enthralled by its world. It's what I've always wanted. Another place to exist.[2]

I was thinking about feelings, about soundtracks. Why does this anime that I watched three years ago still linger in my mind? Why can't I let go of things like that, and why is it so hard to move on? I was having all these questions about emotions that weren't therapeutic questions—they were very abstract … I wanted to feel these things through color, but I didn't know how to express them. That's where my paintings started coming from.[3]

Even an awkward smile can sprout beyond the sun
2021
Oil, oil bar, and acrylic on canvas
78¾ × 66⅞ in.
(200 × 169.9 cm)
CL1477

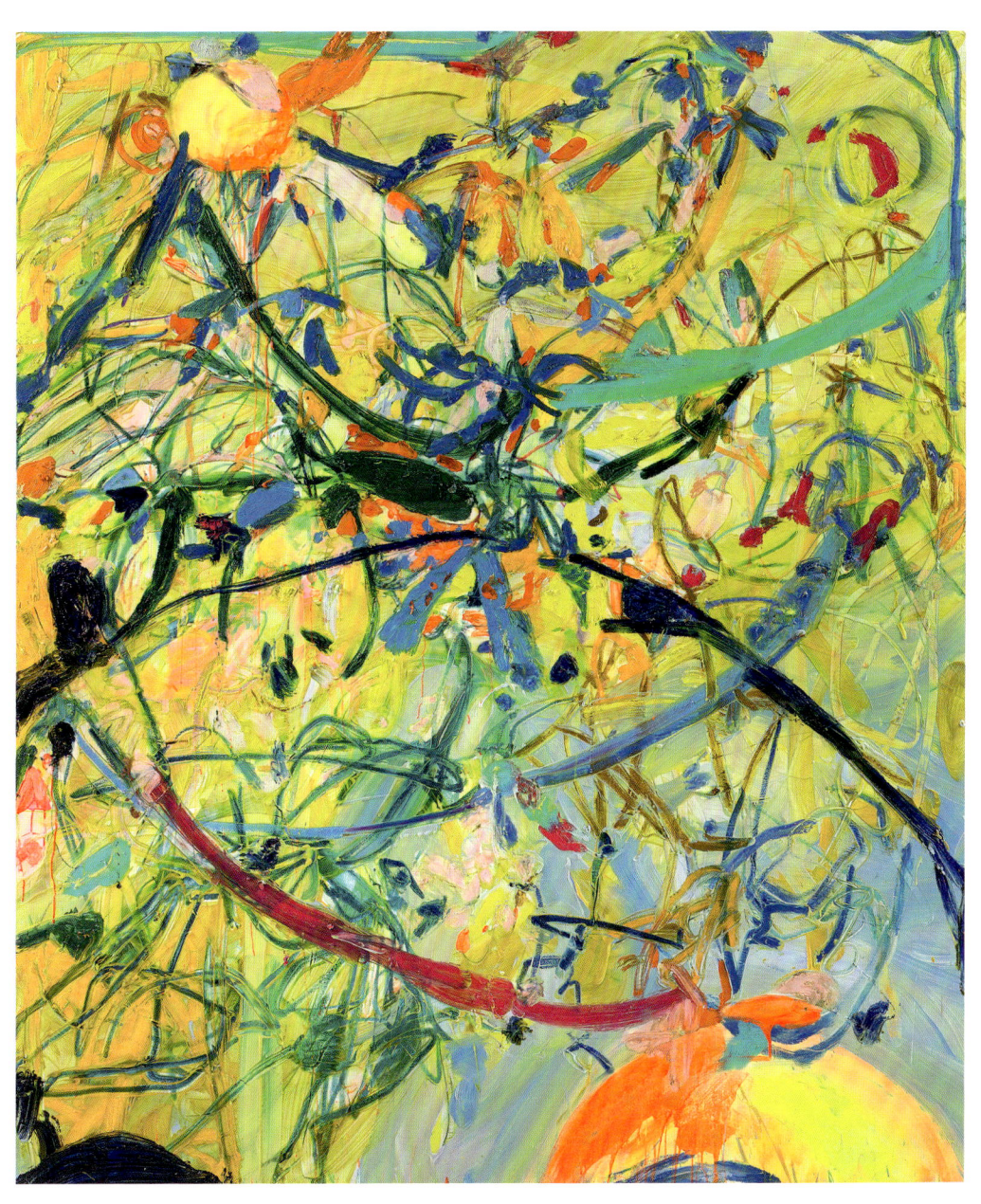

Claire Falkenstein
(1908–1997)

[My] vocabulary consisted of the never-ending screen, the sign and the ensemble, topological structure, lattice structure, and then the combination sometimes of any two or any three ... Topological structure is when the surface becomes the interior. It's the constant motion. But with the lattice, you can have visibility all the time. It isn't a solid ... With the lattice, the wonderful thing is, not only do you have the motion (the moving of the interior to the exterior; the exterior to the interior), but you also have the vision. It's transparent.[1]

An evidence of consciousness, sculpture is structured energy, wherein space-time-mass actualize an organization inherent in existence. An extension of life, sculpture both reveals and changes our perception of reality in the uniting of "duration" and "becoming."[2]

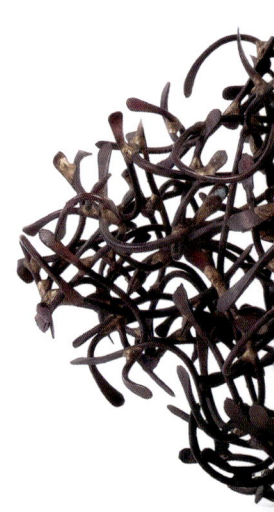

Sign of U (Small Sun)

c. 1959–62
Copper and bronze
10½ × 16¾ × 13½ in
(26.7 × 42.6 × 34.3 cm)

CL924

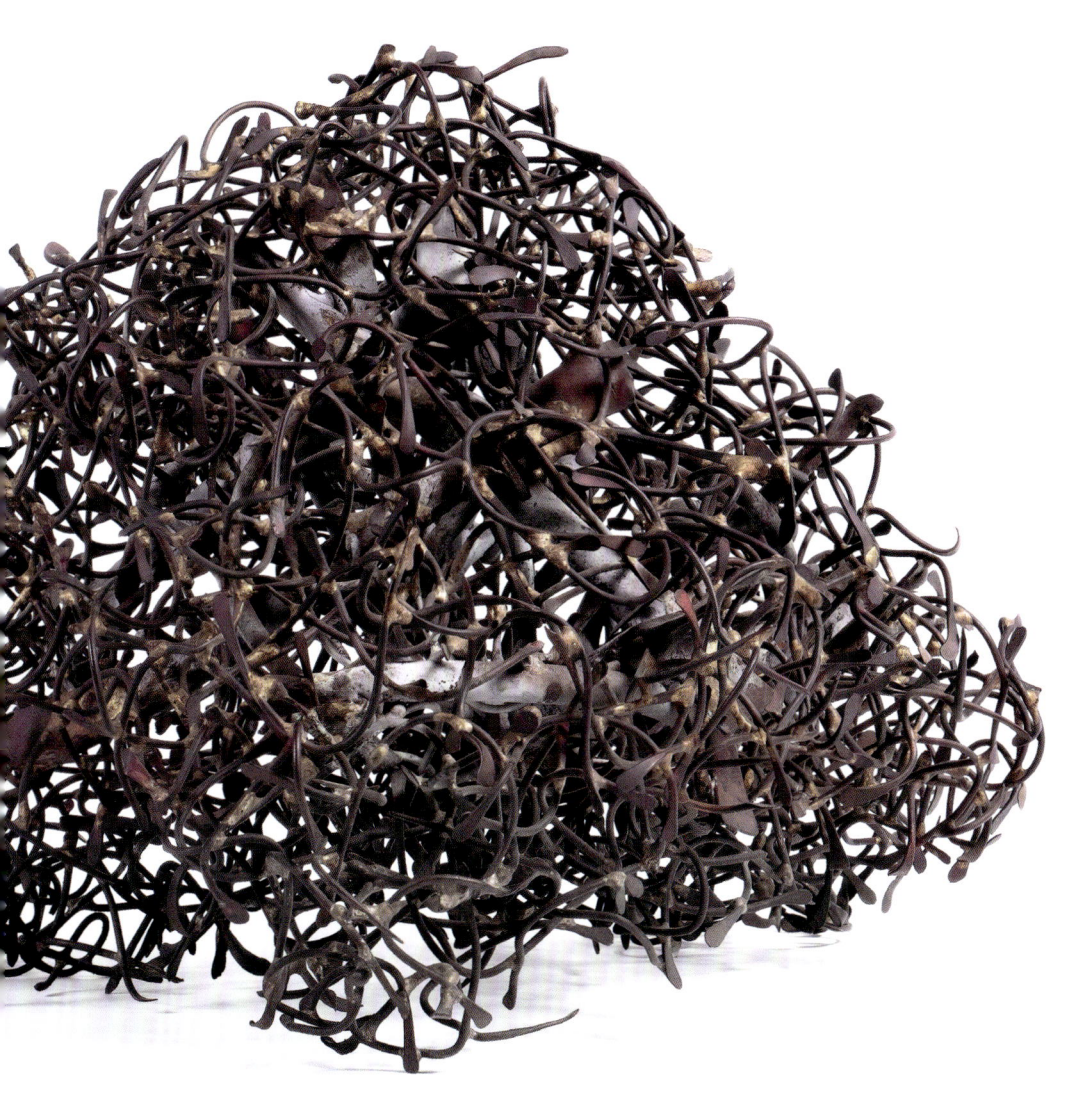

Perle Fine
(1905–1988)

My paintings ... deal not in definition but rather with the art of evocation and suggestion ... Calligraphy remains [in my paintings] to qualify the forms and render a purer, deeper emotion.[1]

The stamp of modern art is "clarity"; clarity of color, clarity of forms and of composition, clarity of determined dynamic rhythm in a determined space. Since figuration often veils, obscures or entirely negates purity of plastic expression, the destruction of the particular (familiar) form for the universal one becomes a prime prerequisite. It is as true in art as it is in life that the purest expression of truth is also the purest expression of vitality. Thus, the new reality, constant, palpable, born of truth, free of oppressive particularities, reveals itself clearly in the continuous and reciprocal play of intrinsic forces in a good modern work of art.[2]

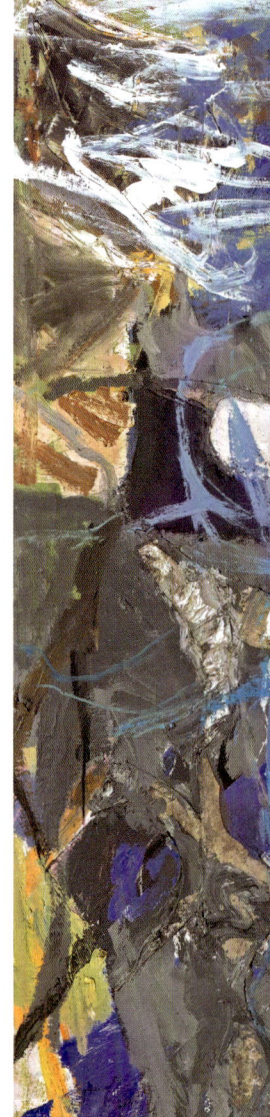

Summer I
1958–59
Oil and collage on canvas
57 × 70 in.
(144.8 × 177.8 cm)
CL881

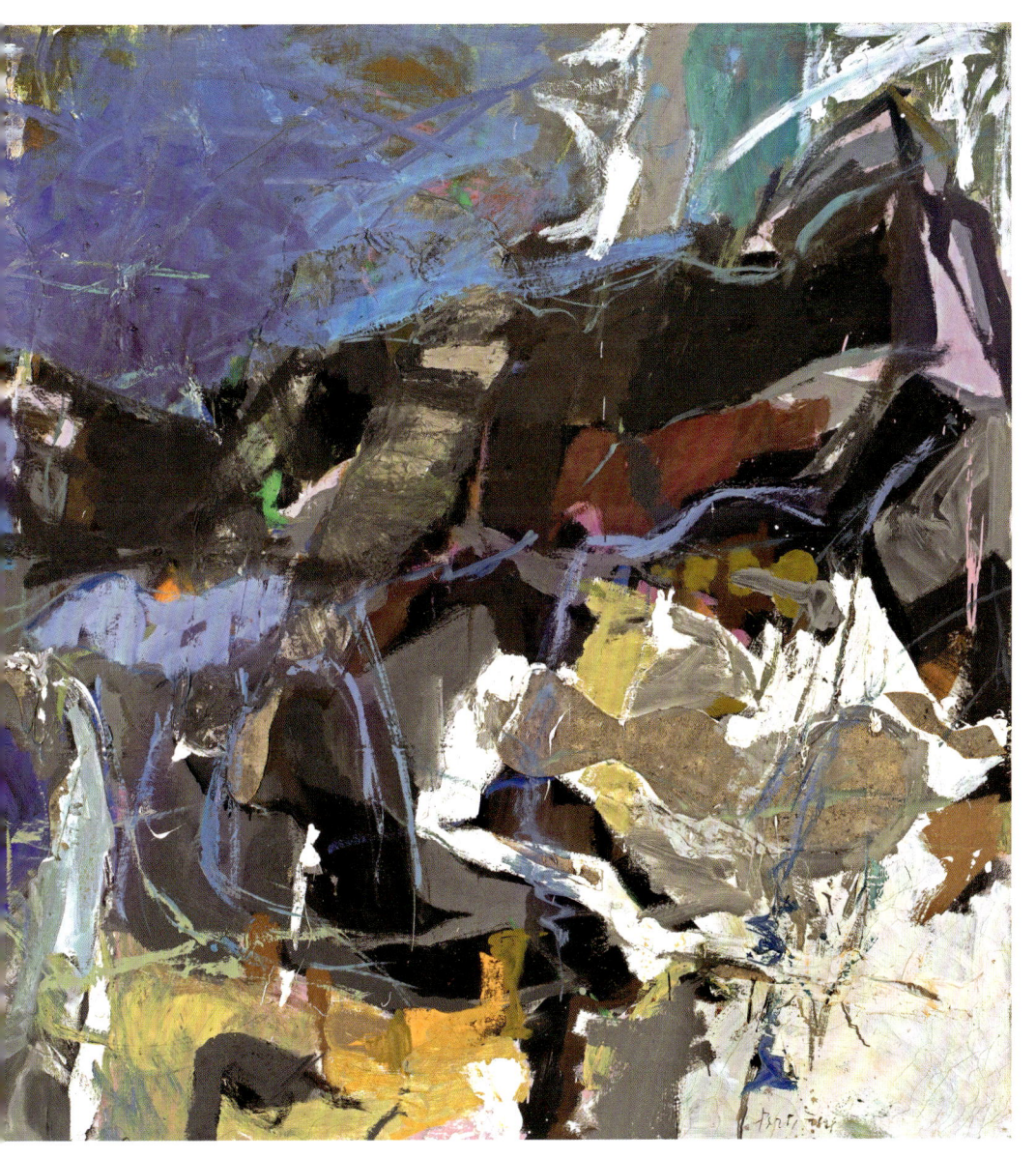

Leonor Fini
(1907–1996)

What are the subjects of my paintings about? Sometimes they spring from a splotch of paint, two splotches, a triangle drawn in a second. I always know, and sometimes this is all I know, that when I begin painting it will be driven by a geometrical form—a triangle, a diamond, a rectangle, a rhombus shape. Human shapes don't begin to appear right away. These figures, which rise up out of the paint, have lives of their own (obviously a part of my life, the part that motivates my dreams, because painting—all art in fact—does not spring just from dreams as some would claim, but follows a lucid, clear path) that often run in parallel to my own. It's like the same sentence but with different words and letters.[1]

I have always been inclined to be motivated by my passions and that is, I think, probably the only "key" to my work. Painting flows directly from my passions because I never attended art school and never took "painting lessons." I just did it.[2]

At twelve or thirteen I was fascinated with the dead. I'd sneak off to the morgue in the main hospital in Trieste. It was divided into two sections: one was used for private and public display of bodies, sumptuously laid out, elegantly dressed, with jewels and covered with flowers.[3]

A painting is something like a spectacle, a theater piece in which each figure lives out her part.[4]

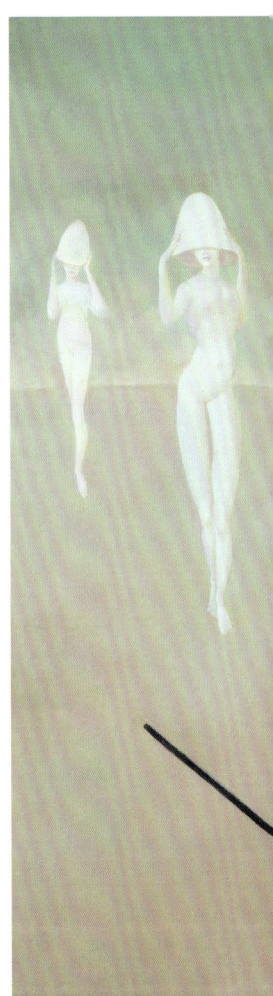

Les Étrangères
1968
Oil on canvas
31⅞ × 43¼ in.
(81 × 109.9 cm)
CL1226

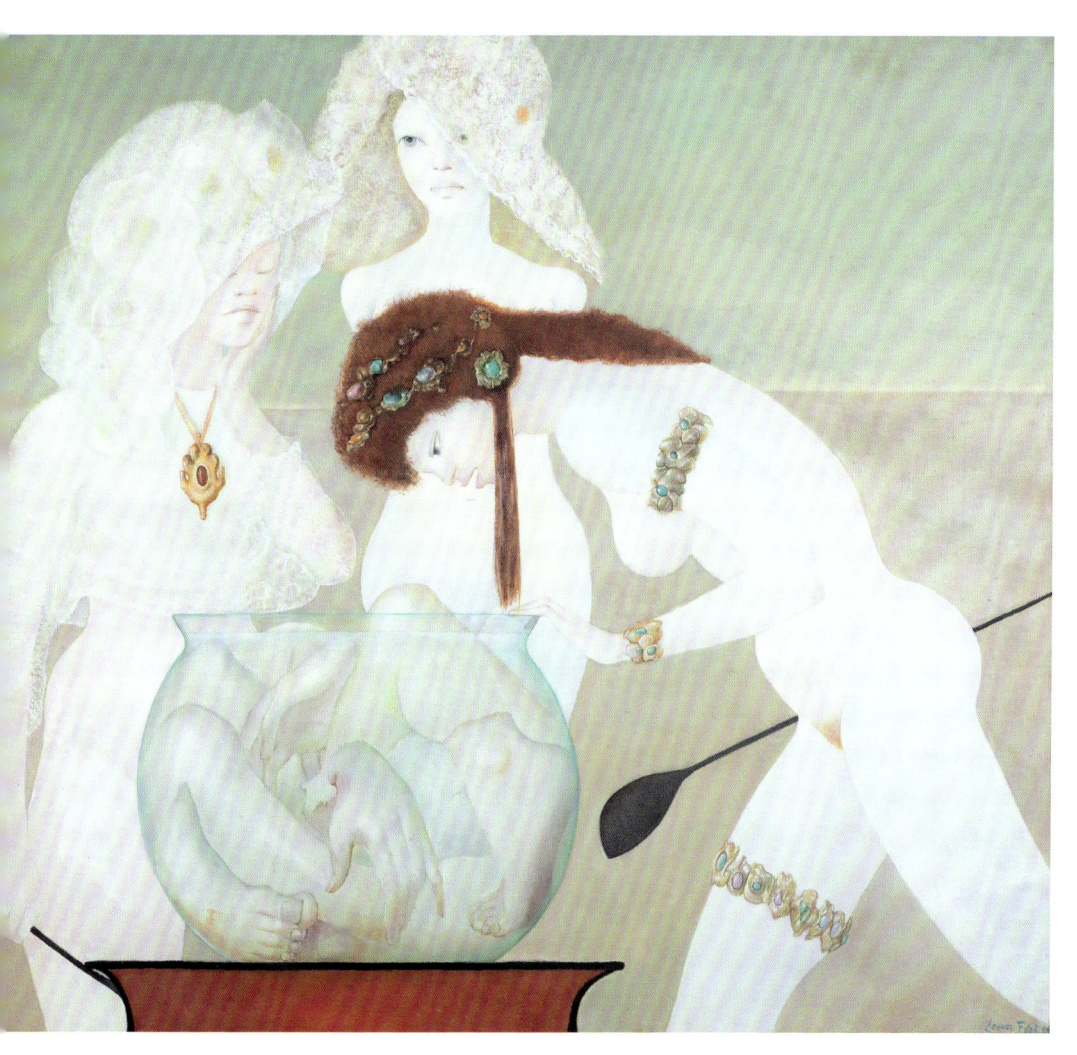

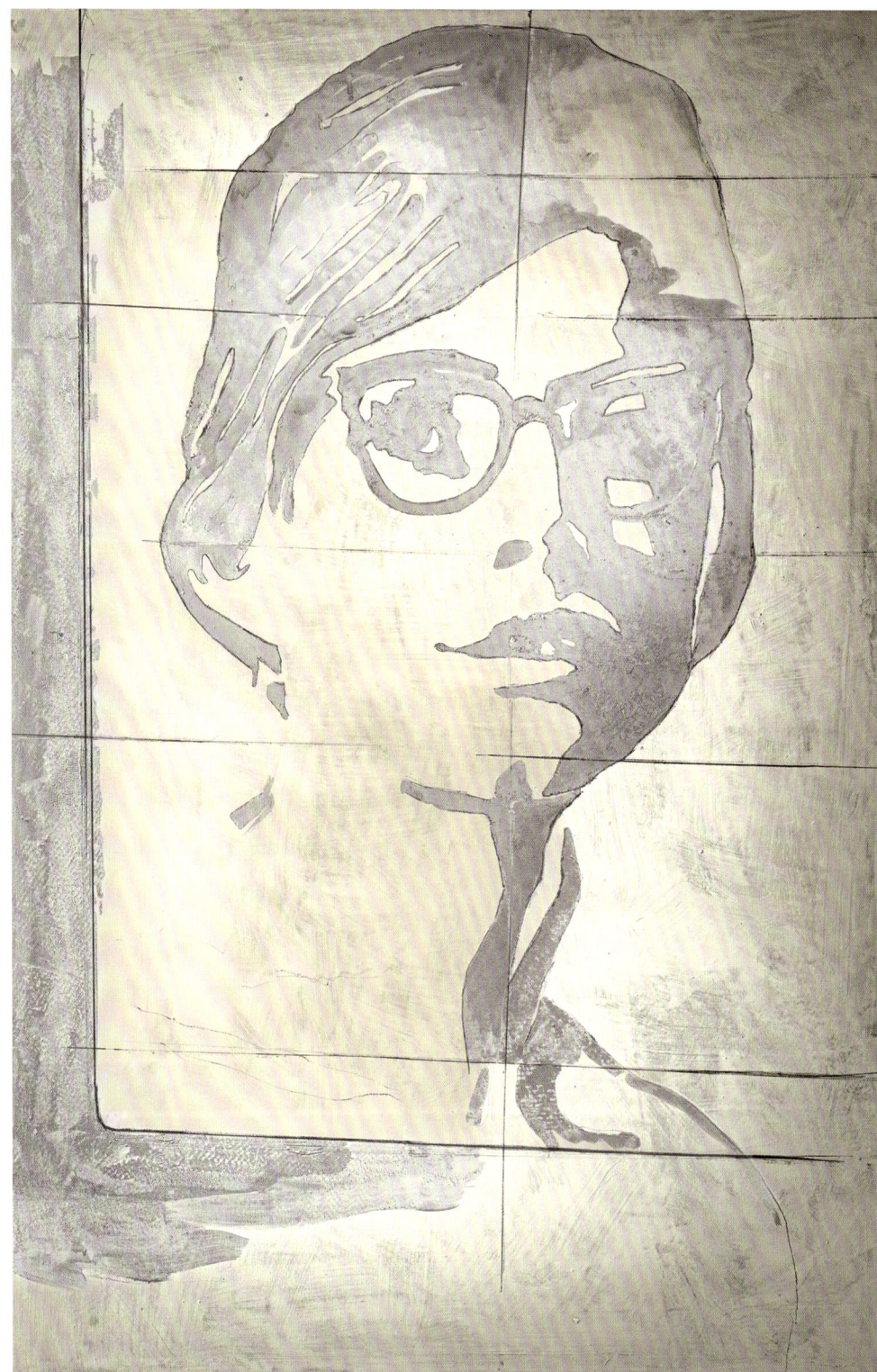

Giosetta Fioroni
(b. 1932)

Many images came from fashion photography; others were simply photos of girls or women of different ages. In any case, in those years of "feminism" I was always more interested in the feminine, in the feelings these women expressed with their eyes, with the movement of a hand, with their body language.[1]

In the 1960s, I was part of a group that had two labels: the "school of Piazza del Popolo" ... And "Roman pop." I accept the first definition, but all these years later, I've come to realise that there was almost nothing in common with American Pop. I think the respective cultures, in the background, [were] far too apart and different. In Rome, in those years, I was struck by the geometrical metaphysical works of Tano Festa. Styli shutters, doors, "geometric spaces" with a bright red colour ... All contained within heavy black raised frames. Large frames with mirrors, where the mirror part was visibly raised by silver varnish. And the obelisks, wooden bas-reliefs, essentially painted white with quick and thick strokes. In other words, a special, very personal interpretation of a new metaphysical art ... Not the "eternal" one of De Chirico.[2]

Gli occhiali (The Glasses)
1968
Pencil, enamel, and aluminum on canvas
51⅛ × 33½ in.
(129.9 × 85.1 cm)
CL1042

Helen Frankenthaler
(1928–2011)

Well … I became, not a connoisseur, but I really learned how to look at [the Old Masters] before 1960. And in a sense that sharpened my eye for abstract pictures. Because it's light in the painting that makes it work … You see the sketches for the Rubens Medici series in the Louvre … it's another world and they are divine.[1]

One quality I try to achieve in a picture is an immediate, allover look … rather than … a labored, made, applied look … I prefer something that looks as if it was born all at once. As if it happened.[2]

For me, as a picture develops, color always comes out of drawing … it's born out of idea, mood, luck, imagination, risk, into what might even be ugly; then I let it tell me what might/should be used next.[3]

After Rubens
1961
Oil and charcoal on unsized, unprimed canvas
93 × 73½ in.
(236.2 × 186.7 cm)
CL1028

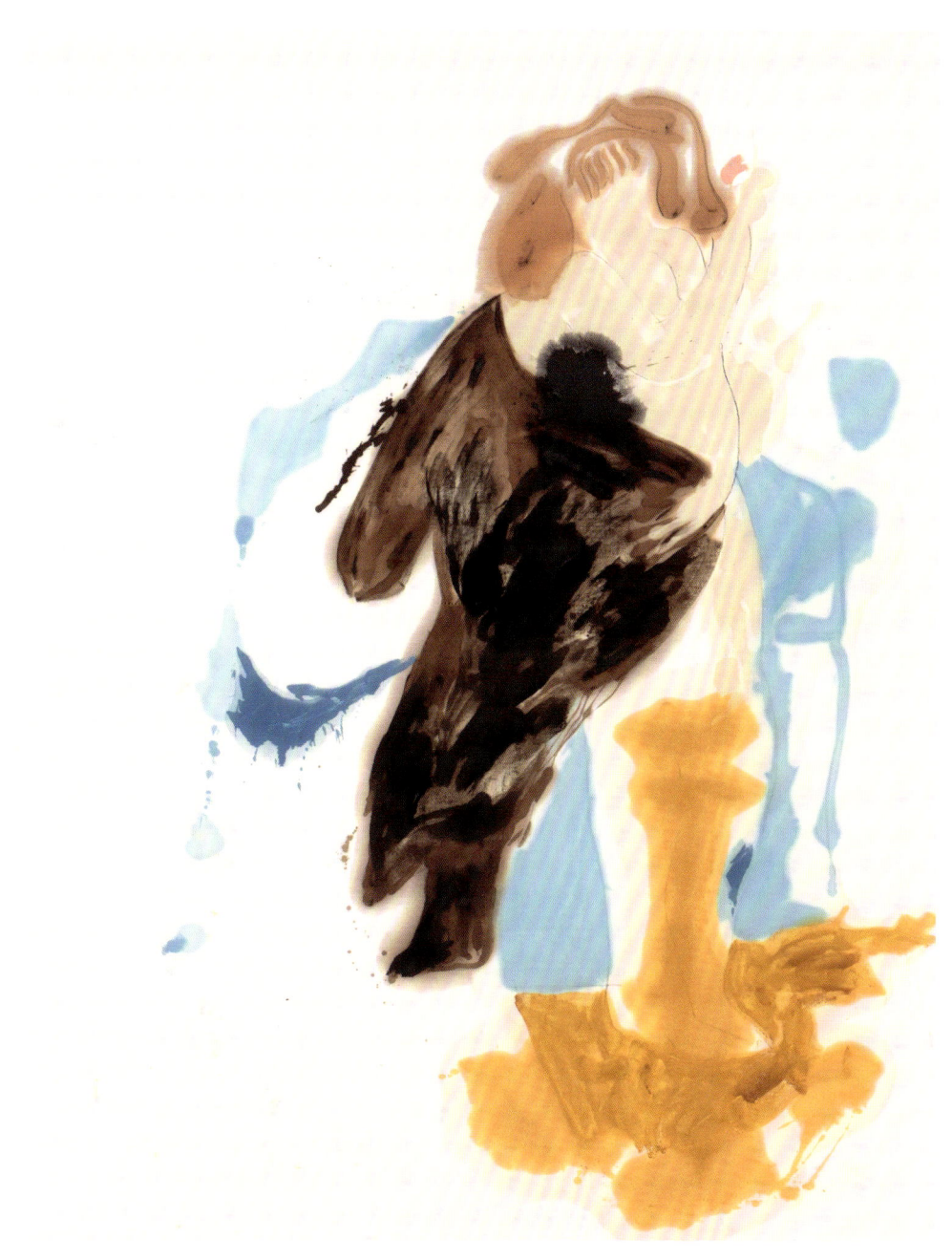

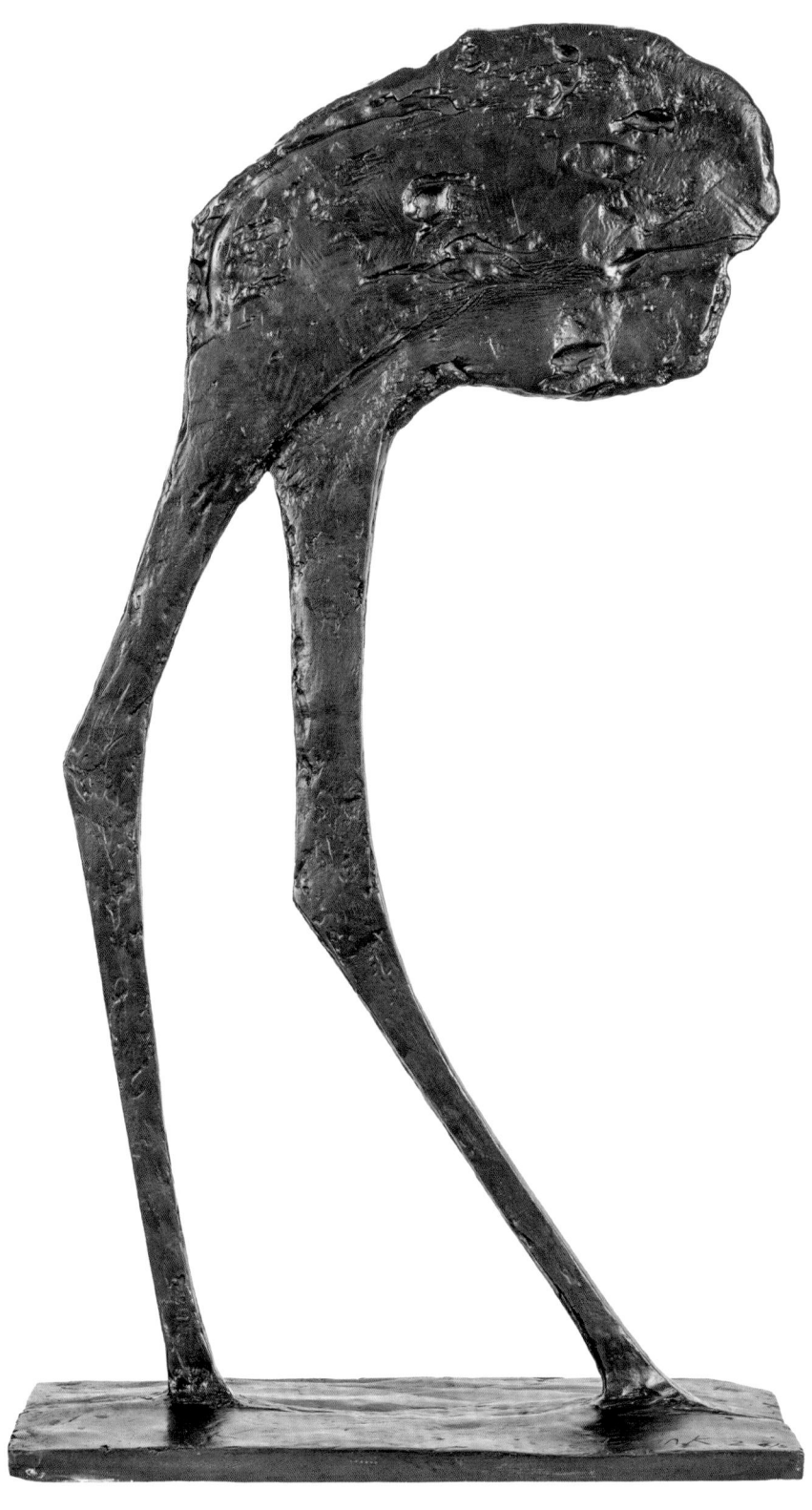

Dame Elisabeth Frink
(1930–1993)

[In the Camargue, southern France] you get these
extraordinary heat hazes and you see these creatures which
seem to be sort of birds, or it could be a person, or a tree.
Any of those make this extraordinary stalking shape that
shimmers across. That's what gave me the original idea. Just
sitting there, watching them. And it's fascinating to see what
will emerge. You'd just look up and sometimes it was a man
on a horse, or it was a bird, one of those long egrets. Or one
of those umbrella pines, distorted. It seemed to have legs.[1]

Mirage II

1967
Bronze with a dark-
brown patina
Height 36 in. (91.4 cm)
No. 4 from an edition
of 5
CL1025

Claire Gavronsky
(b. 1957)

The embrace, a suspended, sustained empathy, either in greeting or bidding farewell, *Present Continuous* could be a perpetual circumstance which talks about the intimacy, love and support between women, in times of both strife and peace. The way that women interact, and their alternative proposals in any circumstance, whether a relationship or a world view. An implicit, tender, immediate recognition between individuals that doesn't rely on words. Painting itself offers an apposite correlation in its ability to speak outside of language, to make meanings that resist narratives, that can be felt and understood viscerally. Through the interplay of fine, detailed drawing, loose merging washes, and subtle color shifts, the figures both dissolve and emerge.[1]

Present Continuous
2023–24
Acrylic on cotton
70⅞ × 59 in.
(180 × 149.9 cm)

CL1379

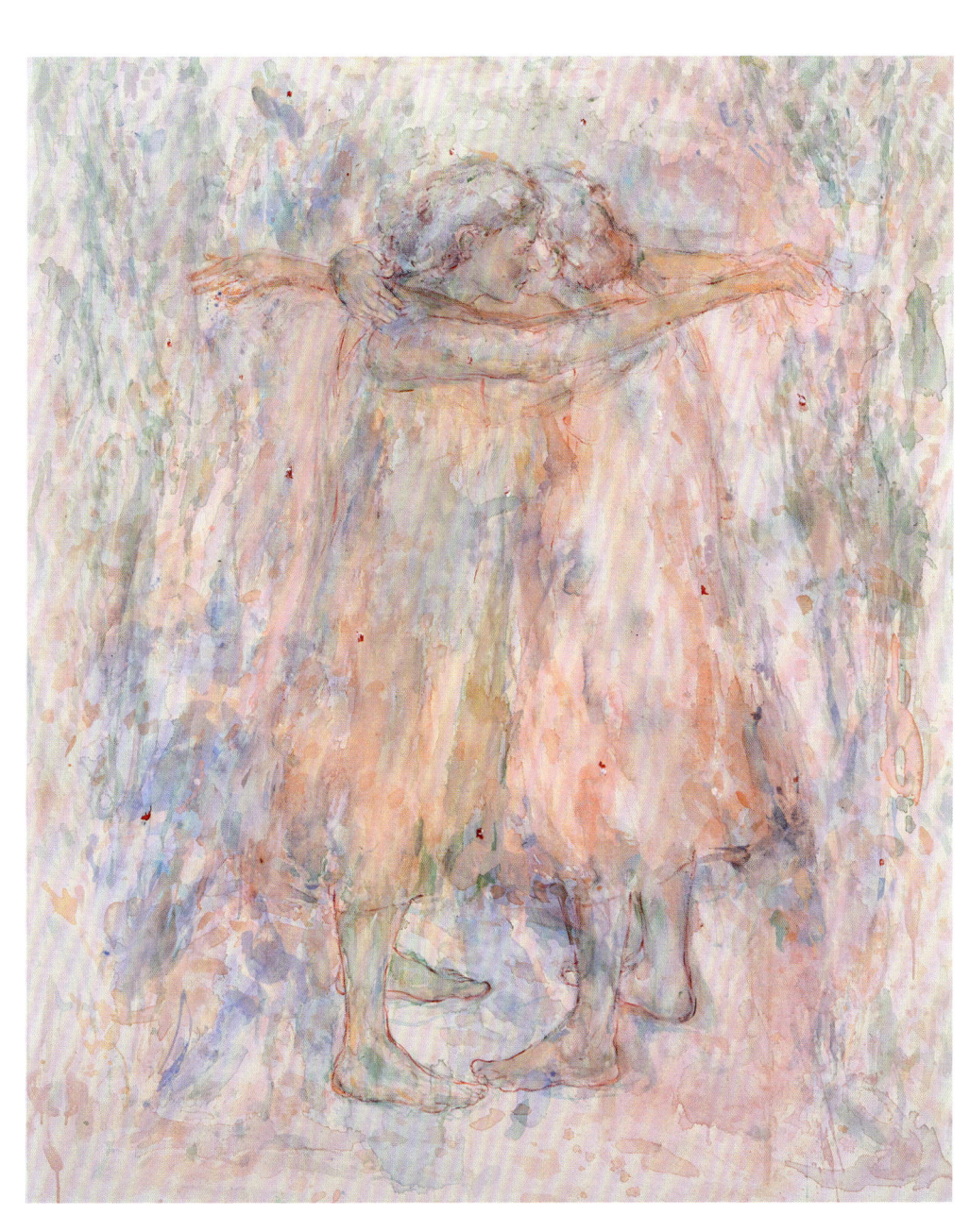

Sonia Gechtoff
(1926–2018)

Ernie Briggs ... talked constantly about [Clyfford] Still's ideas. It all sounded so unique and dramatic and fantastic to me, this whole idea of painting for its own sake and ... the idea of searching for an image went out the window.[1]

Women have complained about the whole macho hang up that New York guys had for years, and for good reason. If it was in San Francisco, I didn't feel it ... they treated us as equals ... they weren't thinking of me as a woman painter, but as another painter.[2]

The Queen
1958
Oil on canvas
84 × 66 in.
(213.4 × 167.6 cm)
CL822

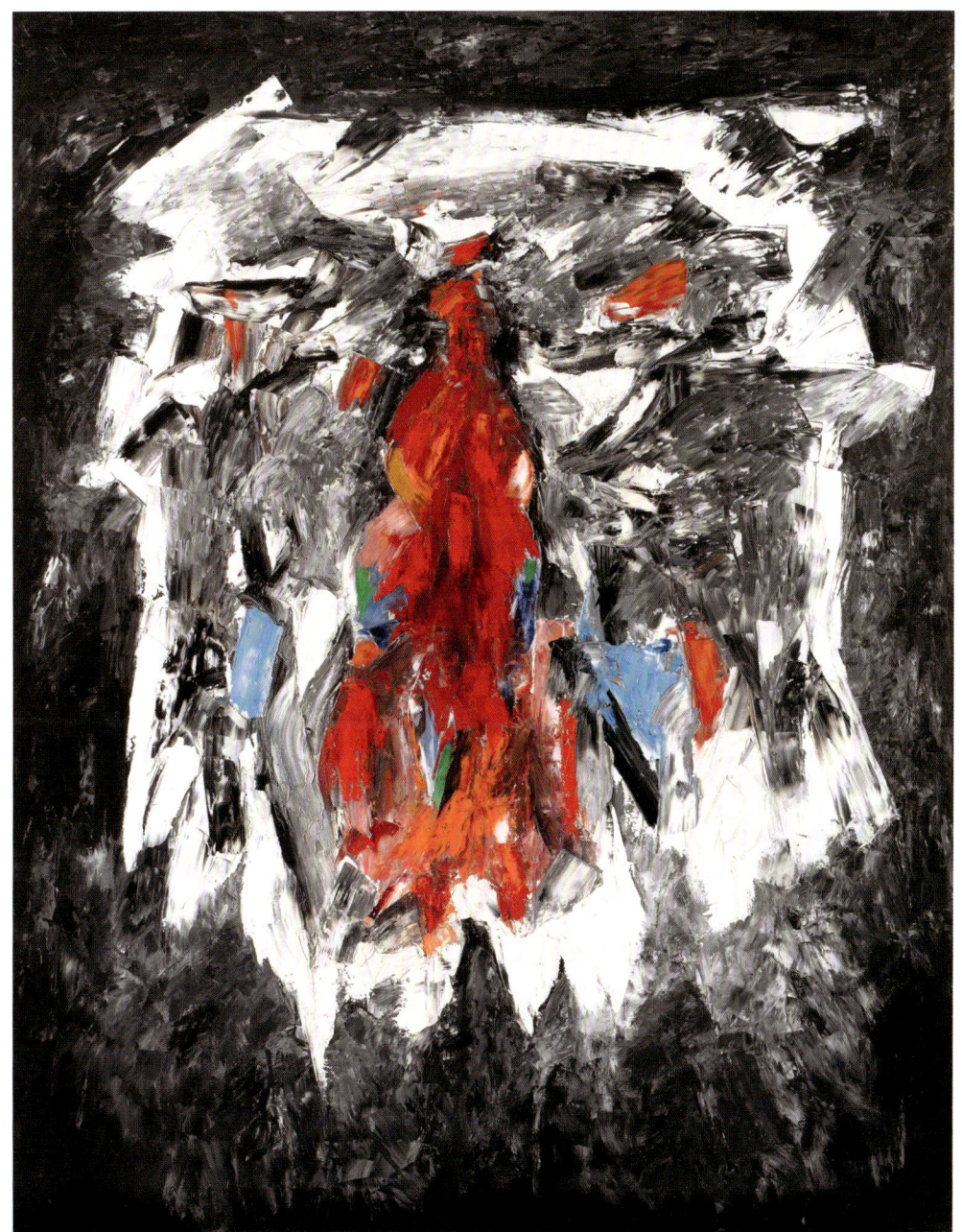

Françoise Gilot
(1921–2023)

I express myself through my paintings, and even then they are still mysterious. When I paint, all my feelings are in there, but not everyone can decipher them.[1]

Since childhood I have searched for ways to seduce painting, to ensnare painting. My eye has measured and compared; at times my gaze was fearful, at others bold. What was not solved consciously was often resolved in sleep through dreams. I had to be brave before the Gorgon-faced painting of others, to decipher riddles, to rework experiences, to study approaches, to play the game, to take on roles and even to follow them along the thread of time in keeping with my own development, or to reject them and venture defenceless into the unknown. The gaze scans future and past, past and future, back and forth, *gradually becoming what it creates*.[2]

I paint with my whole body, with every cell in my body. I can't explain it in any other way. It really is a physical experience, and you need a certain innocence to do it, like a child.[3]

Joueuse de mandoline
c. 1953
Oil on panel
63¾ × 51⅛ in.
(161.9 × 129.9 cm)

CL1412

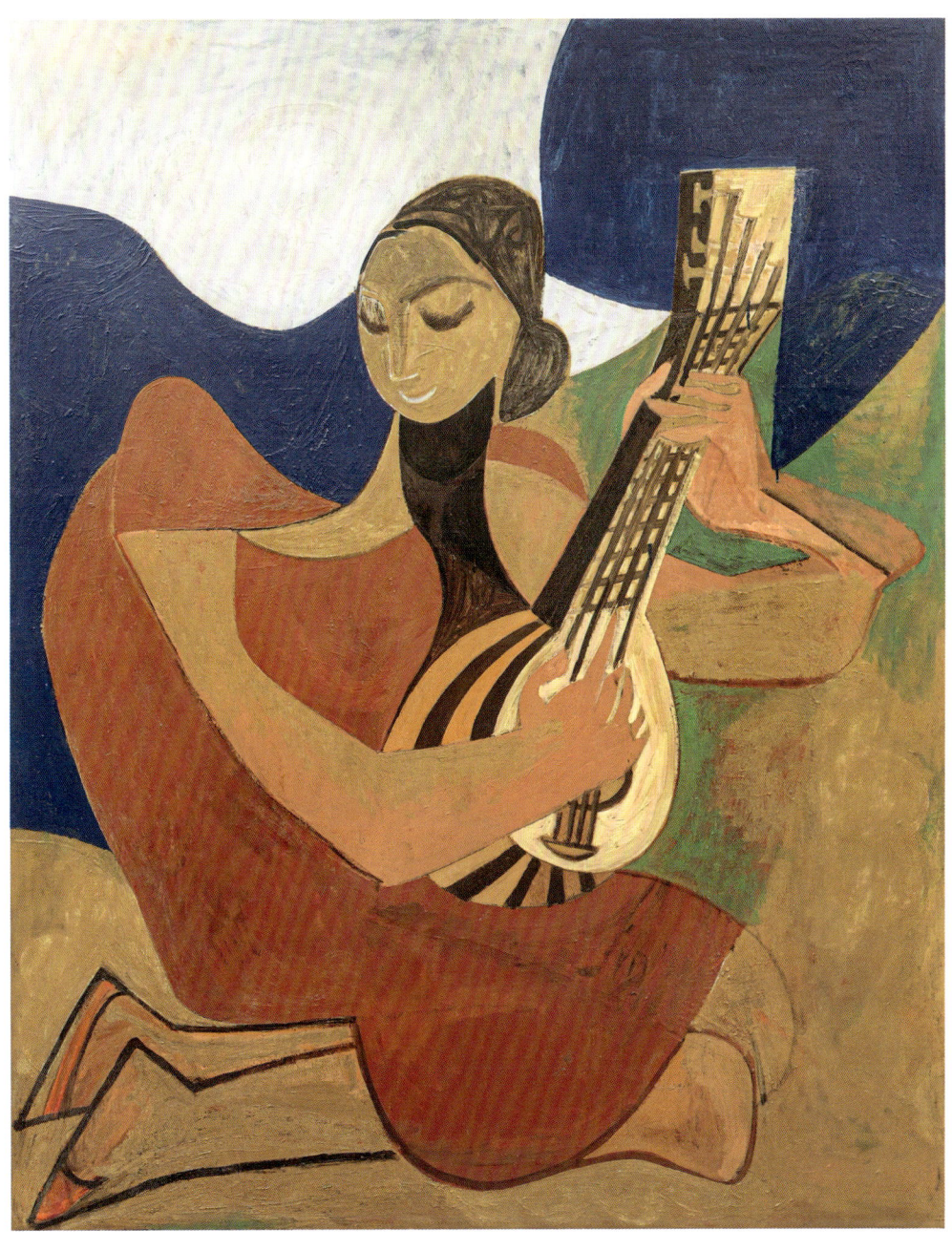

Nan Goldin
(b. 1953)

For me it is not a detachment to take a picture. It's a way
of touching somebody—it's a caress. I'm looking with a
warm eye, not a cold eye. I'm not analyzing what's going
on—I just get inspired to take a picture by the beauty and
vulnerability of my friends.[1]

My work has always come from empathy and love ...
I photograph out of love and out of wanting to touch
someone in a way, in some way. So I only photograph
people who touch me.[2]

I want to show people that I love how beautiful they are,
and I actually have succeeded in doing that sometimes.
People have said that they didn't know they were beautiful
until I photographed them and showed them themselves.[3]

I was given a hard time by male photographers for years,
both for my lack of technical ability and my subject
matter.[4]

Käthe in the Tub
1984
Cibachrome print
29⅞ × 39¾ in.
(75.9 × 101 cm)
No. 7 from an edition
of 25
CL1041

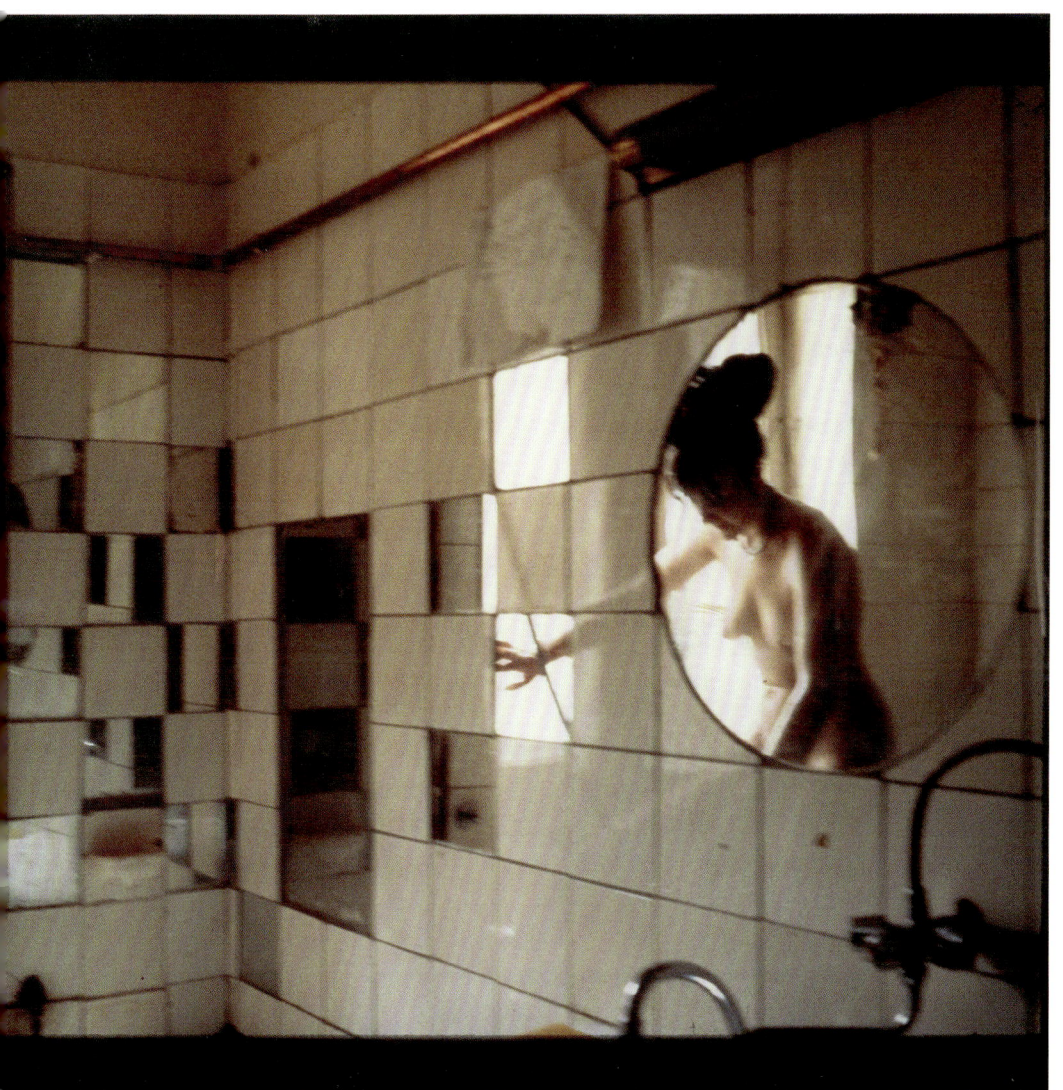

Catherine Goodman
(b. 1961)

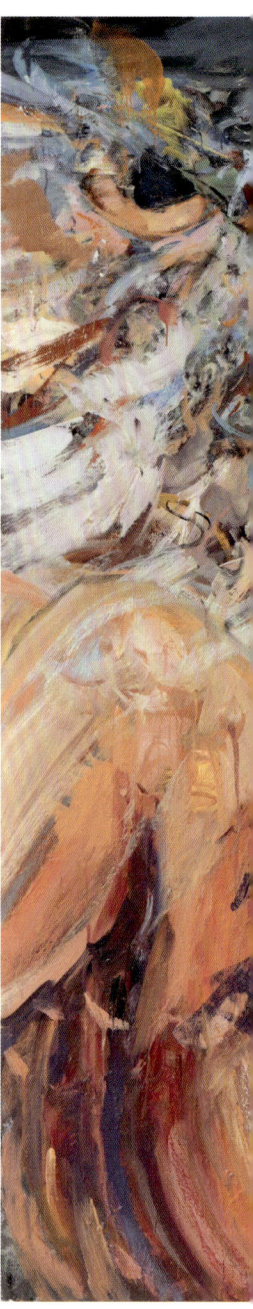

Isley is a result of both outward observation and deep introspection. This painting was developed from drawings that I created of the American-born, London-based playwright and poet Isley Lynn. For me, the daily practice of drawing serves as an important tool of expression that unifies thinking and feeling, and connects me to my subject. Painted several years after my initial sketches, *Isley* bears an imprint of my own memory, permeated through spontaneous expressive gestures and dynamic colour combinations that have long been a signature of my visual language …

While drawing and painting, I am always fascinated by the tiny shifts in feeling that happen when you're looking at light falling on the subject, how memories can be triggered by changes in light, colour or smell, and how this is then integrated into the experience of painting and communicated beyond that. Painting is always an escape, but it's also a way of inhabiting the presence more deeply. Mostly it's a way of processing and holding many different experiences together in one image.

The woman in this painting is Isley Lynn, now an award-winning playwright, but then a friend who was life-modelling to support their practice. Isley was born on the East Coast of the USA before coming to London and staying here. The painting is based on drawings I did in my studio. I remember Isley talking about childhood in the States while we listened to the entirety of John Steinbeck's *The Grapes of Wrath*, which was set during the Great Depression in the USA. Isley's memories of childhood, the atmosphere of the Great Depression and Steinbeck's compassionate writing and humour all seemed to work their way into the final image.[1]

Isley
2023
Oil on linen
80¼ × 84 in.
(203.8 × 213.4 cm)
CL1317

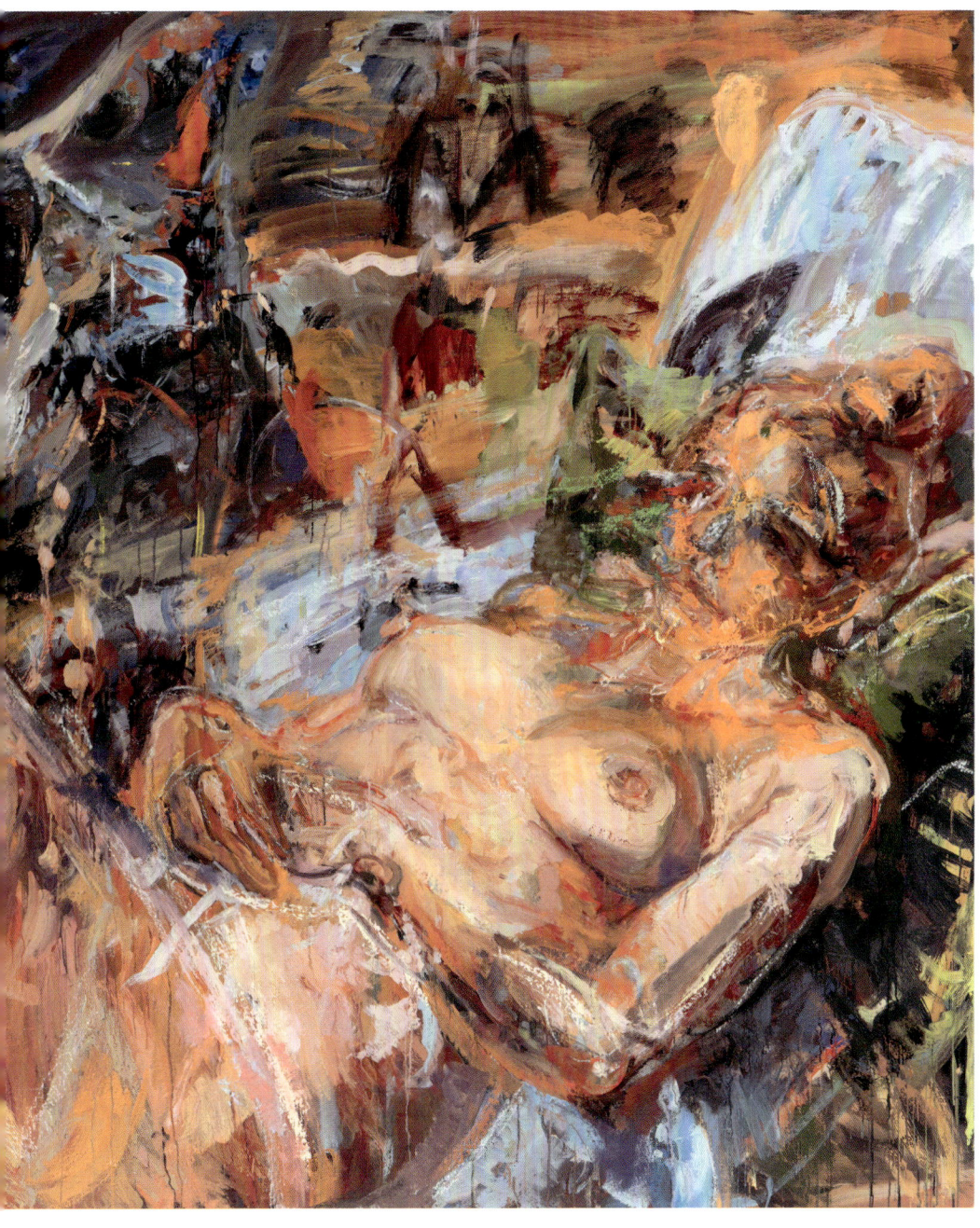

Jane Graverol
(1905–1984)

[I have] always led a double existence, a dream deeply intertwined with what we call everyday reality.[1]

To be a Surrealist is a state that one carries within oneself or not.[2]

To talk about my painting is to talk about my skin.[3]

I'm not a butcher, nor a postman, nor a naive painter, nor a profitable schizophrenic; I simply need to create something that allows me to escape above the crowd and to think that the world could have been different from what it is.[4]

Untitled

1959
Oil on canvas
27½ × 19¾ in.
(69.9 × 50.2 cm)

CL1328

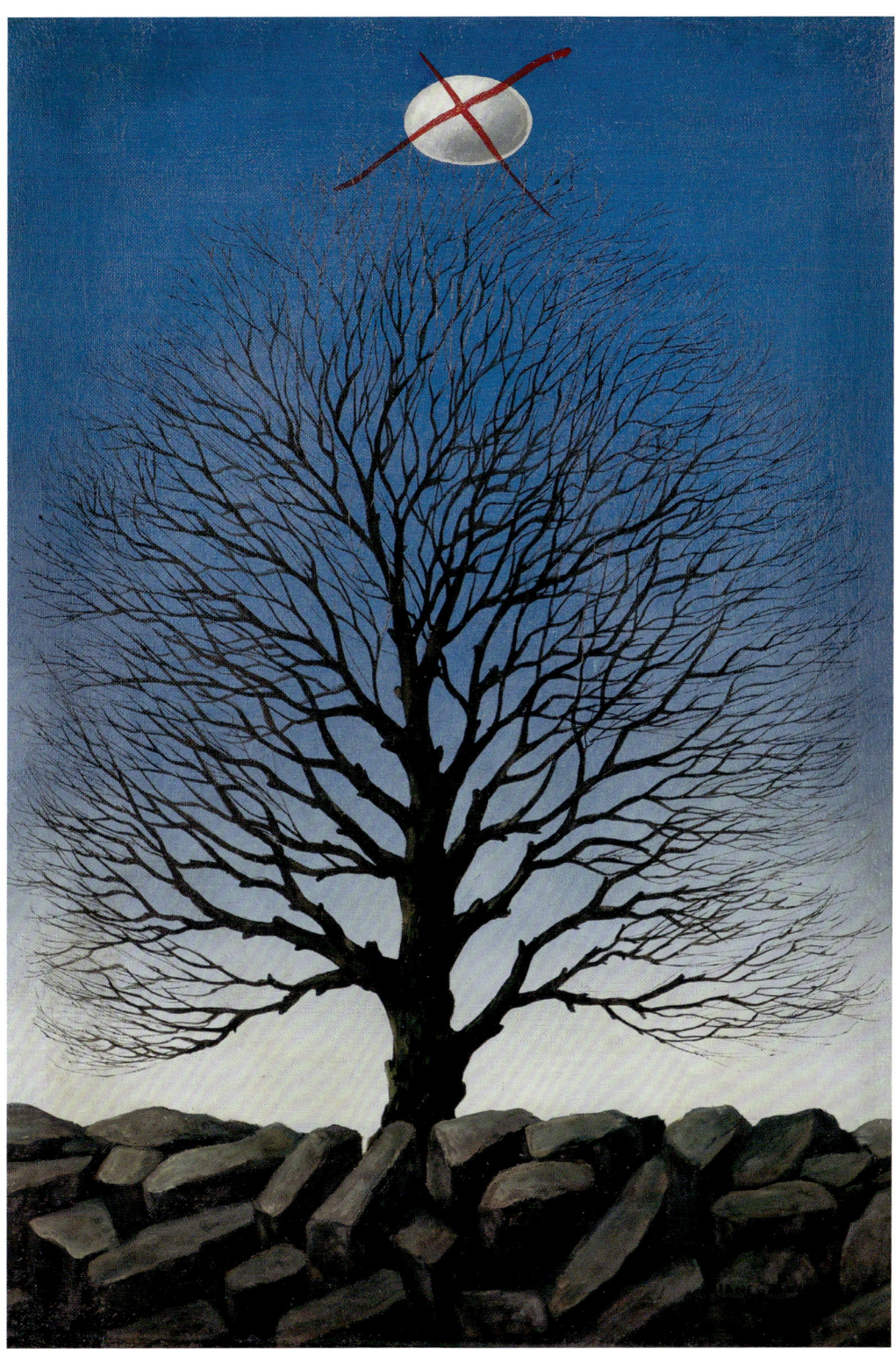

Jenna Gribbon
(b. 1978)

This is a painting of my wife, Mackenzie, and my dog Sylvia, in what appears to be a stage setting, though Mackenzie's state of undress is unconventional for a live theatrical performance. The spotlight and velvet curtains are meant to highlight the role of the subject as performer. My work is often concerned with the triangulation of the dynamics of engagement between the subject, the viewer and the artist. In *The Magician's Assistant*, we're left to wonder, who is the magician? Who is the assistant?[1]

The Magician's Assistant

2023
Oil on linen
93 × 71 in.
(236.2 × 180.3 cm)

CL1336

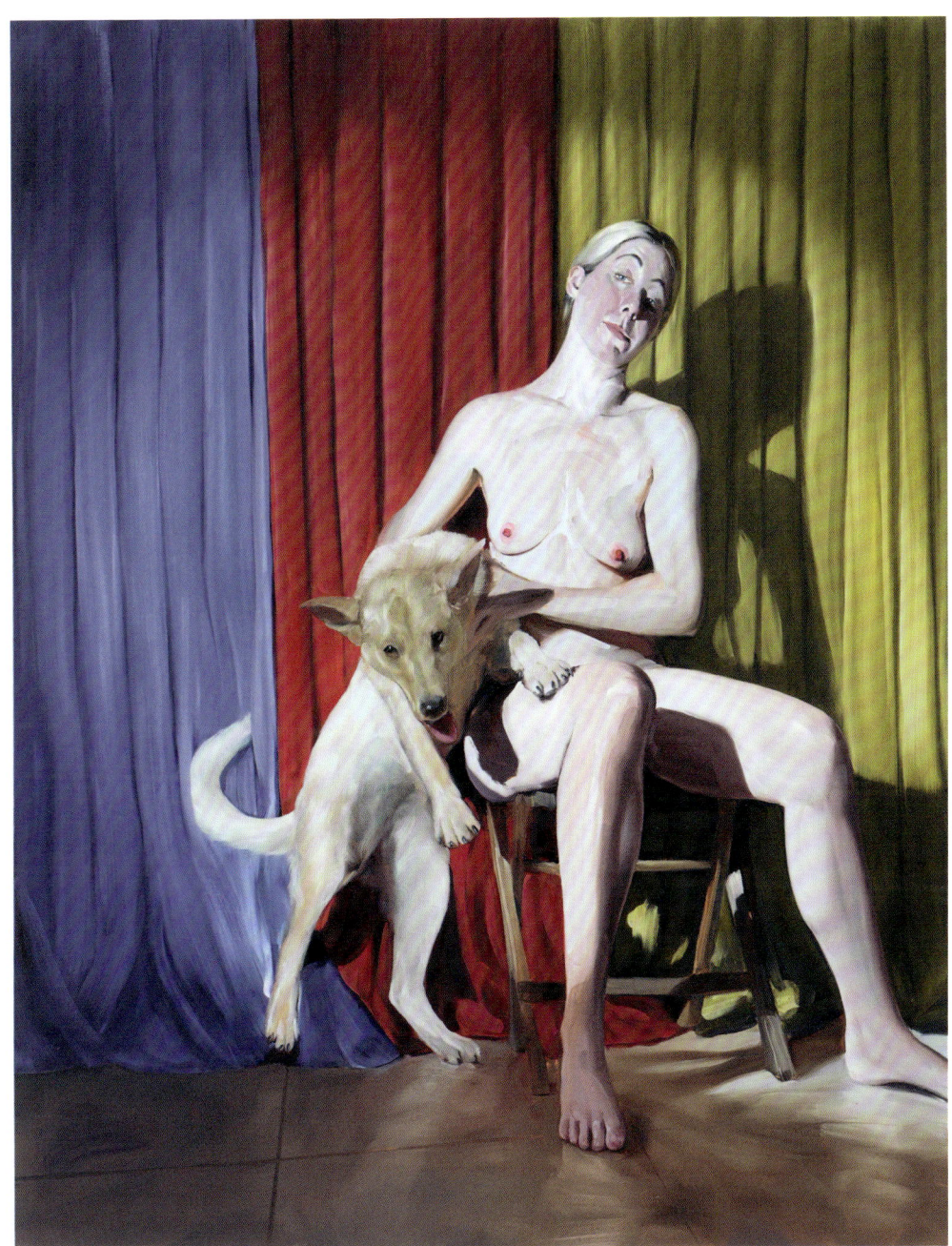

Wenhui Hao
(b. 2000)

She curls into a fetal position within the fissures of light.
The pond is not water, but a glazed scab crusted over
    festering wounds.
Gloss is the veneer of violence.

Wildflowers and weeds are microscopic instruments of
    torture:
Dandelion fluff becomes silver needles inverted into the
    hollow of her waist,
nettles branding honeycombed scars on her scapulae.
Ivy vines entwining her ribs tame breath into tides of
    submission.

She is hidden within a vegetal gallows, veiled by the guise
    of tender care.
Each petal enacts microscopic colonization—the more
    vibrant the blooms,
the closer they approach ornamental homicide. Saw-edged
    reeds drown her chest,
redefining the contours of breasts; metallic dust in the
    pond's depths are shrapnel-stars dredged from her
    wounds.

"Concealment" is society's slow-motion violence against
    women:
Moss smothers her final whimper with a velvet shroud,
while the pond secretes a bronze-toned, silent dawn from
    its festering wounds.[1]

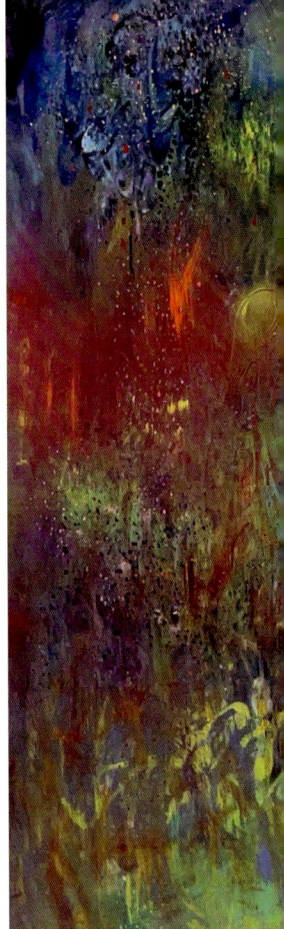

Glossy Pond

2024
Oil on linen
47¼ × 70⅞ in.
(120 × 180 cm)

CL1479

94

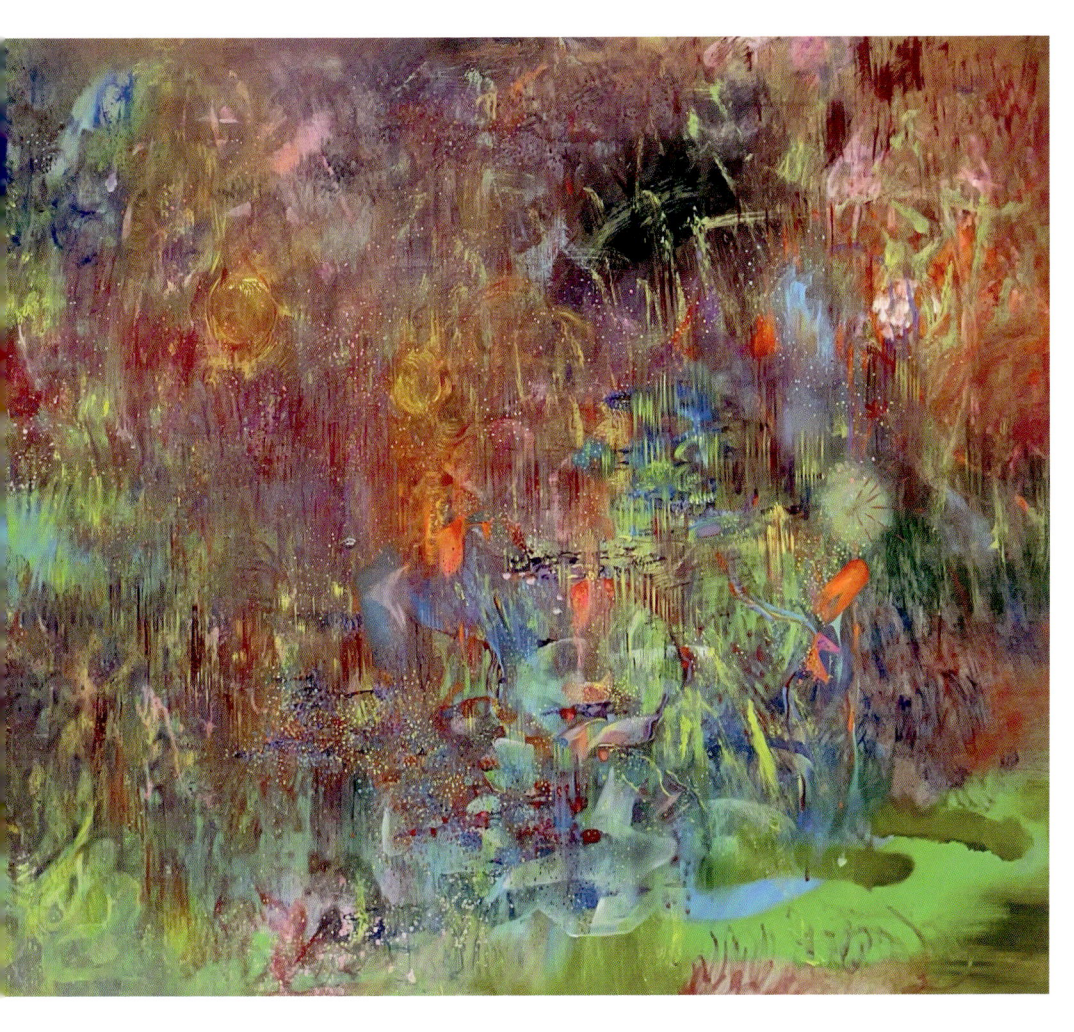

Grace Hartigan
(1922–2008)

You know you don't go into the studio and say, "Oh here I am this marvelous heroine, this wonderful woman doing my marvelous painting so all these marvelous women artists can come after me and do their marvelous painting." There you are alone in this huge space and you are not conscious of the fact that you have breasts and a vagina. You are inside yourself, looking at this damned piece of rag on the wall that you are supposed to make a world out of. That is all you are conscious of. I simply cannot believe that a man feels differently … Inside yourself, you are looking at this terrifying unknown and trying to feel, to pull everything you can out of all your experience, to make something. I think a woman or a man creating feels very much the same way. I bring my experience, which is different from a man's, yes, and I put it where I can. But once that is done, I don't know if it's a woman experience I'm looking at.[1]

The only way to discover oneself is to paint from the areas of blind, inspired feeling. How to reach into there is the problem … I must not paint pictures which are comforting to my eyes. To shock the bourgeois is easy—to shock the "avant-garde," that's the thing. To shock oneself is the most important of all.[2]

I didn't choose painting. It chose me. I didn't have any talent. I just had genius.[3]

Portrait of W.
1951–52
Oil on canvas
85 × 58 in.
(215.9 × 147.3 cm)
CL816

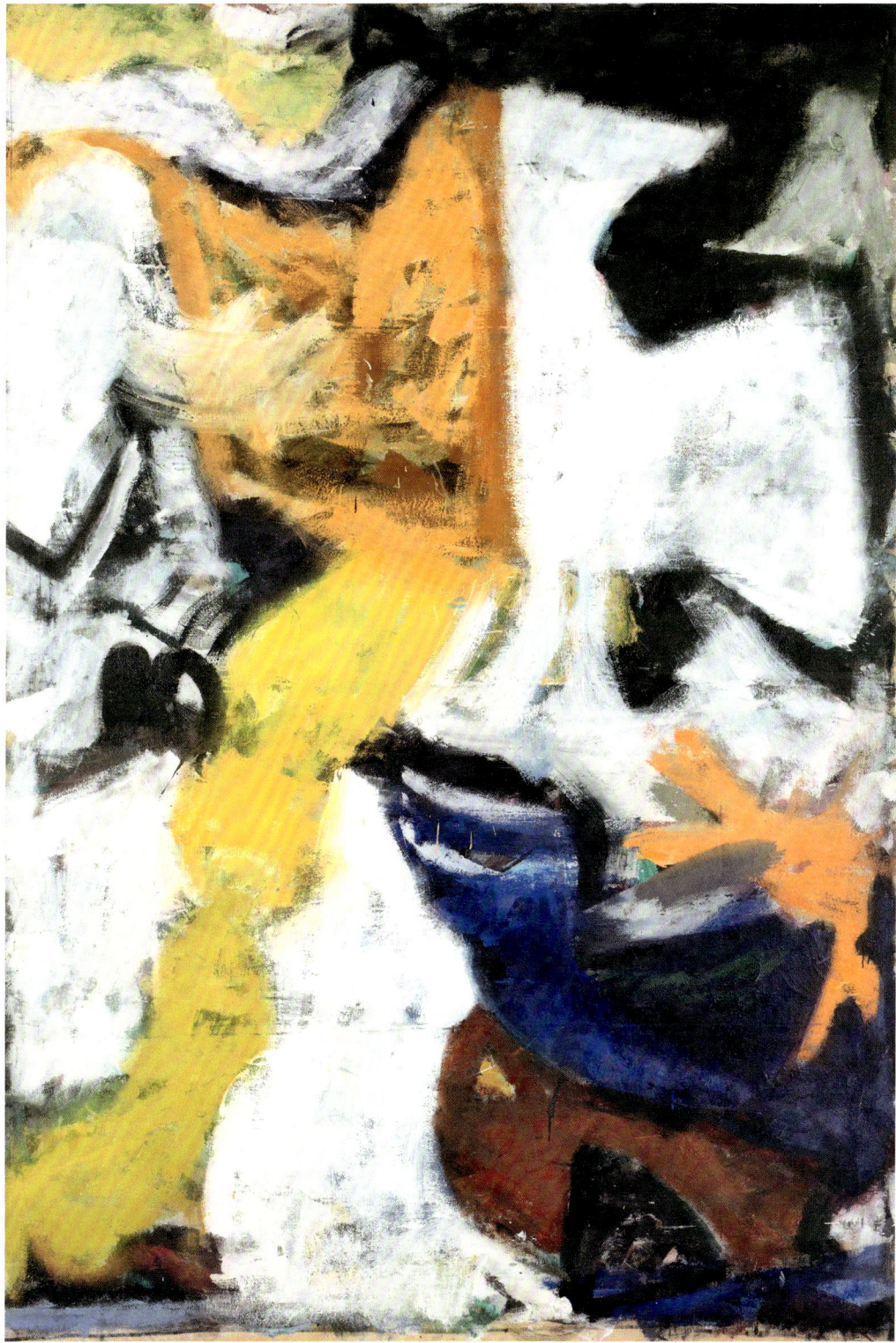

Dame Barbara Hepworth
(1903–1975)

"Abstract" is a word which is now most frequently used to express only the type of the outer form of a work of art; this makes it difficult to use it in relation to the spiritual vitality or inner life which is the real sculpture. Abstract sculptural qualities are found in good sculpture of all time, but it is significant that contemporary sculpture and painting have become abstract in thought and concept. As the sculptural idea is in itself unfettered and unlimited and can choose its own forms, the vital concept selects the form and substance of its expression quite unconsciously.[1]

From the sculptor's point of view one can either be the spectator of the object or the object itself. For a few years I became the object. I was the figure in the landscape and every sculpture contained to a greater or lesser degree the ever-changing forms and contours embodying my own response to a given position in that landscape.[2]

I find it easier now I'm more free to make forms and move around them. I don't feel so personally involved—I'm not exactly the sculpture in the landscape any more. I think of the works as objects which rise out of the land or the sea, mysteriously.[3]

They are bronze sculptures, and the material allows more openness of course. I was a comparative newcomer to bronze, so I used it extravagantly to see how far I could go. It has a presence, but it doesn't look at you in the way that a carving does. There is a stronger sense of participating in the form—you want to go in and out as you look at a sculpture like *Trezion* or *Porthcurno*. Maybe it's not big enough to do this, but you don't need to be physically entangled if you've got a pair of hands. If you feel something, you know what the experience is.[4]

Six Forms on a Circle
1967
Polished bronze on a revolving bronze base
Height 23¾ in. (60.3 cm)
No. 6 from an edition of 7
CL1054

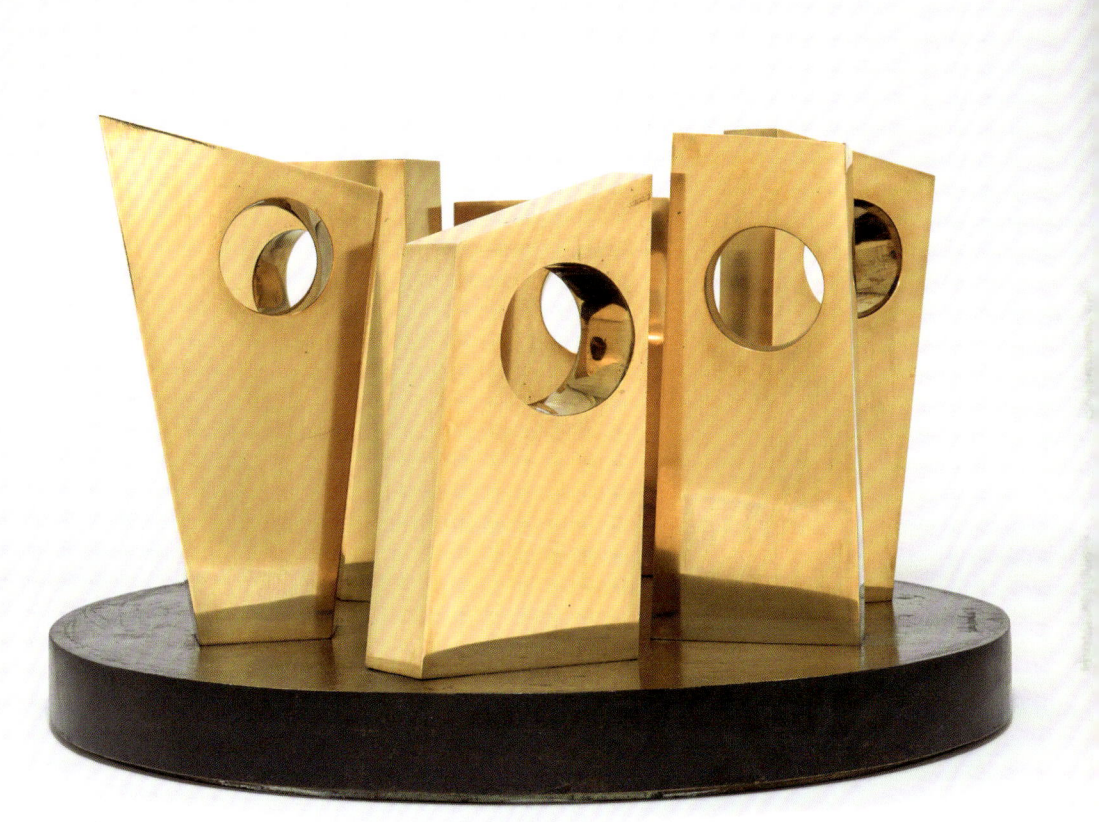

Martha Jungwirth

(b. 1940)

My pictorial reality is charged with passion, a language tied to the body, to dynamic movement. Painting is a matter of form, and then it receives a soul—through me.[1]

My art is like a diary, seismographic. That is the method of my work. I am completely related to myself. Drawing and painting are a movement that runs through me.[2]

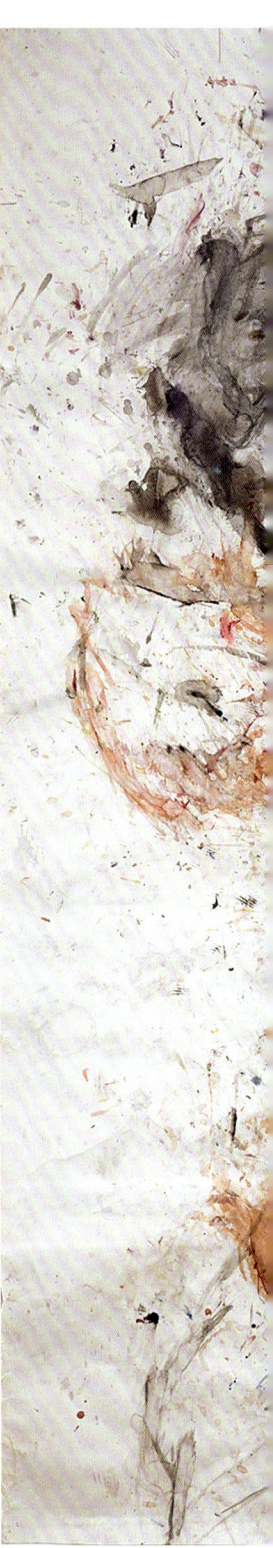

*Hier und jetzt und
nie wieder II*

1982–83
Watercolor on paper
90½ × 84⅝ in.
(229.9 × 215 cm)

CL206

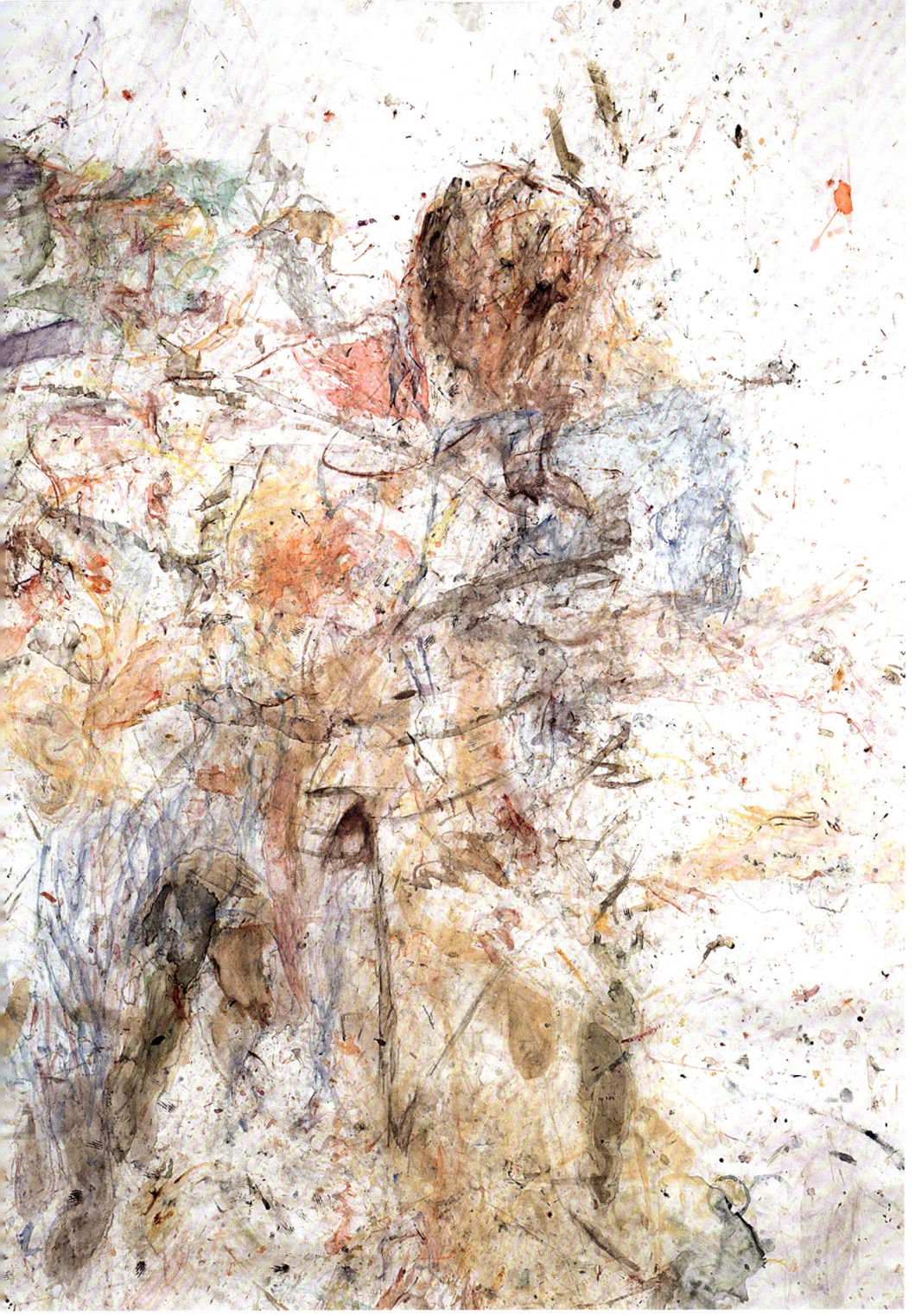

Frida Kahlo
(1907–1954)

I want to turn [my work] into something useful; until now I have managed simply an honest expression of my own self, but one which is unfortunately a long way from serving the [Communist] Party. I must struggle with all my strength to ensure that the little positive that my health allows me to do also benefits the Revolution, the only real reason to live.[1]

I adore surprise and the unexpected. I like to go beyond realism ... Surrealism is the magical surprise of finding a lion in a wardrobe, when you were "sure" of finding shirts ... I use surrealism as a means of poking fun at others without their realizing it and of making friends with those who do realize it ... I paint my own reality. The only thing I know is that I paint because I need to, and I paint always whatever passes through my head, without any other consideration.[2]

There have been two great accidents in my life. One was the trolley [bus] and the other was Diego [Rivera]. Diego was by far the worst.[3]

Hammer and Sickle (and unborn baby)

c. 1950
Dry plaster and mixed media
16¼ × 13 × 6 in.
(41.3 × 33 × 15.2 cm)
CL1324

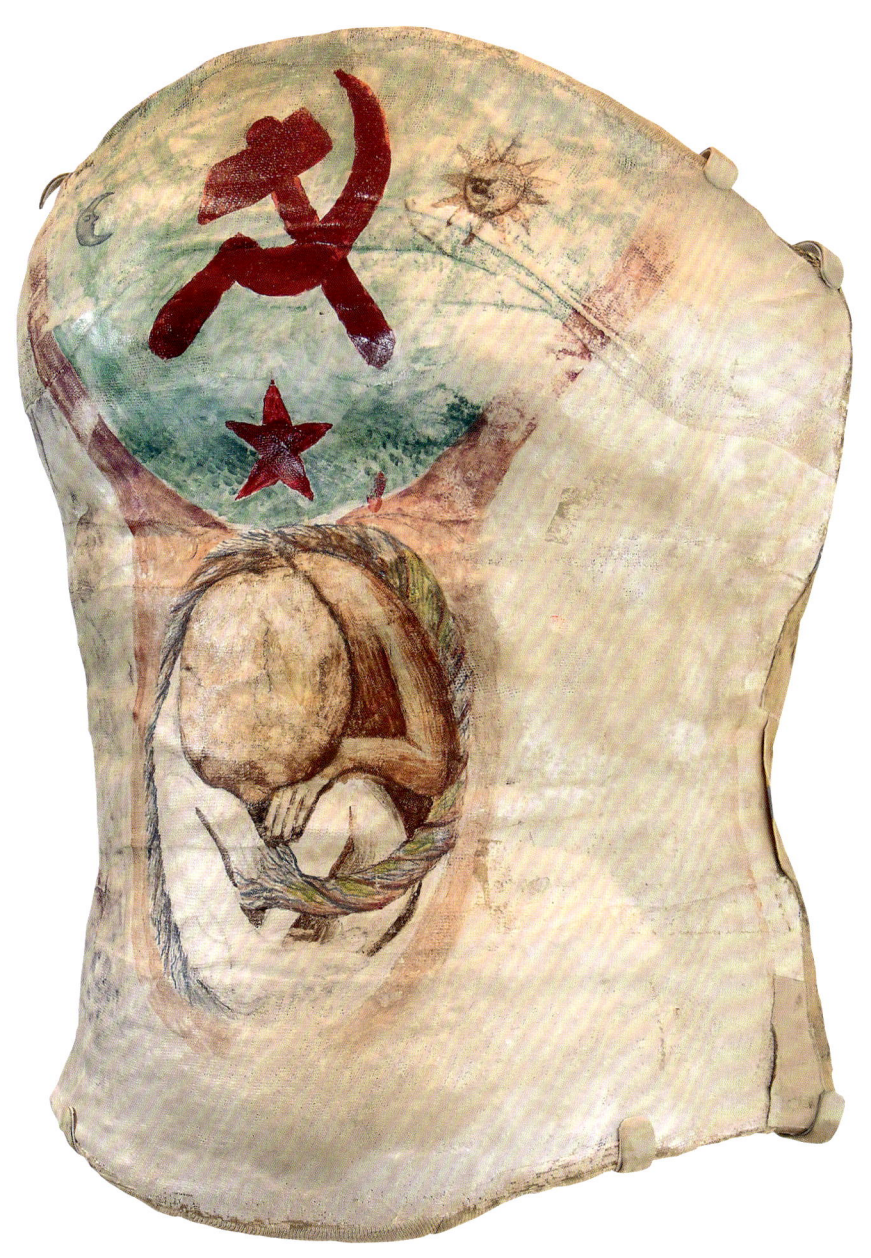

Lee Krasner
(1908–1984)

Prophecy was fraught with foreboding. When I saw it, I was aware it was a frightening image, but I had to let it come through.[1]

I keep thinking about the painting called *Prophecy* which I painted just before I took off for Europe. The painting disturbed me enormously, and I called [my husband] Jackson in to look at it. He assured me it was a good painting, and said not to think about it, just continue—do another one. Not tie into what my reaction to it was, the way I was doing. Then Pollock died, I got back from Europe and this painting—once more I had to look at it and deal with it. *Prophecy* still frightened me enormously. I couldn't read why it frightened me so, and even now would be hard put to do so. And so in that sense the painting becomes an element of the unconscious—as one might bring forth a dream.[2]

There is a painting called *Prophecy* which I did just before I left for Europe. Every time the work broke it sent me into a tailspin because I couldn't tell what was happening. I asked Jackson to come and look at this painting and he did and said I needn't be nervous about it. He thought it was a good painting and the only thing that he objected to was this image in the upper right hand which I had scratched in with the back of a brush. It made a kind of an eye form. He advised me to take it out. I said that I didn't agree with him and left it in … Jackson was killed in the automobile accident while I was [in Europe] and when I came back I had to confront myself with this painting before I was able to start again. I went through a rough period in that confrontation.[3]

Painting is not separate from life. It is one. It is like asking—*do I want to live?* My answer is yes—and I paint.[4]

Prophecy
1956
Oil on cotton duck
58⅛ × 34 in.
(147.6 × 86.4 cm)

CL108

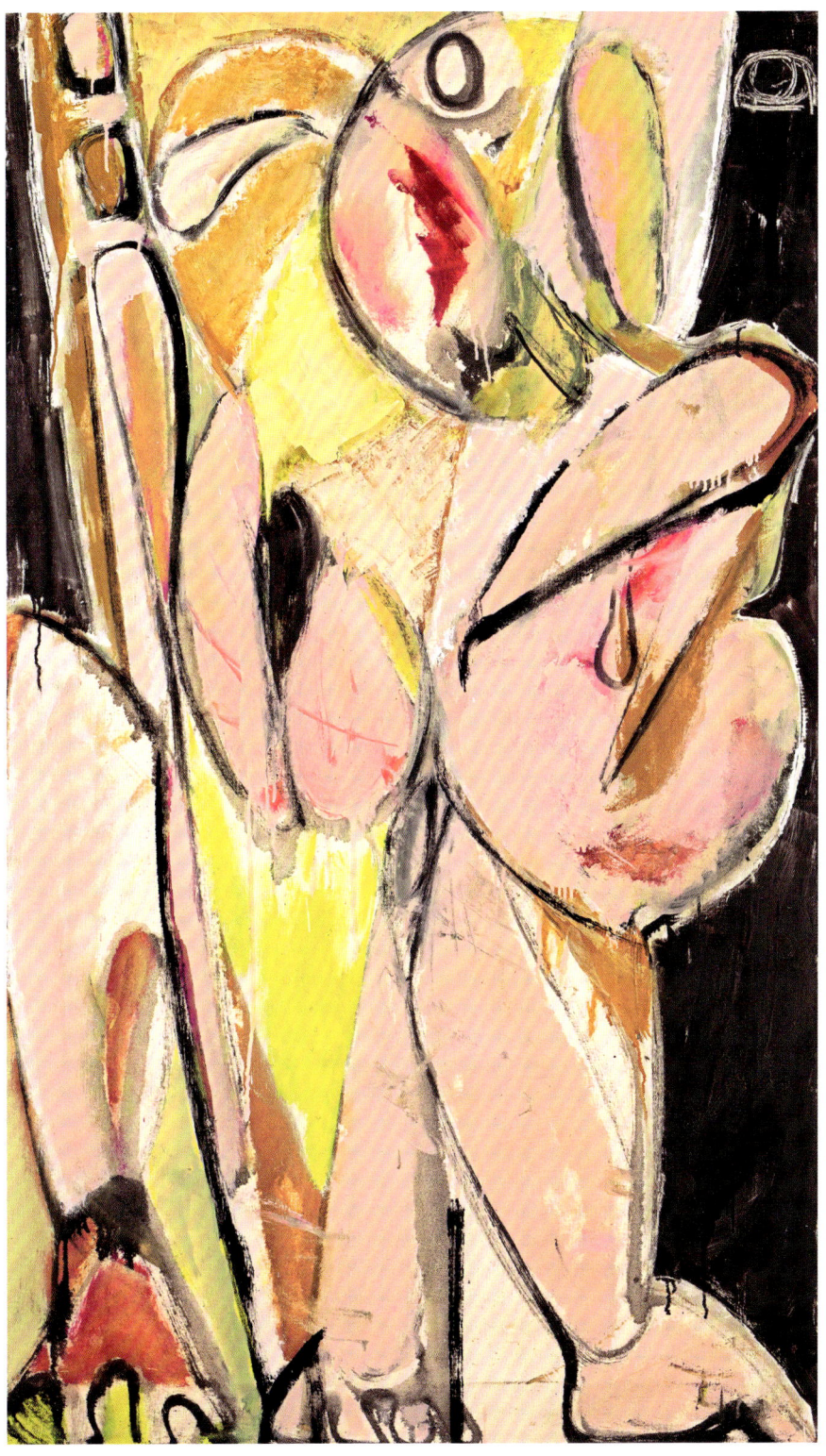

Lalan (born Xie Jing-Lan)
(1921–1995)

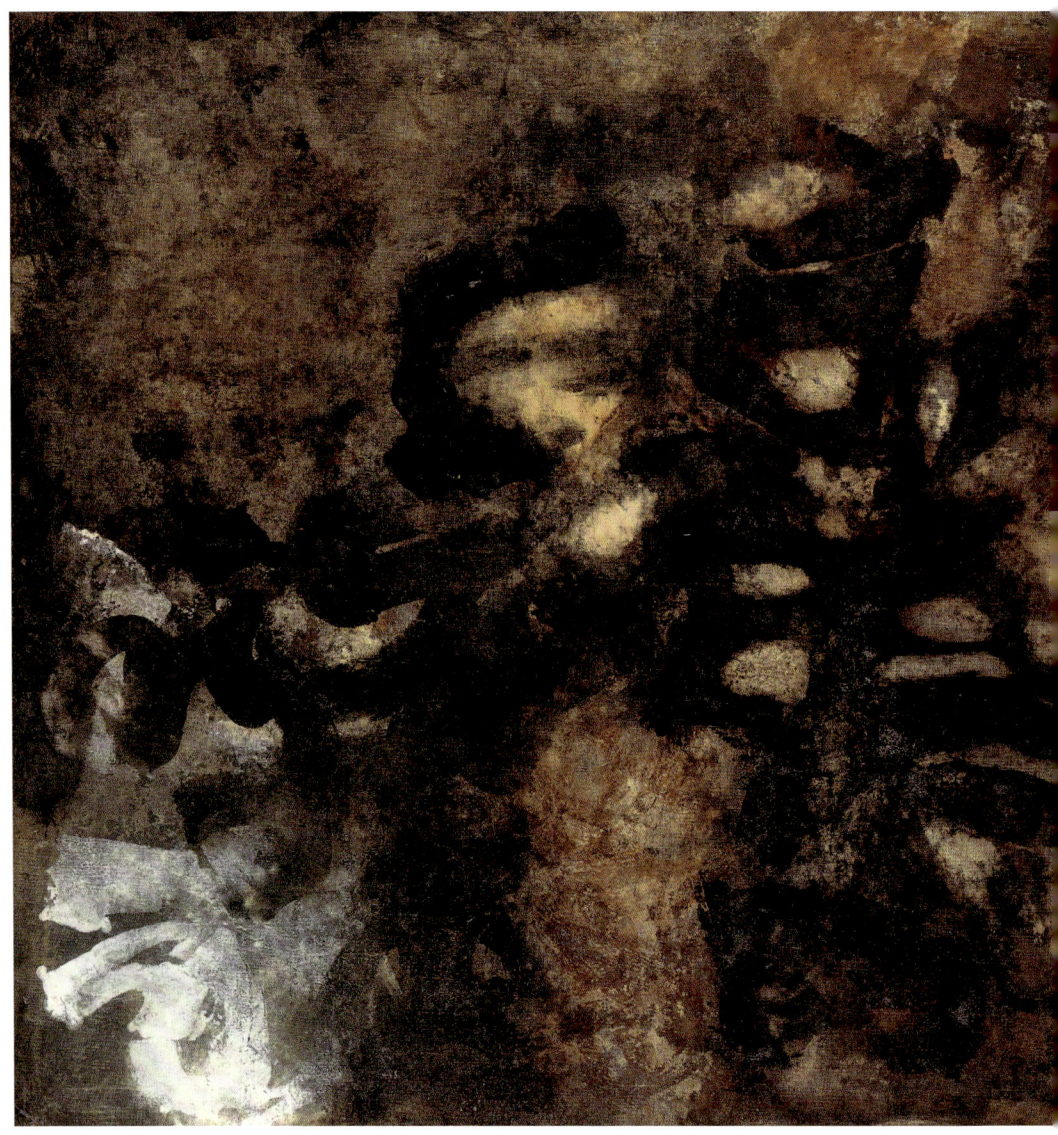

I never confine myself in [the] ivory tower.[1]

My early works are somewhat lyrical. Their colors are vibrant. They are abstract paintings, akin to writing, completed by movements led by the hands.[2]

In my own creation, the action of painting is carried by the sound and inner movement of the body.[3]

Through the Trees
1965
Oil on canvas
44⅞ × 57¼ in.
(114 × 145.4 cm)
CL.1241

Marie Laurencin
(1883–1956)

If I feel so far removed from painters it is because they are men, and in my view men are difficult problems to solve ... But if the genius of men intimidates me, I feel perfectly at ease with everything that is feminine.[1]

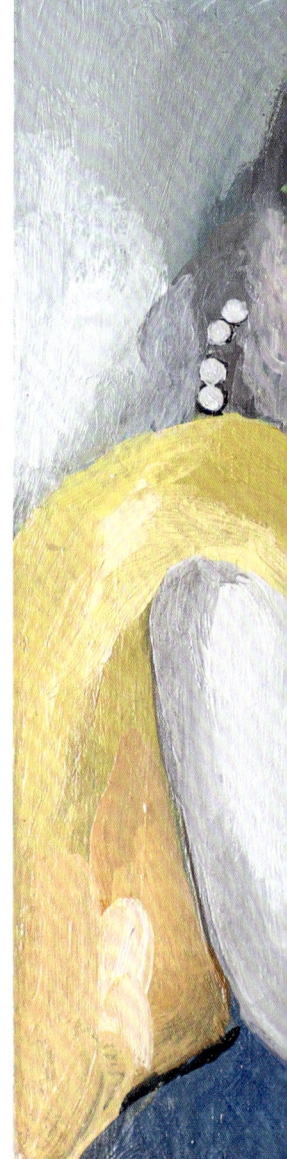

Jeune femme à la guitare (Young Woman with a Guitar)

c. 1935
Oil on canvas
15 × 18¹⁄₈ in.
(38.1 × 46 cm)

CL1309

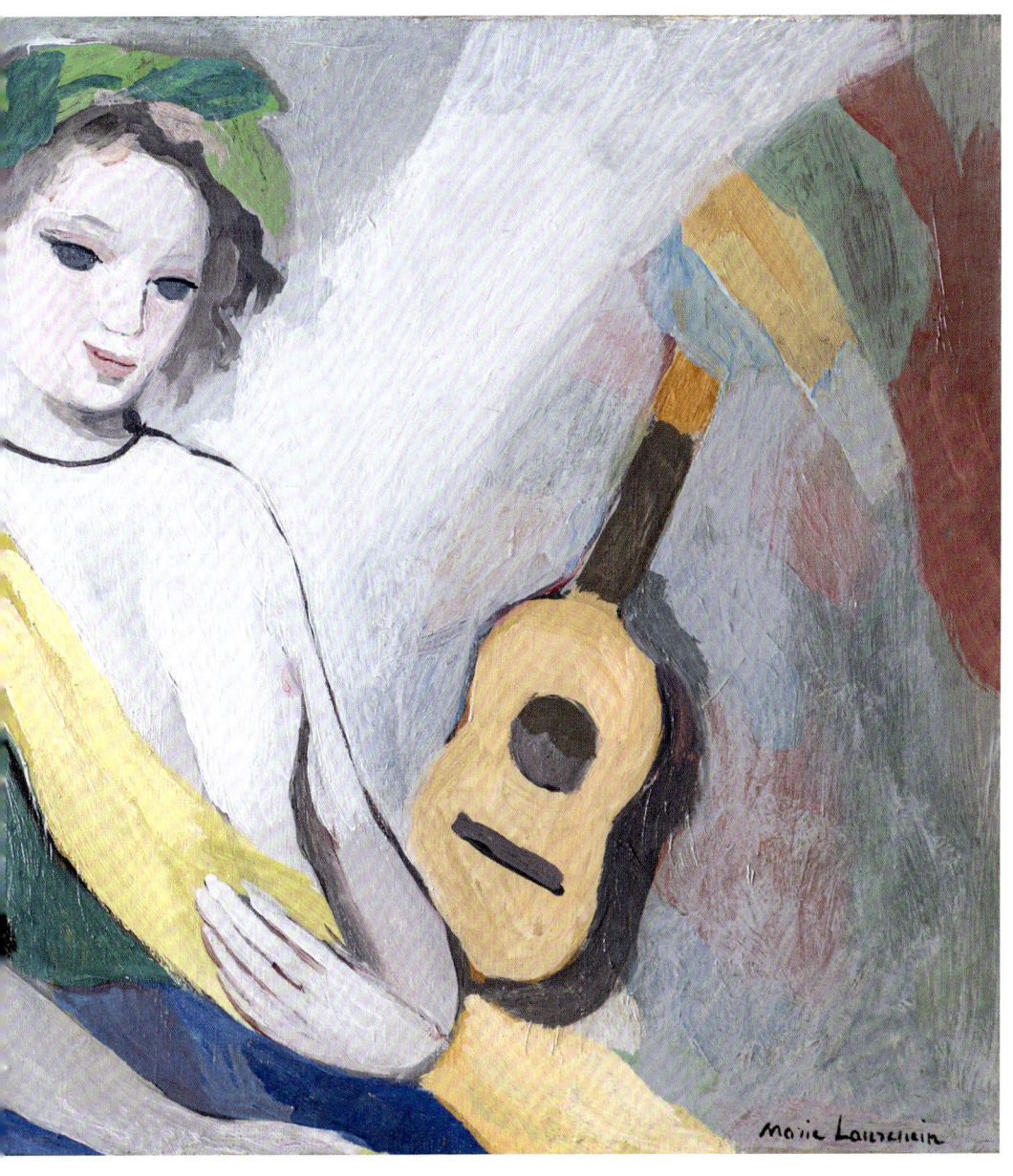

Lifang (also known as Li Fangzhi)
(1933–2020)

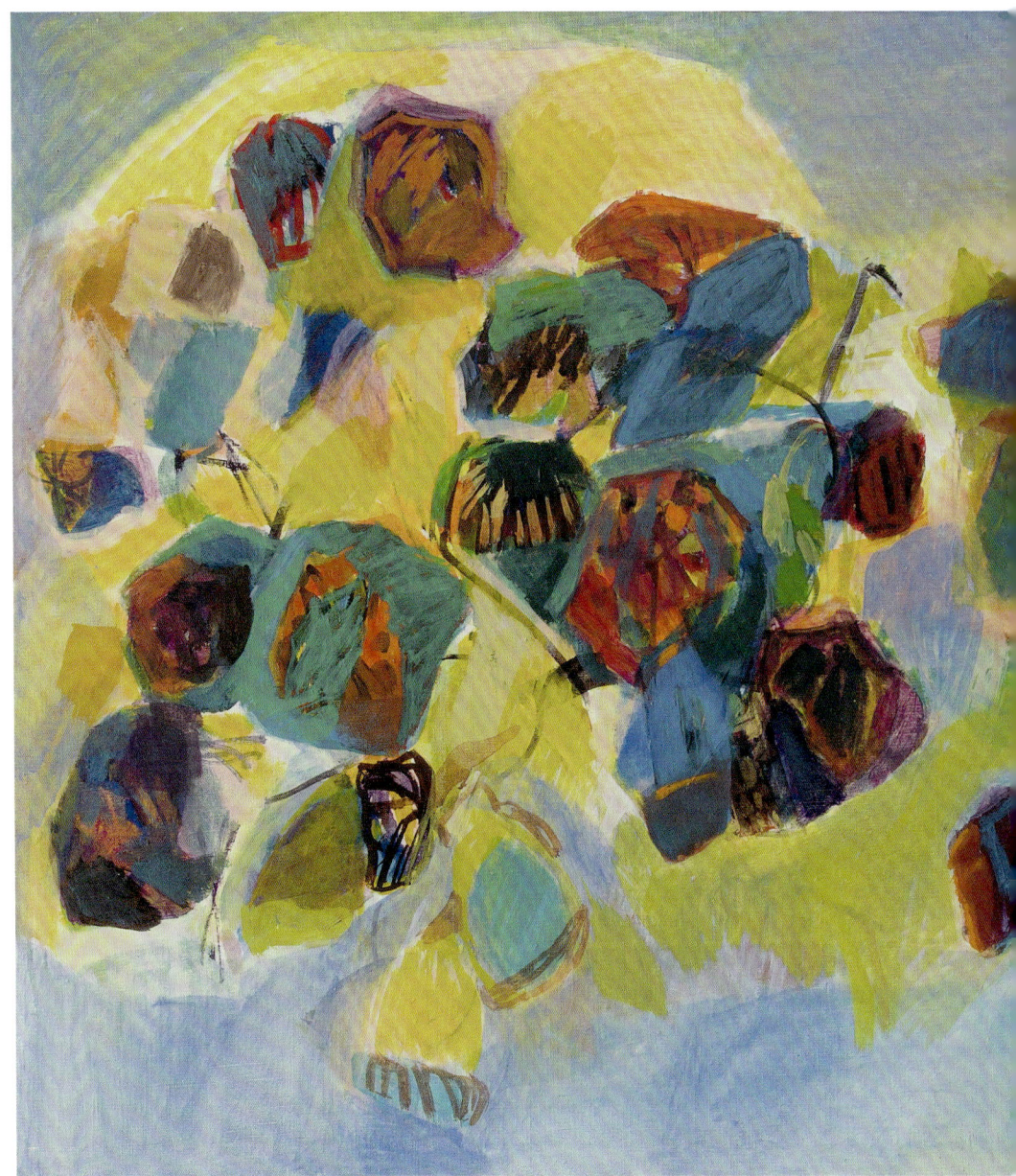

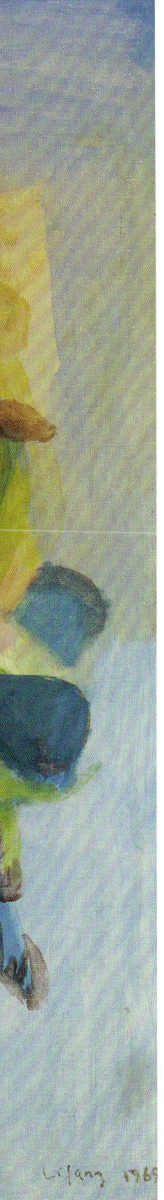

When I paint, my heart is full of appreciation of the scene in front of me. My heart is also full of affection for my people. It is my sincere wish that I could record my feelings so that others can experience this joy too.[1]

When a person is insightful she cannot fear nature.[2]

Even in difficult times I have never stopped painting. When my child was ill, I held him in one arm and painted with the other hand.[3]

On being asked why she changed her painting style from abstract to landscapes:

I discovered that abstract drawing was much too dependent on randomness. Randomness could not satisfy my search for truth. When I lived in nature once more, I felt the need to paint nature more directly. So the change was obvious for me and not unusual.[4]

Untitled

1969
Oil on canvas
27⅛ × 29½ in.
(68.9 × 74.9 cm)
CL1239

Sahara Longe
(b. 1994)

I would like to see more black portrait artists—
representation is extremely important, and growing up
I never saw representations of myself in museums and
galleries and it had a very profound effect on me. That
want of being able to see black people depicted in paintings
(and not holding a bowl of fruit in the background) really
propelled me to choose the path I did.[1]

I know when a work is finished because of an immediate
response to the painting. It doesn't have to be "perfect," it
will just come down to the feeling I get once seeing it with
fresh eyes the next day, or after some time apart from the
work. All you need is a split second to know whether you
have an emotional connection with the work. Painting
should be enjoyable, it can't just be about the conceptual
or symbolic analysis. It has to be visually interesting too.[2]

Ode to the Dog Rose
2021
Oil on jute
55⅛ × 35⅜ in.
(140 × 89.9 cm)

CL1236

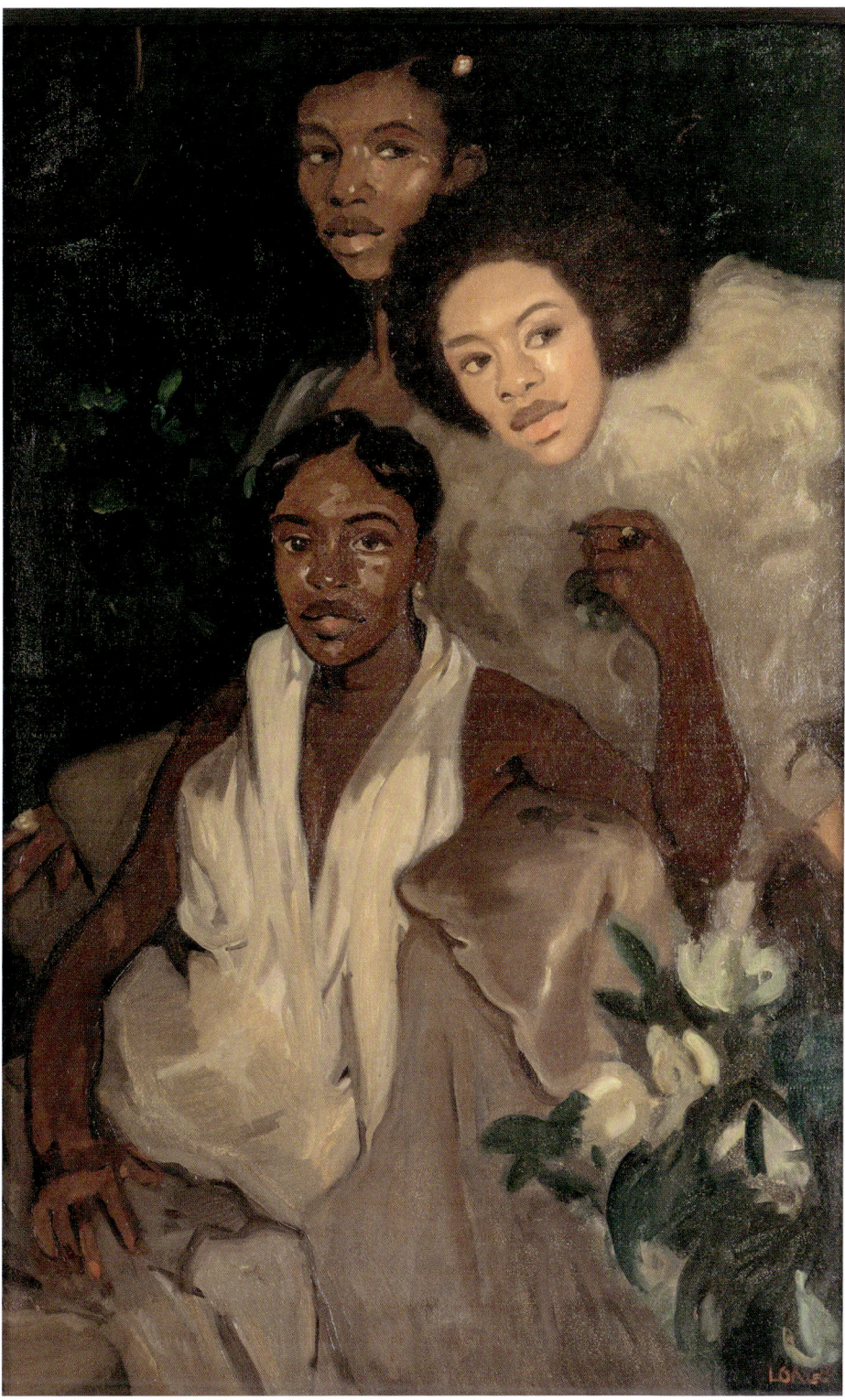

Sarah Lucas
(b. 1962)

Description of work and the artist's thoughts on it:

Obsidiana consists of eight ambiguous biomorphic forms made of nylon tights filled with fluff, emerging from a ceramic household toilet. Their nylon multitude evokes an expulsion or suggestive spurt from the womb-like black toilet, their shape suggesting breasts or sperm. The title of the work references the naturally occurring black glass formed by a volcano and was specific to the exhibition ... in Mexico City in 2012. Set in the spectacular context of the archaeological Museo Anahuacalli, *Obsidiana* explores the themes of fertility and sexuality reflected in the collection's Mexican antiquities which were shown alongside Lucas's work.

I thought there was something so human about them ... something quite sexy.[1]

People come up with all sorts of fantasies about who I am, and what my life must be like. I'm habitually honest, but that has nothing to do with my art being confessional or about myself. I think my works, particularly my sculptures, are true to themselves, to materials: that's what really matters. In sculpture more than painting, materials want to do what they want to do. You can't torture them into something they don't want to be. This principle always stuck with me. At some point, I introduced that logic to content as well. I don't want to make it feel like I'm imposing a meaning or that I am preaching anything. I'd like to be true to what the thing is.[2]

I enjoy being a woman, I enjoy being a hard-hitting angry woman.[3]

Obsidiana
2012
Bricks, ceramic toilet, natural cotton, and Lycra tights
28⅜ × 25 × 22¼ in.
(72.1 × 63.5 × 56.5 cm)
CL1393

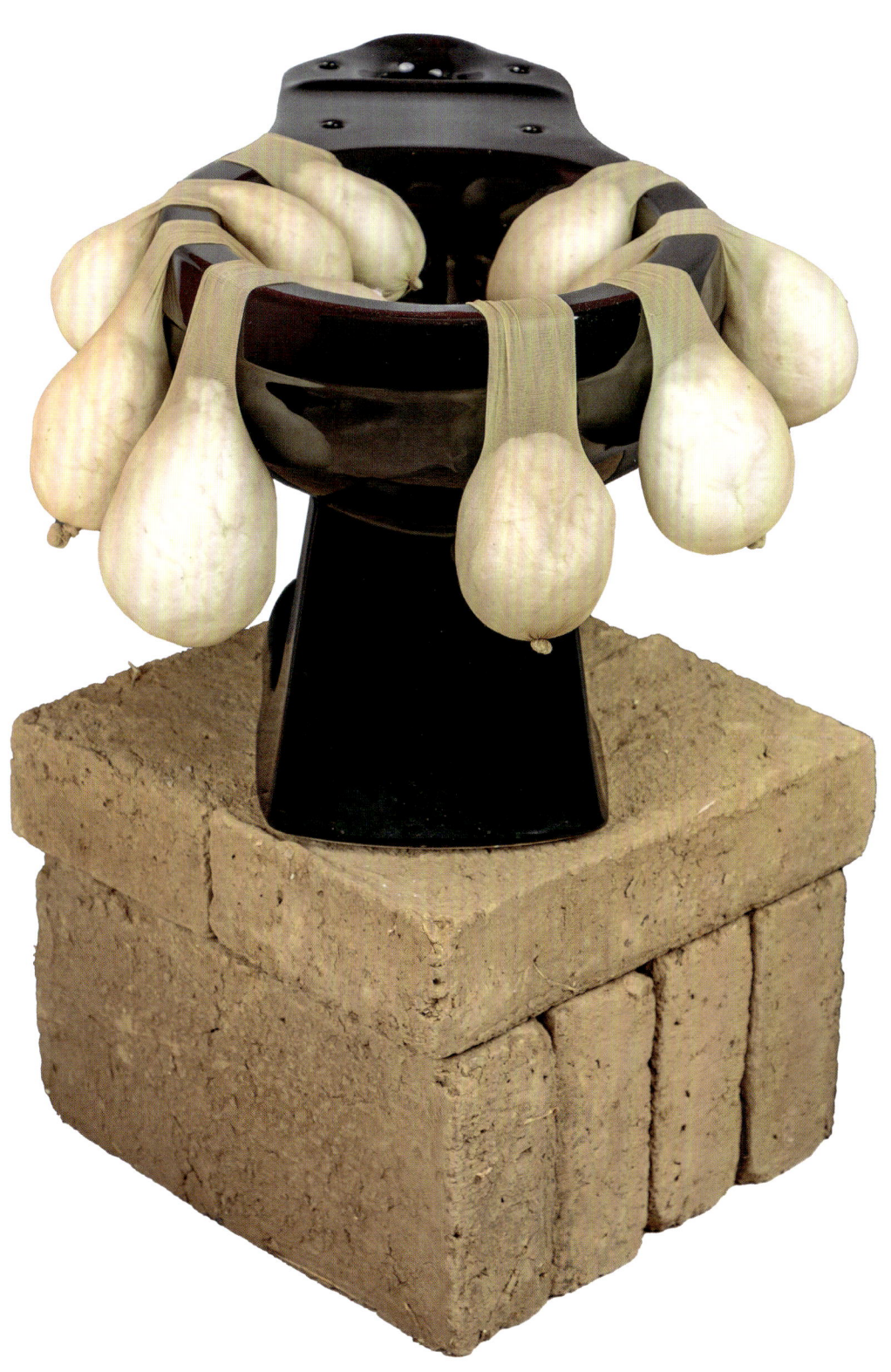

Dora Maar
(1907–1997)

I must dwell apart in the desert. I want to create an aura of mystery about my work. People must long to see it. I'm still too famous as Picasso's mistress to be accepted as a painter.[1]

On being told by the writer James Lord that she would never be forgotten because Picasso's depictions of her were hung in museums across the world:

Do you think I care? Does Madame Cézanne care? Does Saskia Rembrandt care? Remember that I, too, am an artist. I, too, am familiar with the auspices of posterity.[2]

Portrait de Jacqueline Breton-Lamba
1939
Oil on canvas
36¼ × 28¾ in.
(92.1 × 73 cm)

CL1397

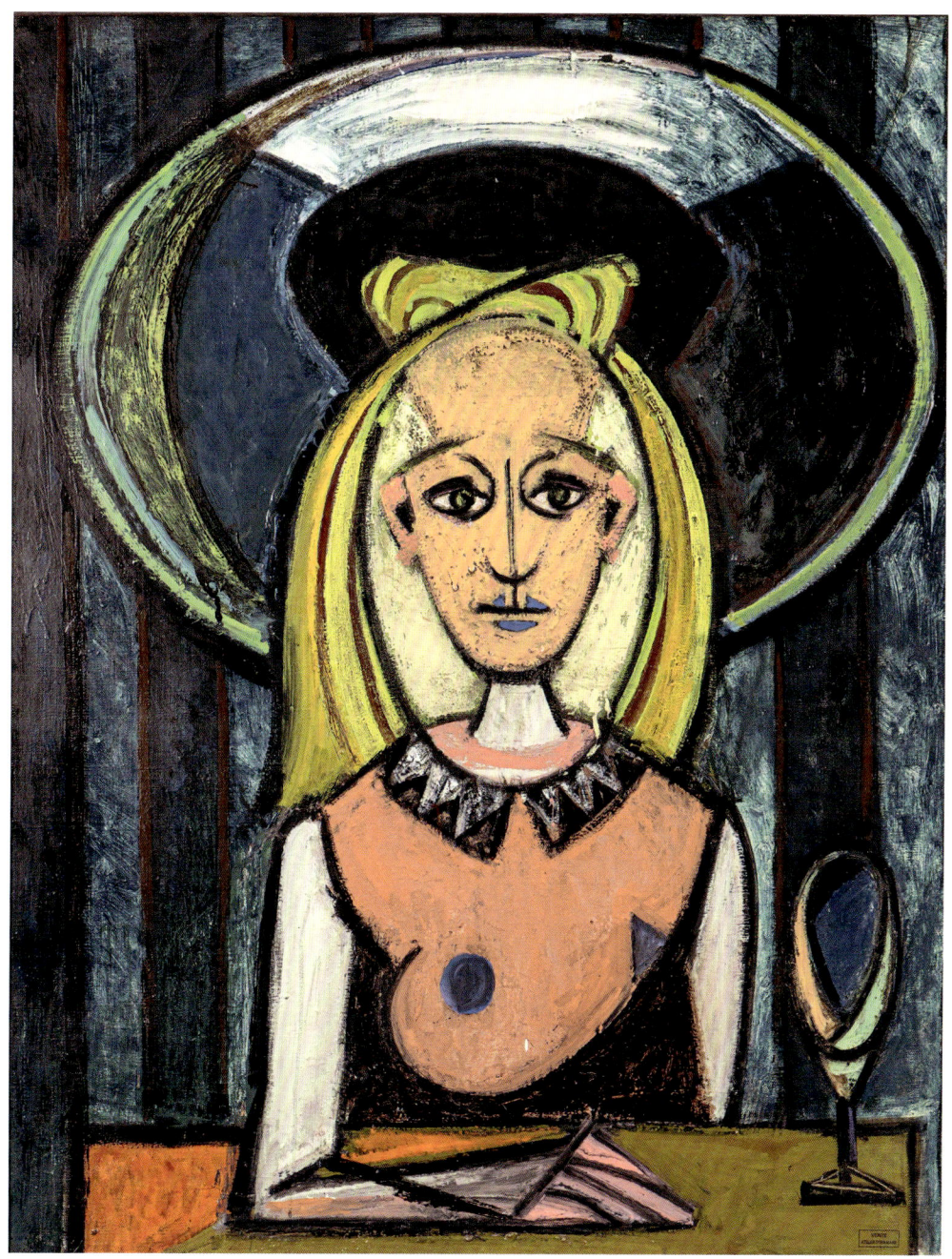

Jacqueline Marval
(1866–1932)

I touch my art only when I am in a state that we call,
I believe, subconscious. In these moments I think I will
say sublime things. I sing the most beautiful hymn to
the sun ... but immediately I realize that, having wanted
to be the nightingale, I am voiceless. I then become
completely discouraged. I cry. My hair turns white in just
a few minutes. I dye it immediately. To be prettier, I put
a blindfold on my eyes, and I go on beautiful trips.

After all this wantonness, I start again and I don't say
anything ...

I never thought about wearing a blouse for work.
I need freedom of movement. When it's hot, I work naked,
out of humility, because I came into the world like this.
The women, children, and flowers that I encounter often
feature in my paintings, but they are only secondary
elements. Above all, it's the light that falls on them that
I love, and that's the only reason for my art.[1]

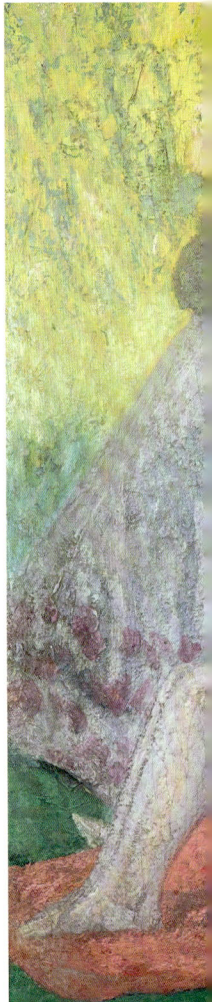

Le Fils du roi
(The King's Son)
1906
Oil on canvas
38¼ × 51⅛ in.
(97.2 × 129.9 cm)
CL1354

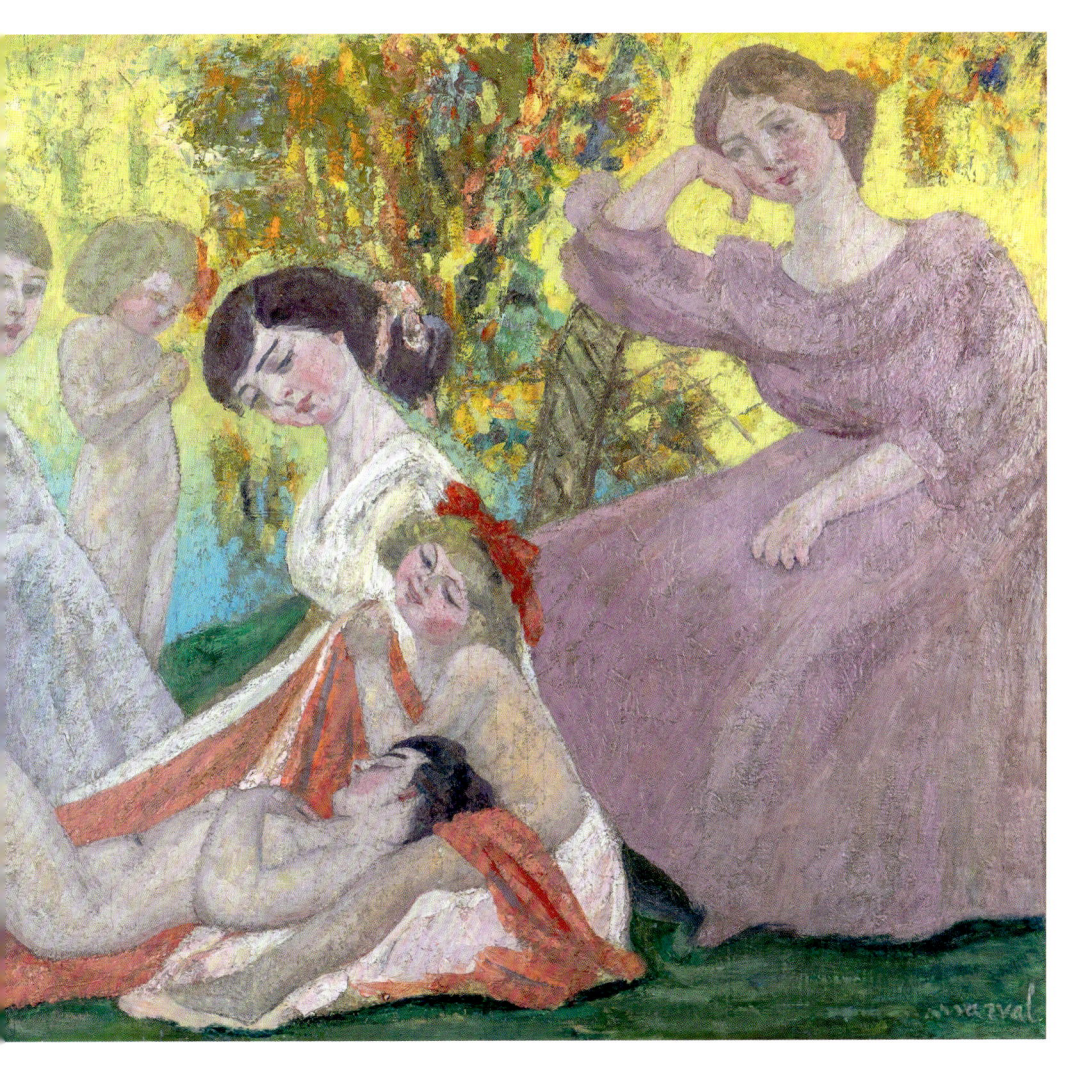

Joan Mitchell
(1925–1992)

We arrived about 4 am—and I sat at that quay—the light was fabulous—and the black rubber tires under the quay looked like something [Robert] Motherwell should have seen ... also there was a mad rock that Rufus took photographs of—little bits of ideas—strange light.[1]

My sister is always putting the past behind her—Well I use the past to make my pics and I want all of it and even you and me in candlelight on the train and every "lover" I've ever had—every friend—nothing closed out—and dogs alive and dead and people and landscapes and feeling even if it is desperate—anguished—tragic—it's all part of me and I want to confront it and sleep with it—the dreams—and paint it.[2]

The painting is just a surface to be covered. Paintings aren't about the person who makes them, either. My paintings have to do with feeling, yet it's pretentious to say they're about feelings, too, because if you don't get it across, it's nothing.[3]

Painting is a way of forgetting oneself ... I am not there any more. It is a state of non-self-consciousness. It does not happen often ... It is lovely.[4]

Rufus' Rock
1966
Oil on canvas
76⅝ × 51⅛ in.
(194.6 × 129.9 cm)
CL100

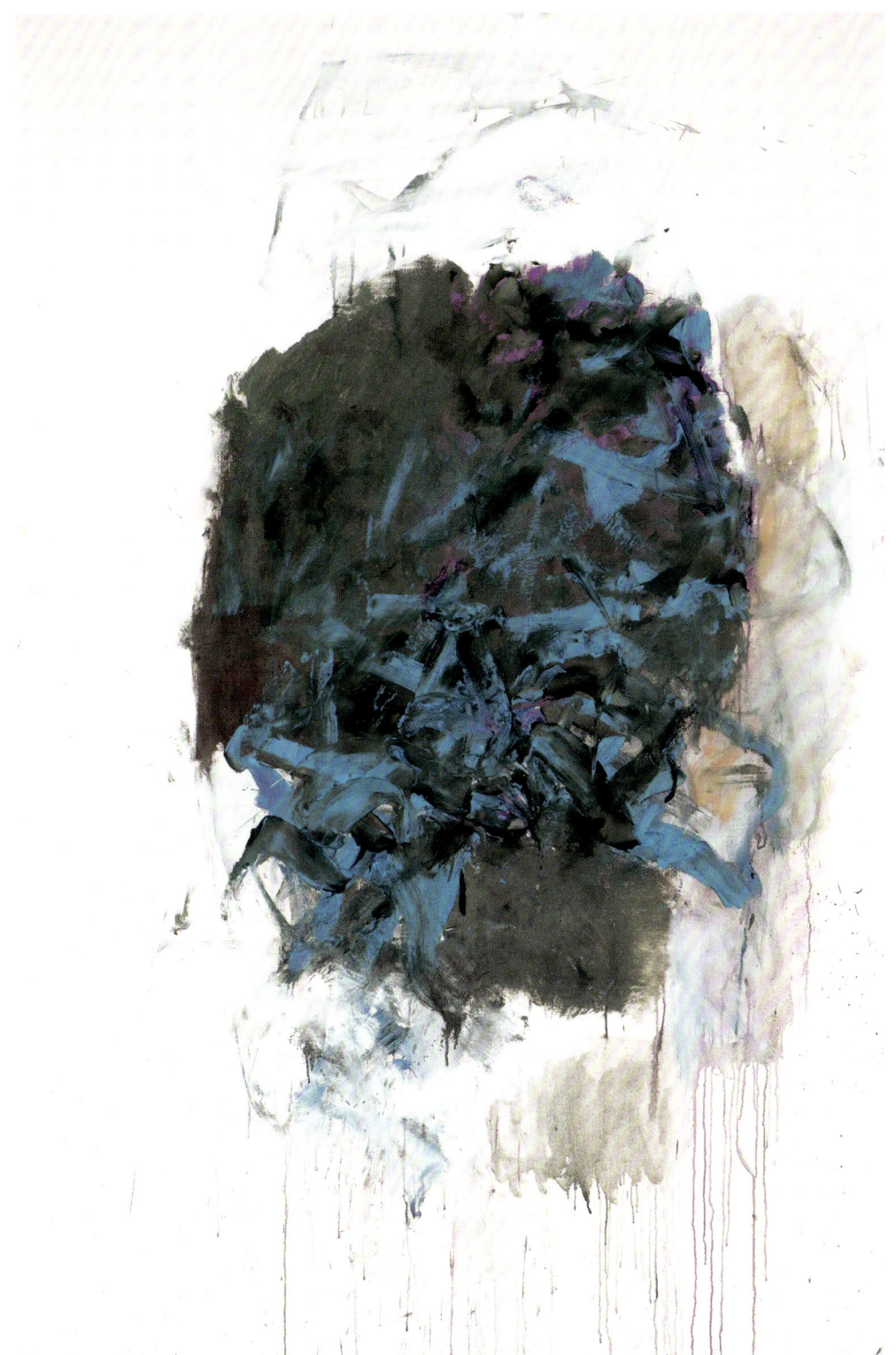

Jesse Mockrin
(b. 1981)

Biblical and mythological stories have provided myriad narrative outlets in which to present the female nude. Historically, the goddess of love is often portrayed— largely by male artists—as the source of all lust. Venus is a powerful woman whose desires cause problems and moral quandaries for others.

The "Venus effect" is an art-historical term for the tradition of images that depict Venus gazing into a mirror. It's a perceptual phenomenon wherein the viewer is fooled into believing that Venus is looking at her own reflection— in reality, her line of sight in the mirror connects both with the contemporary viewer and with the painter who created the work. This is an apt metaphor for historical paintings themselves, which profess to portray women's self-obsession, but instead depict female subjects gazing adoringly at the male painters who fashioned them.[1]

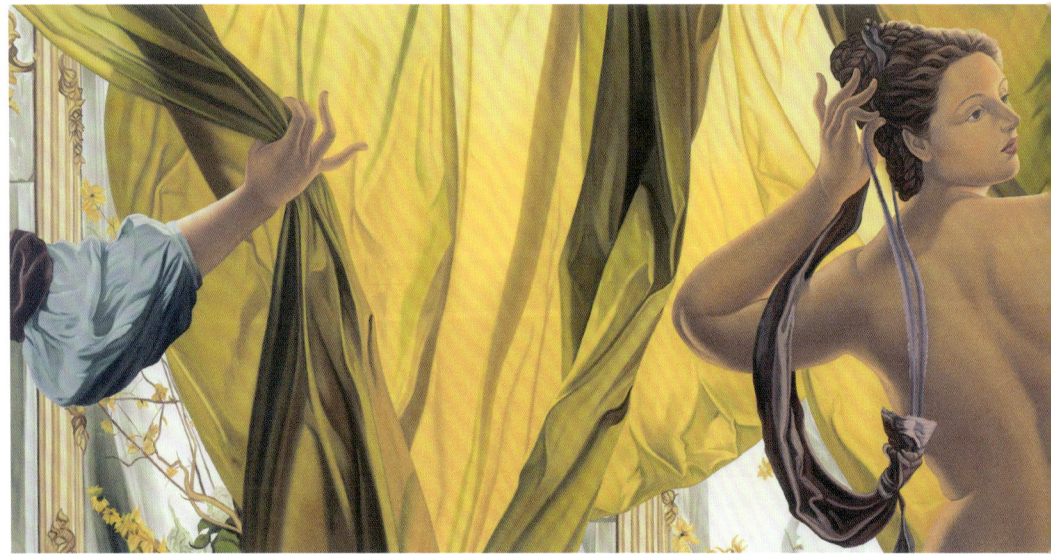

Hands are a huge part of the images from the very beginning. I think they're really interesting stand-ins for the body and how expressive they can be. Other than the face, there's really no other part of the body that's as expressive as the hands. So I like the idea of these hands communicating gestures that we've lost access to … these ambiguous signs that are pointing at some kind of meaning, but that meaning is lost or we're lacking translation … When I started drawing freehand, the fingers started getting weird. They're almost like these rubbery tentacles, they're missing some knuckles. That's partly from looking at Mannerism, which I love, looking at Fragonard and Boucher, who always have this curly little pinky that's sticking up in all the hands …[2]

The Venus Effect
2023
Oil on cotton
36 in. × 12 ft
(91.4 × 365.8 cm)
CL1308

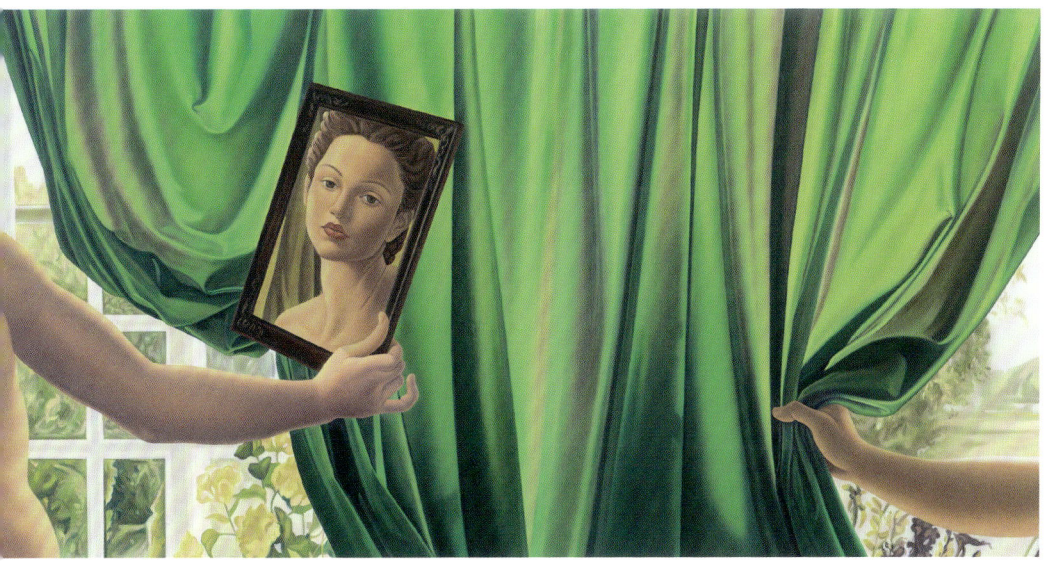

Berthe Morisot
(1841–1895)

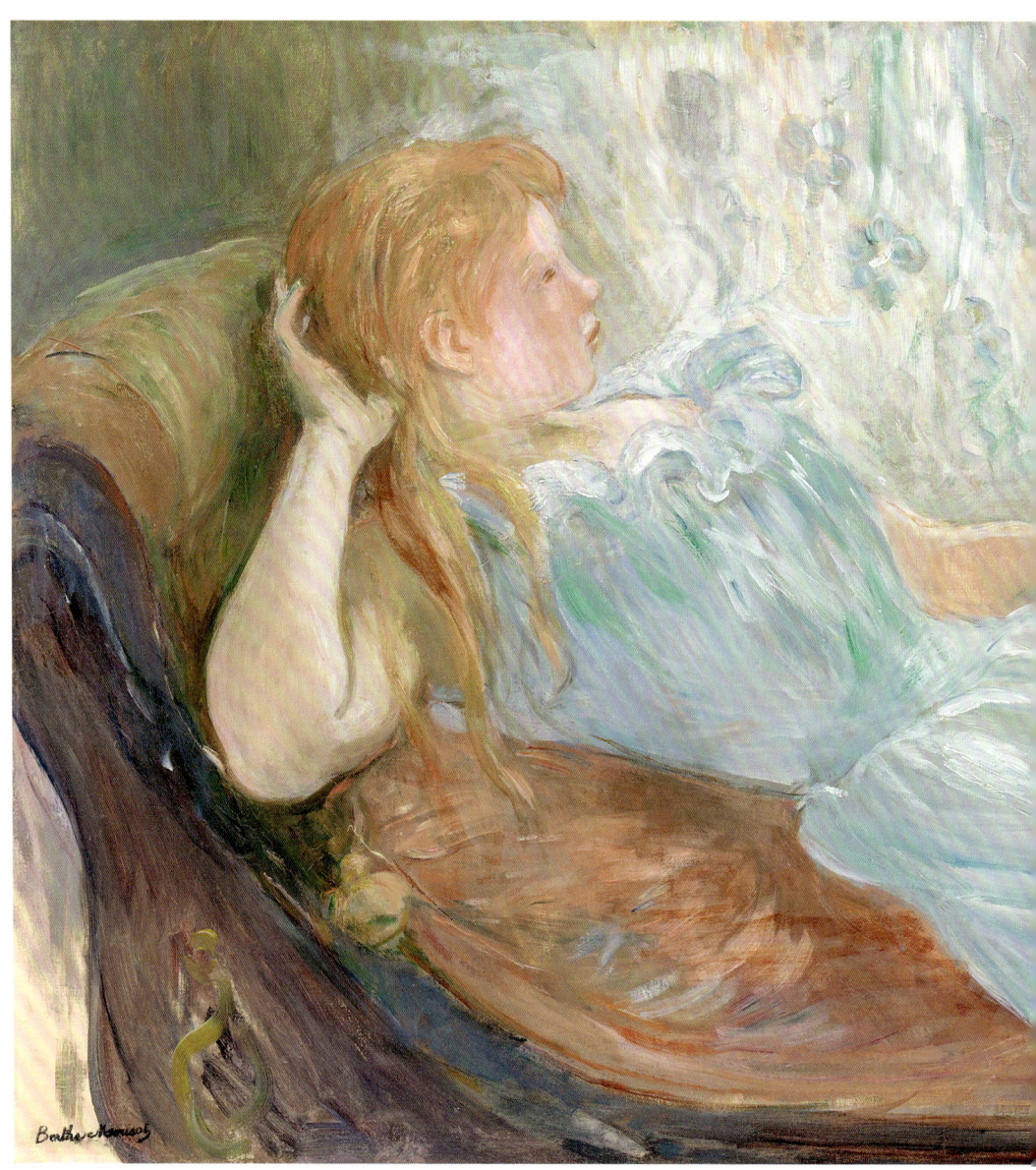

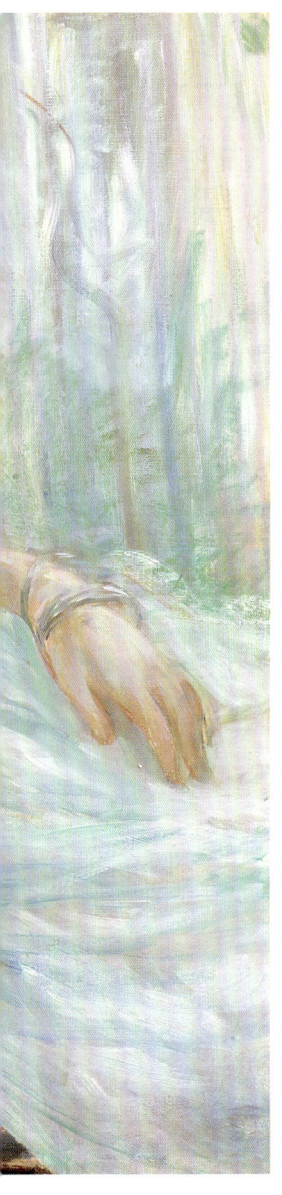

To me, it seems that Rubens is perhaps the only painter to have completely rendered beauty: the moist gaze (the shadows of eyelashes), the transparent skin, the silky hair, the graceful posture ... It is, however, right to add those of the last century, who have also rendered it with more affectation but plenty of charm. Look at the graces in Boucher's great painting of Venus and Vulcan, the portraits of Madame de Pompadour by Boucher and La Tour, the admirable Perronneaus from the Groult collection, and also (some of) the English Masters—Reynolds, Romney.[1]

I don't think there has ever been a man who treated a woman as an equal, and that's all I would have asked for—I know I am worth as much as they are.[2]

Jeune fille étendue
(Young Girl Lying
Down)
1893
Oil on canvas
25¾ × 32 in.
(65.4 × 81.3 cm)
CL1251

Sabine Moritz
(b. 1969)

Ferragosto II is characterized by its complex and reactive painting style ... Blue and red as the dominant colors are reflected and reinforced by their complementary colors yellow and green. The strong contrasts are nuanced by pink and white. A brushstroke often places several colors on the canvas at the same time, so that the tones remain next to one another or mix in the movement of the paint. The parallelism of the colors creates shades and surfaces that give the impression of three-dimensionality.

In the upper half, slightly to the left of center, a bright color shines—a focal point of the painting, around which the other tones play in gradations, repeating its form. The composition is reminiscent of the golden ratio proportions of antiquity and the Renaissance, proportions that have since been considered particularly calm and harmonious. What diverges from this is the versatile application of the paint, whose brushstrokes are in constant flux. Narrow or wide, thick or thin, the lines continuously change direction ... The lower half shows darker tones that lighten toward the center and top. This creates another dynamic.

Ferragosto II symbolizes midday. The image's strong colors of red, yellow, and white and the meandering lines convey much of the impression of shimmering heat and the rising haze of a charged city. At the same time, the darker, cool complementary colors convey a longing for the more relaxed afternoon and evening hours ... The idea ... of imaginary peace and freshness in the Italian south flows into the painting of the work just as much as the actual surroundings of a hot summer.

The *Ferragosto* series is named after the Italian holiday that celebrates the Assumption of the Virgin Mary, but its tradition dates back to the Roman emperor Augustus and his victory over the Egyptians. The day marks the peak of the holiday season in Italy, when cities empty and residents head to the sea or the countryside because of the heat.[1]

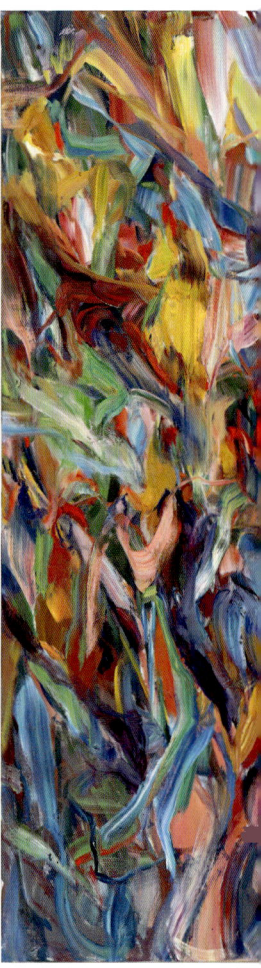

Ferragosto II
2023
Oil on canvas
78¾ in. × 9 ft 10⅛ in.
(200 × 300 cm)

CL.1262

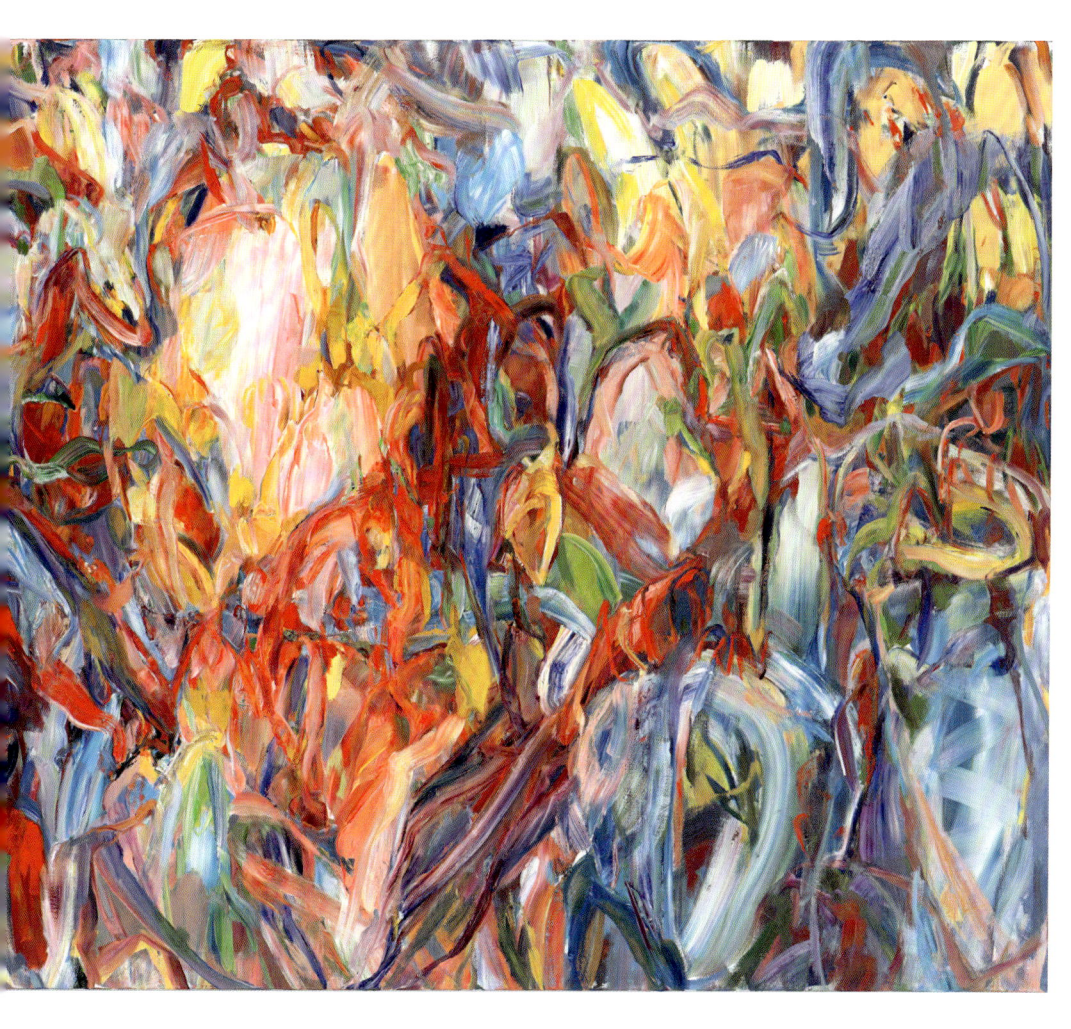

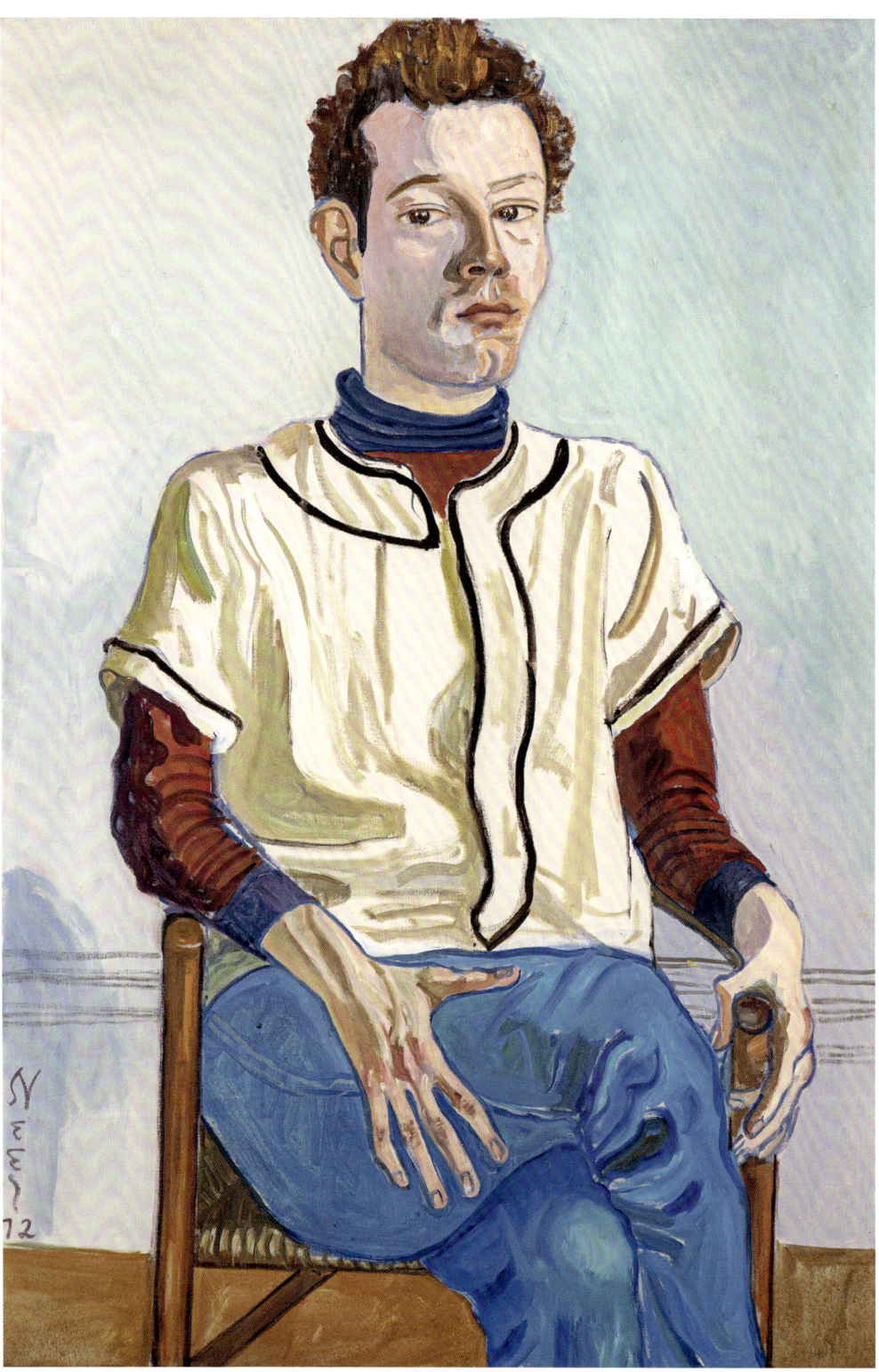

Alice Neel

(1900–1984)

I do not pose my sitters. I never put things anywhere.
I do not deliberate and then concoct. I usually have people
get into something that's comfortable for them. Before
painting, when I talk to the person, they unconsciously
assume their most characteristic pose, which in a way
involves all their character and social standing—what the
world has done to them and their retaliation. And then I
compose something around that. It's much better that way.[1]

I am a collector of souls ... I paint my time using the people
as evidence.[2]

I represent the 20th century. I was born in 1900, and I've
tried to capture the zeitgeist.[3]

I try to capture the essence of the person and of the times—
life as it goes by. I believe in the historical importance of art
and that more is communicated about our era and its effect
on people by a revealing portrait than in any other way ...
    As for people who want flattering paintings of
themselves, even if I wanted to do them, I wouldn't know
what flattery is. To me, as Keats said, beauty is truth, truth
beauty. Altered noses always look much worse. I paint to try
to reveal the struggle, tragedy and joy of life.[4]

*Jackie Curtis as
a Boy*
1972
Oil on canvas
46¾ × 30 in.
(118.8 × 76.2 cm)
CL1330

Shirin Neshat
(b. 1957)

In 1993–97, I produced my first body of work, a series
of stark black-and-white photographs entitled *Women
of Allah*, conceptual narratives on the subject of female
warriors during the Iranian Islamic Revolution of 1979.
On each photograph, I inscribed calligraphic Farsi text on
the female body (eyes, face, hands, feet, and chest); the
text is poetry by contemporary Iranian women poets who
had written on the subject of martyrdom and the role of
women in the Revolution. As the artist, I took on the role of
performer, posing for the photographs. These photographs
became iconic portraits of willfully armed Muslim women.
Yet every image, every woman's submissive gaze, suggests
a far more complex and paradoxical reality behind the
surface.[1]

Untitled, from
Women of Allah
series

1995
Gelatin silver print
60 × 40 in.
(152.4 × 101.6 cm)
No. 2 from an edition
of 3

CL1395

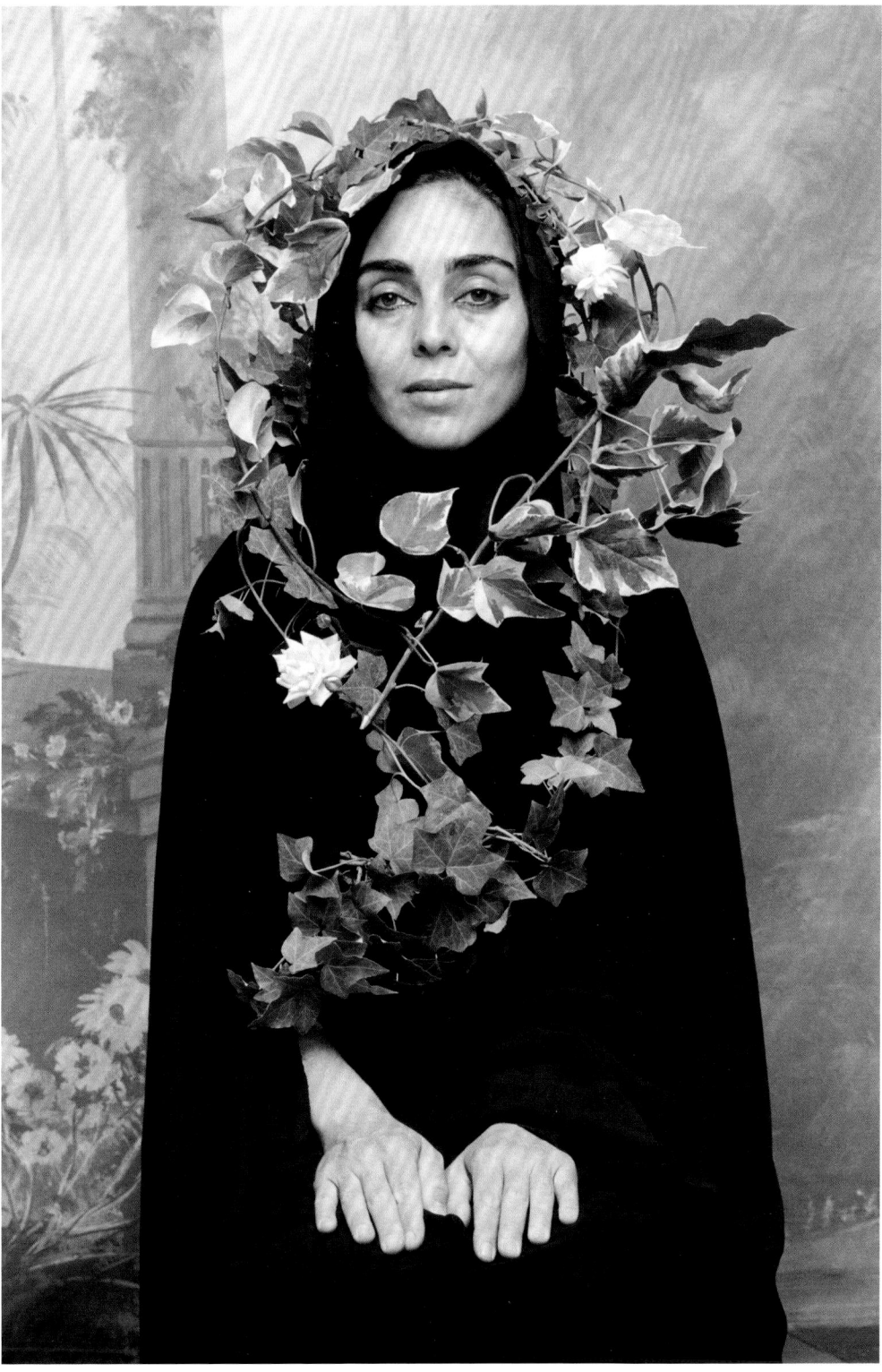

Louise Nevelson
(1899–1988)

Now when I take these old woods that have nails in them or are scratched and have texture, that to me is drawing. Where they're dented—that's a drawing, or where it sucks up space and becomes darker ... When I put pieces together, that means that I'm applying drawing as well. Every piece is not just a piece, it's a connection. It seems I make all my work *just to draw*.[1]

The only reality that I recognize is my reality, and through the work.[2]

It's funny that no matter what one does in life, it hasn't got the vitality or the excitement of really living ... But when you're creating, there's an added energy that surpasses anything else.[3]

I feel that my works are definitely feminine ... The dips and cracks and details fascinate me, my work is delicate: it may look strong, but it is delicate ... My work is the creation of a feminine mind—there is no doubt ... Now I feel that a woman's work will always be a little different than that of a man's.[4]

Untitled
1950s
Painted wood
31 × 12 × 11½ in.
(78.7 × 30.5 × 29.2 cm)
CL855

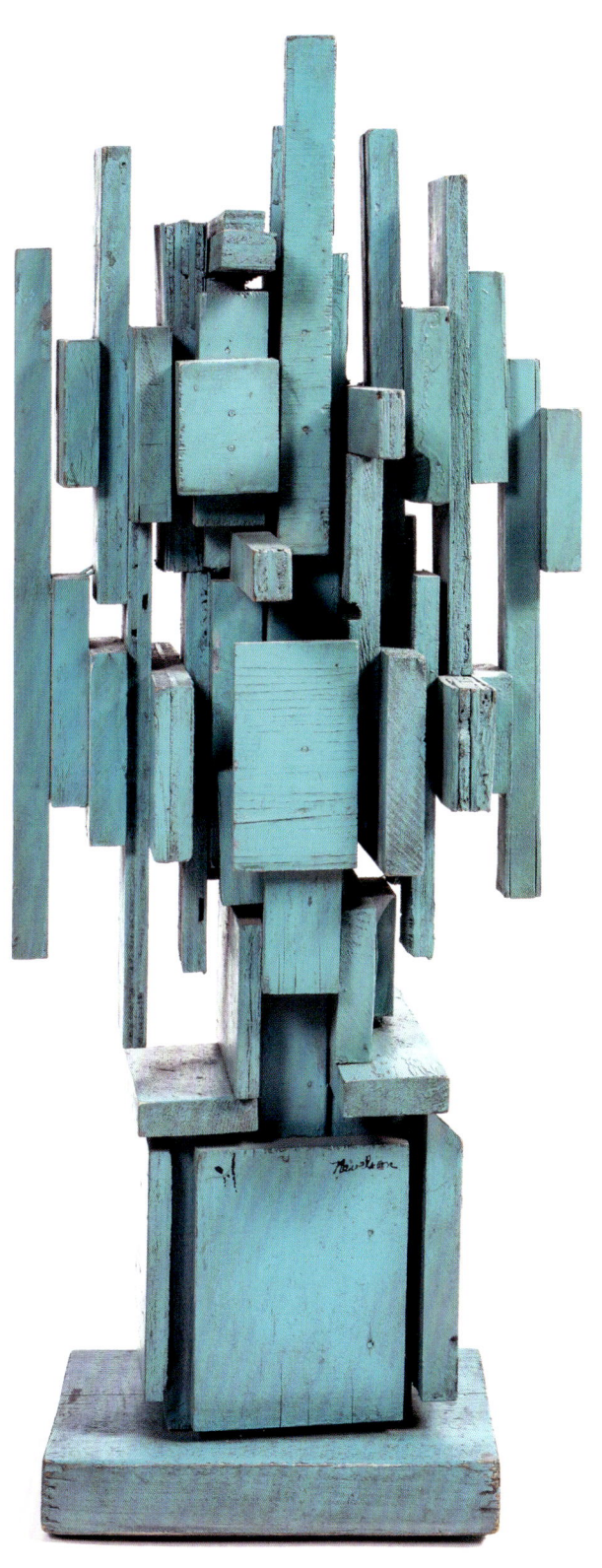

Pat Passlof
(1928–2011)

[Painting] offers the richest, most direct, most plastic of all vehicles. I can do anything with it.[1]

Push back the limits—be willing to risk or sacrifice what you have—throw the cards to the winds and see where they come down. Look for new and unexpected combinations.[2]

I tell students, "If you can think it, don't bother doing it. Think with a brush—the finger of your brain."[3]

Art is a surprise. It is beautiful, but often doesn't seem so at first because it goes against the grain.[4]

Stove
1959
Oil on linen
77 × 69 in.
(195.6 × 175.3 cm)
CL853

134

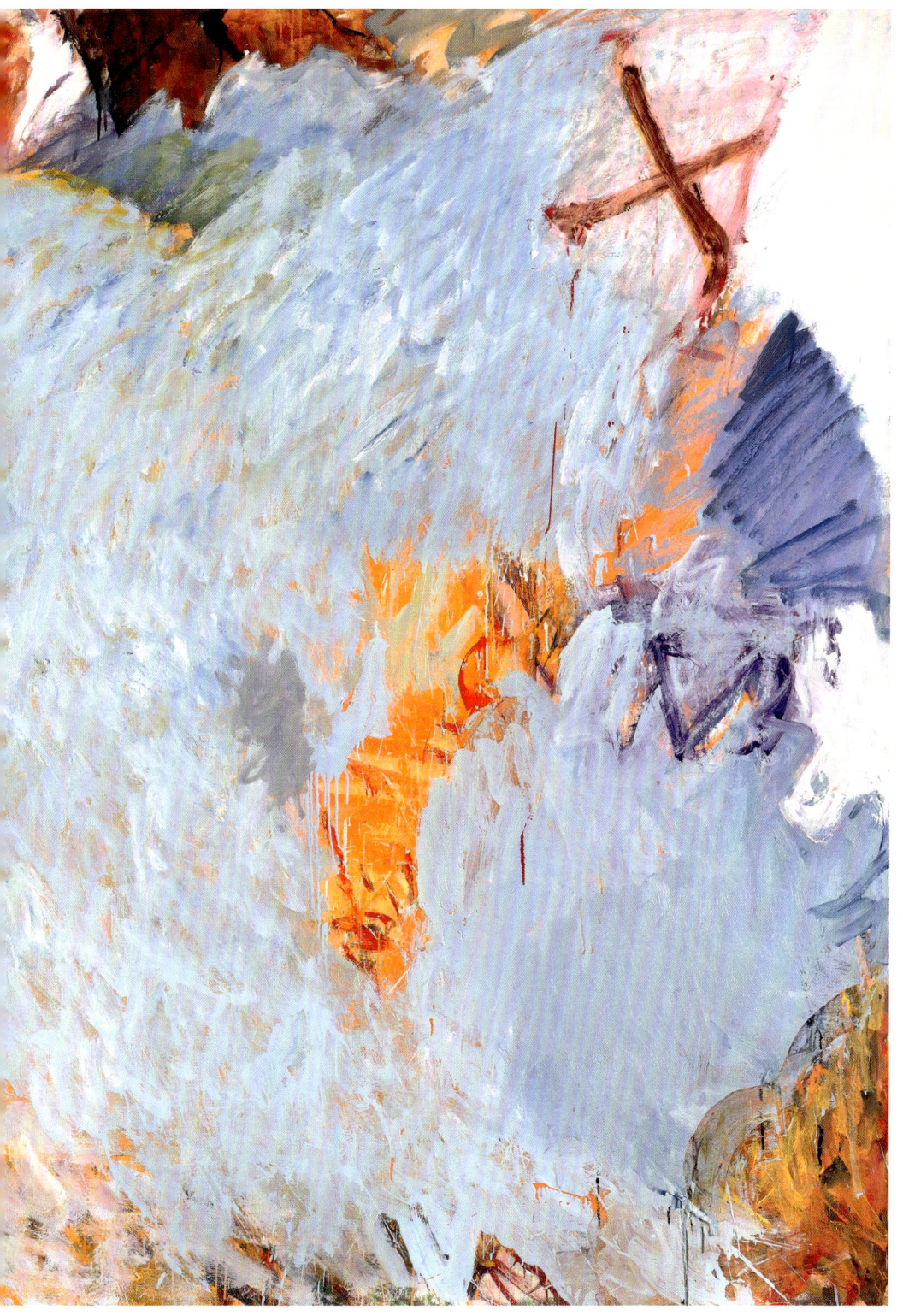

Celia Paul
(b. 1959)

My husband, Steven Kupfer—poet and philosopher—was
my most devoted sitter. We never lived together. Twice a
week, he walked from his house in Camden to my studio
in Bloomsbury, arriving promptly at 8.30 in the morning;
he would leave at 1 pm. After he left, I would work more
on the portrait in his absence. I made many paintings of
him throughout the 28 years we were together. I work
in silence, never speaking during sitting sessions. Steve
would think about philosophy. I think this portrait of him
captures his spirit and his presence. He died in March 2021.
I miss him.[1]

Steve in the Studio

2007
Oil on canvas
59⅞ × 49⅞ in.
(152.1 × 126.7 cm)

CL1249

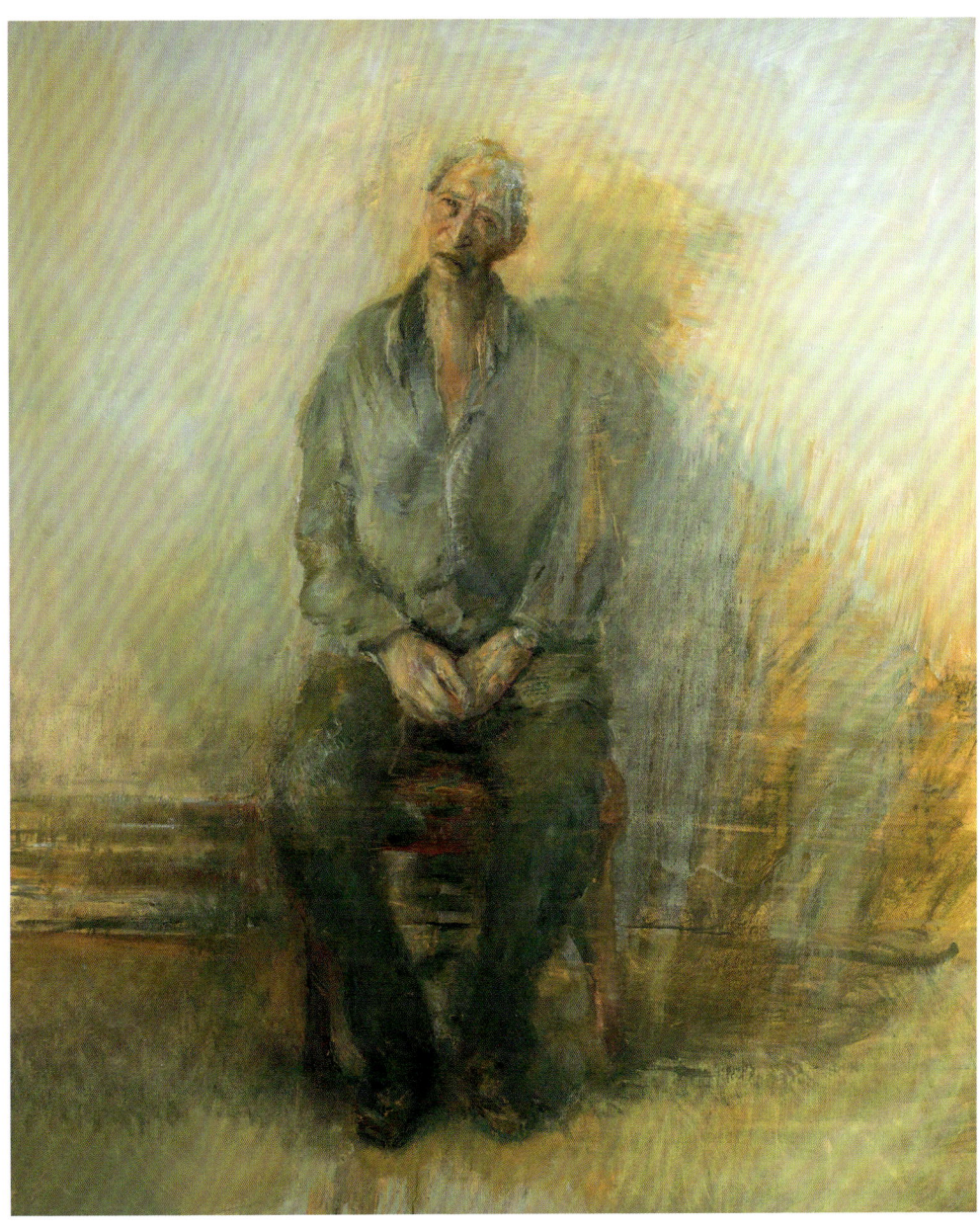

Lilla Cabot Perry
(1848–1933)

If you are to be a true painter, you must approach nature in a mood of humility and love. Nothing else will do. The painter must first choose something that he finds interesting or beautiful and then try to paint it exactly as it appears to him. He must not think about how anyone else painted other subjects or might paint this one; his task is to be utterly true to his own vision. And above all he must not paint to make an impression or an easy sale. If he will go with humility and love, and be true, he will give that rendering of nature which Octave Feuillet or some other French writer called "Nature seen through a temperament."[1]

Girl on a Balcony
1894
Oil on canvas
32 × 20¾ in.
(81.3 × 52.7 cm)

CL1240

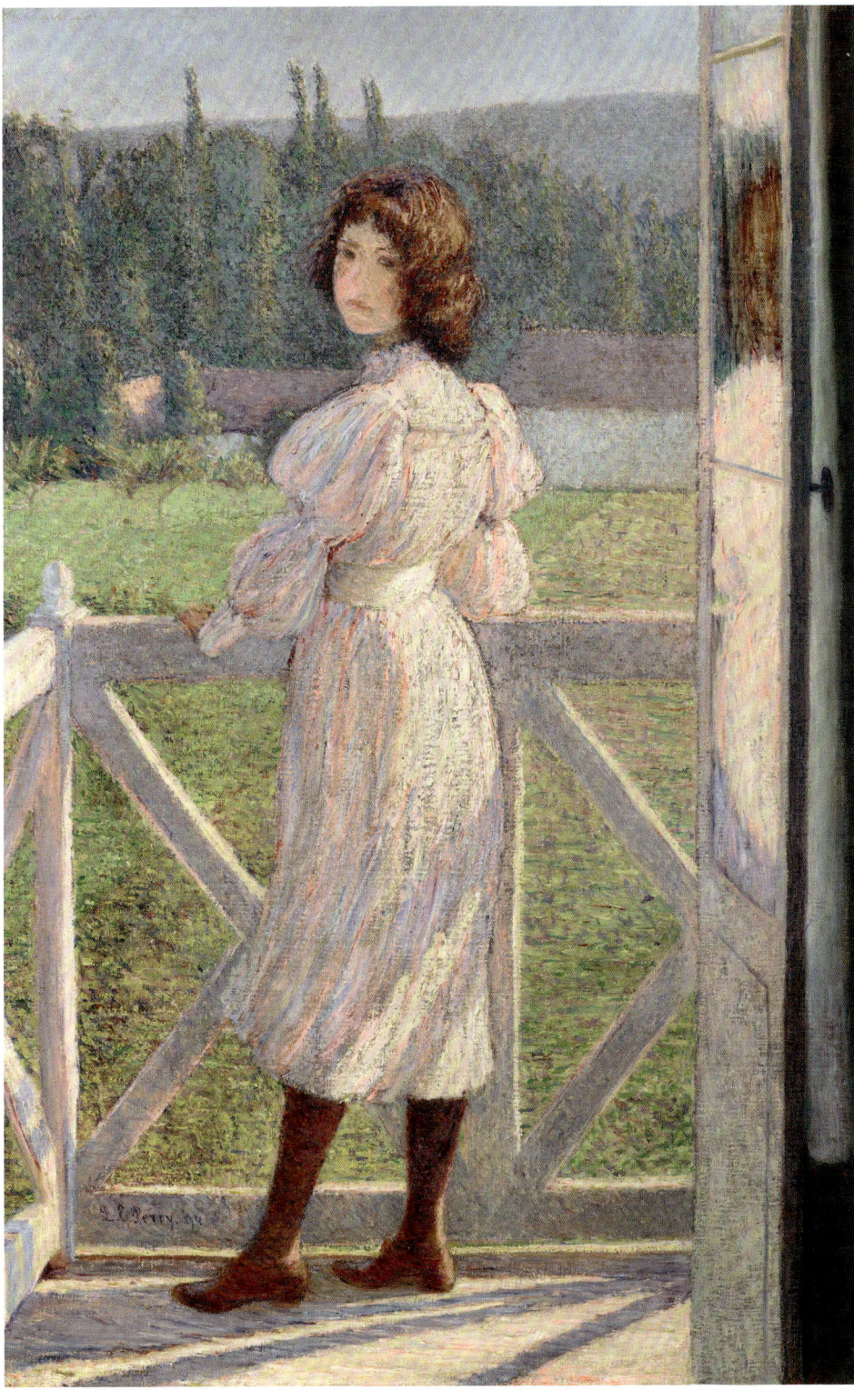

Howardena Pindell
(b. 1943)

I became fascinated by the circle in my last year at graduate school at Yale University's School of Art and Architecture. The circle for me as a point of interest started when I saw the work of a classmate, Nancy Murata. As a child the circle was an indication that the glass or plate, etc. was only to be used by people of colour. I was very young, and my father took me to a root beer stand in northern Kentucky. At the time we were with my grandmother who lived in southern Ohio. It was a symbol used during segregation and Jim Crow. I think on some level I was undoing the hurt during those years.[1]

There's something more I wanted to say about painting. When I teach my students I refer to an exercise I found in a book where you sign your name and then you have a list of feelings. So, for example, for anger you have to think of what makes you angry. You start signing your name, and as you feel that emotion in the moment, you cover it up. Then having thought of something that evokes anger and other emotions, you find the signature keeps changing, though it's still yours. That's what painting is about, a fabric of sensations, emotions and feelings are all there in a tapestry. That's why I'm not a hard-edge painter. There is a tapestry of emotions, and people understand that your feelings come through the hand. Every time I touch the brush, I write my signature, and I am in a certain mood so it's different.[2]

Untitled
1971
Acrylic on canvas
68½ in. × 9 ft 10½ in.
(174 × 301 cm)
CL1172

Alice Rahon
(1904–1987)

On recalling a visit in 1933 to the prehistoric cave paintings in Altamira, Spain:

In earliest times painting was magical; it was a key to the invisible. In those days the value of a work lay in its power of conjuration, a power that talent alone could not achieve. Like the shaman, the sybil and the wizard, the painter had to make himself humble, so that he could share in the manifestation of spirits and forms. The rhythm of our life today denies the primordial principle of painting: conceived in contemplation, the emotional content of the picture cannot be perceived without contemplation.[1]

The true value of the image ... consists in projecting a new realization, which does not necessarily have to be related to an existing object.[2]

Chats nocturnes

1957
Oil on board
30 × 22⅝ in.
(76.2 × 57.5 cm)

CL1427

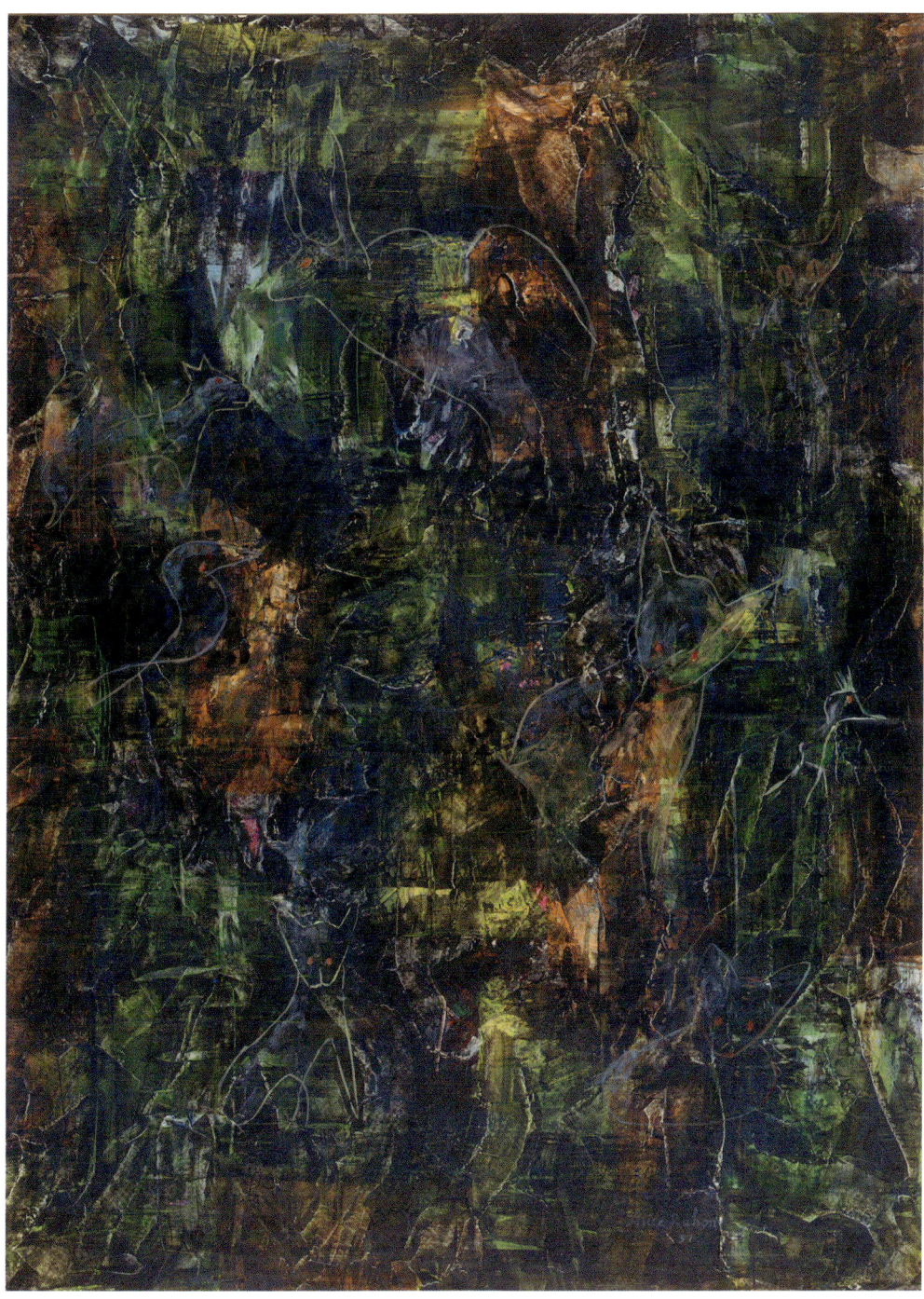

Marie Raymond
(1908–1988)

Life slides into things and light makes it sensible to us.
In the light, images are born that are mirrors of the inner
self and that place before our eyes, within reach of our
senses, a fiction that contains the details and the whole,
the interior and the exterior, the desires and the realities
that thoughts are made of, the ideas (the thrust of vitality
that has taken shape in the dream), the power that creates
the spiritual forms from which the constant process of
becoming is nourished.[1]

I just came up with an idea! [Could] it be that the feminine
expression is focused on life, the harmony between beings
and things expressed long ago by Vermeer?

    The masculine, like time, [is] the one that concludes in
order to compose? And the feminine state [is] the one that
prolongs life through duration? From time immemorial,
woman weaves and embroiders and paints, protects
the offspring, prolongs life. Man, through war, aimed at
conquest and [expansion], provides spirit. This double
state of mankind through harmony and disharmony
transcends time towards the equalization of their forces,
within which the transient and already unreal reality will
have stamped its mark. But do not they tend, one and the
other, to interfering with their initial tendencies towards
an equilibrium of their innate qualities, towards the
androgenic reality of a future?[2]

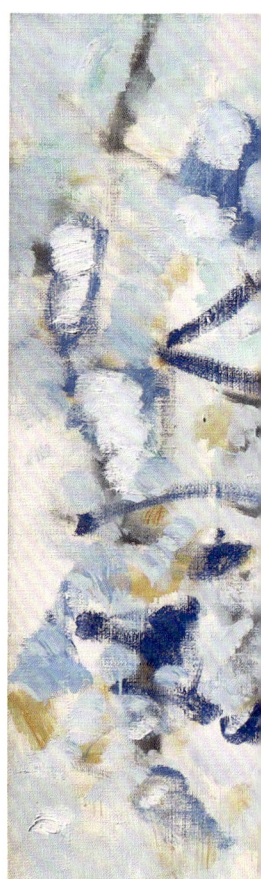

Montagne
1961
Oil on canvas
35 × 57⅛ in.
(88.9 × 145.1 cm)
CL1348

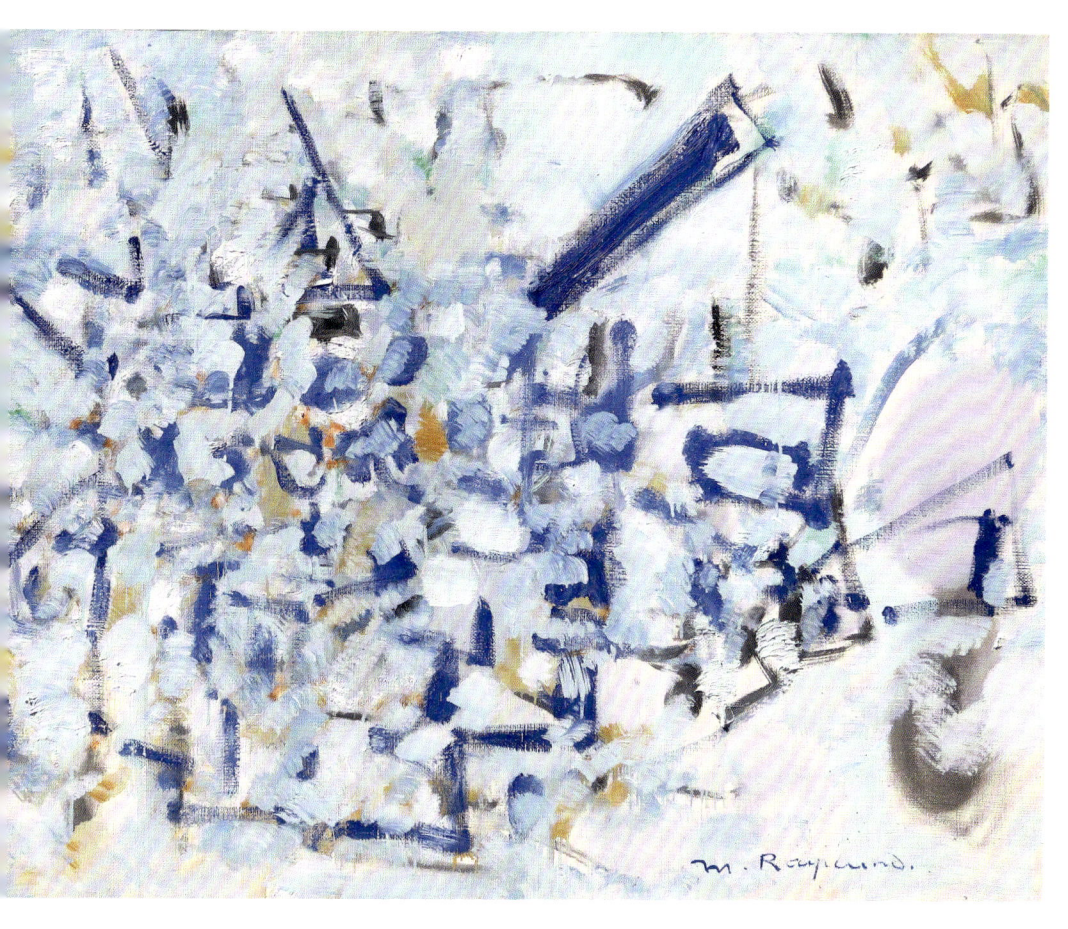

Judit Reigl
(1923–2020)

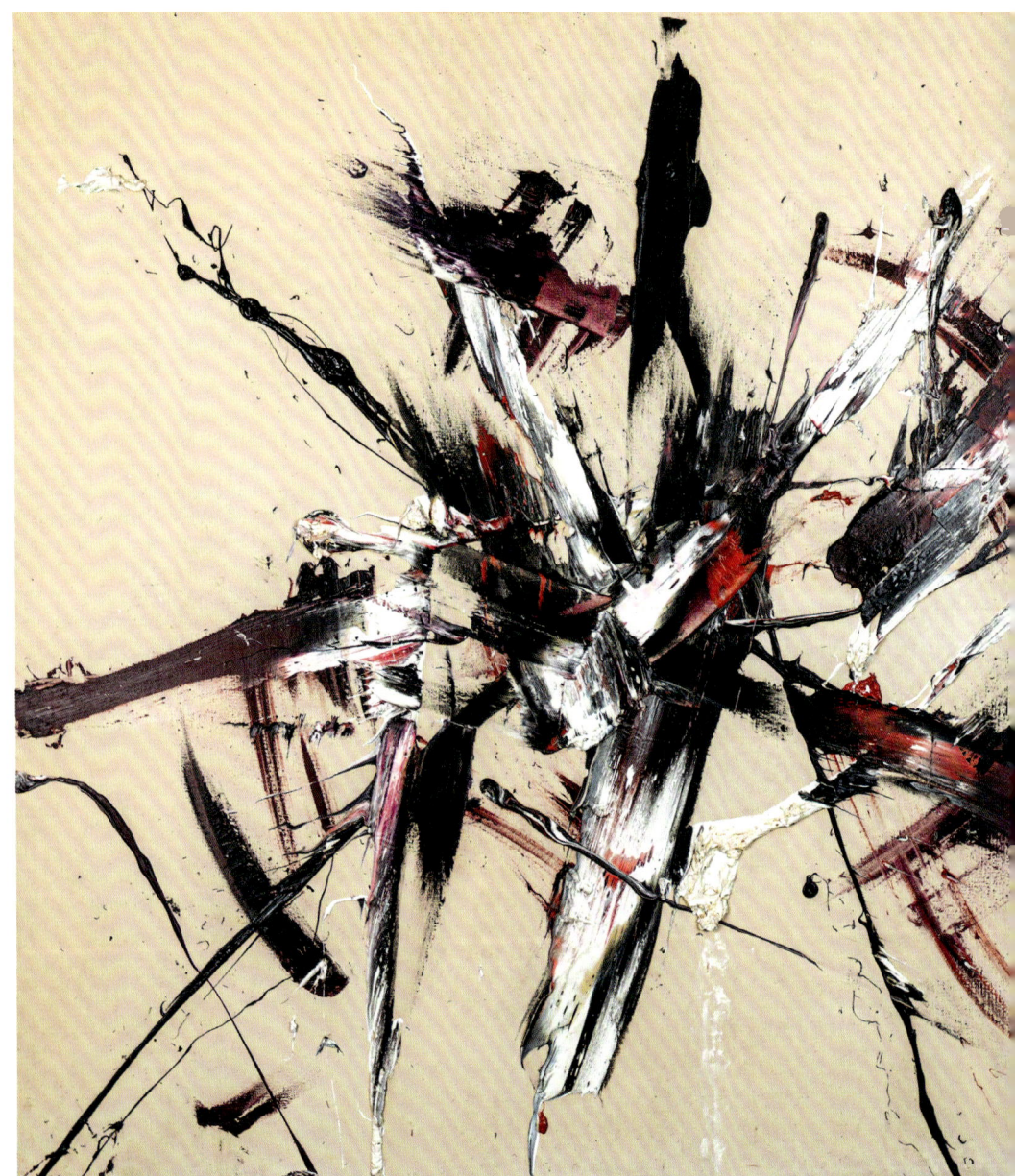

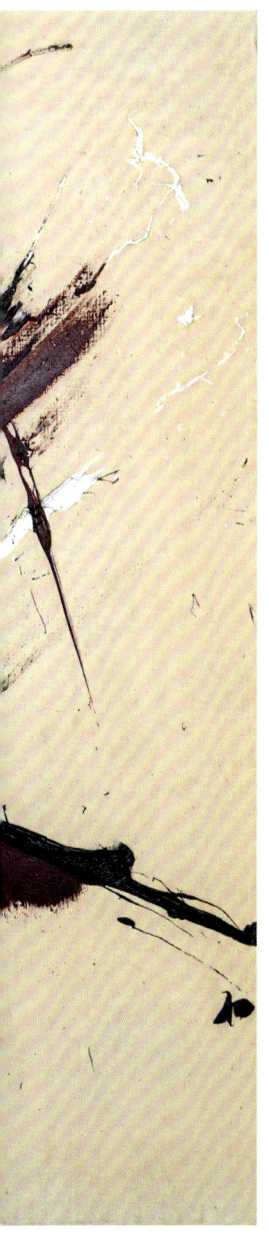

On painting the Éclatement *series:*

The delicate, polished canvas disappears. This brutal white canvas appears, though it has got a bit gray with time. It is almost without a [base]. I bought very cheap paint, not in tubes but large tin boxes. It was also a matter of money. So the paint was thrown up by my hand, as you can see. Somehow I got into this cosmic movement in a way that my whole body moved in. It was a kind of outburst for the world, for myself. Like a supernova ... those large stars that explode. First they are compressed as tiny red constellations, constellations of thousands and thousands of stars together. They are compressed so much that they finally burst out. It is the same here on a small scale. The feelings are the same. It corresponded to my difficult life circumstances at that time. The death of my mother and a lot of other things why it had to be exactly the ... way ... it is.[1]

I visited the Museum of Fine Arts every single day. Come to think of it, I was already one with the craft in my teens, I saw and tried everything. I am in intimate dialogue with the old masters ... I regard them as gifts, heaven-sent. Evoking the old masters solved my painterly problems. I didn't have to look back at the past, I could look into myself ...[2]

Éclatement
1956
Oil on canvas
57¼ × 67⅛ in.
(145.4 × 170.5 cm)
CL1246

Deborah Remington
(1930–2010)

I studied painting with Clyfford Still, David Park, Elmer Bischoff and Hassel Smith at the San Francisco Art Institute ... After my sophomore year, I saw that representation was not my direction ... I wanted my own shapes and space.[1]

The forms I invent become the natural elements of a landscape of an interior world, and it is towards a more intense awareness of that world and an increasingly sensitive depiction of that landscape that I work.[2]

Mine is a very personal imagery with no history except my own history.[3]

I didn't expect anything from the art world, just from myself ... All that ever mattered to me is the work, and the work just speaks for itself.[4]

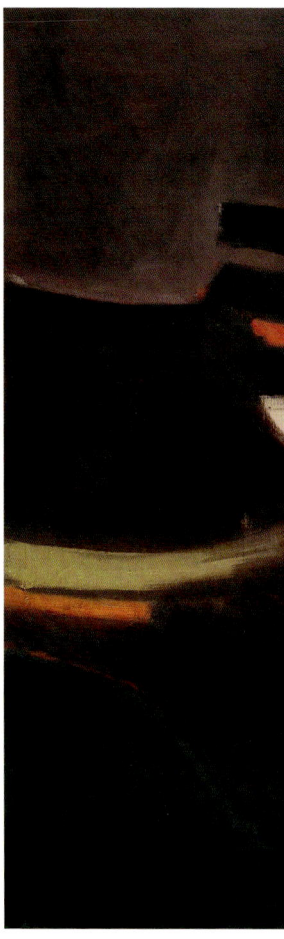

Eleusian
1951
Oil on canvas
43¼ × 71½ in.
(109.9 × 181.6 cm)
CL863

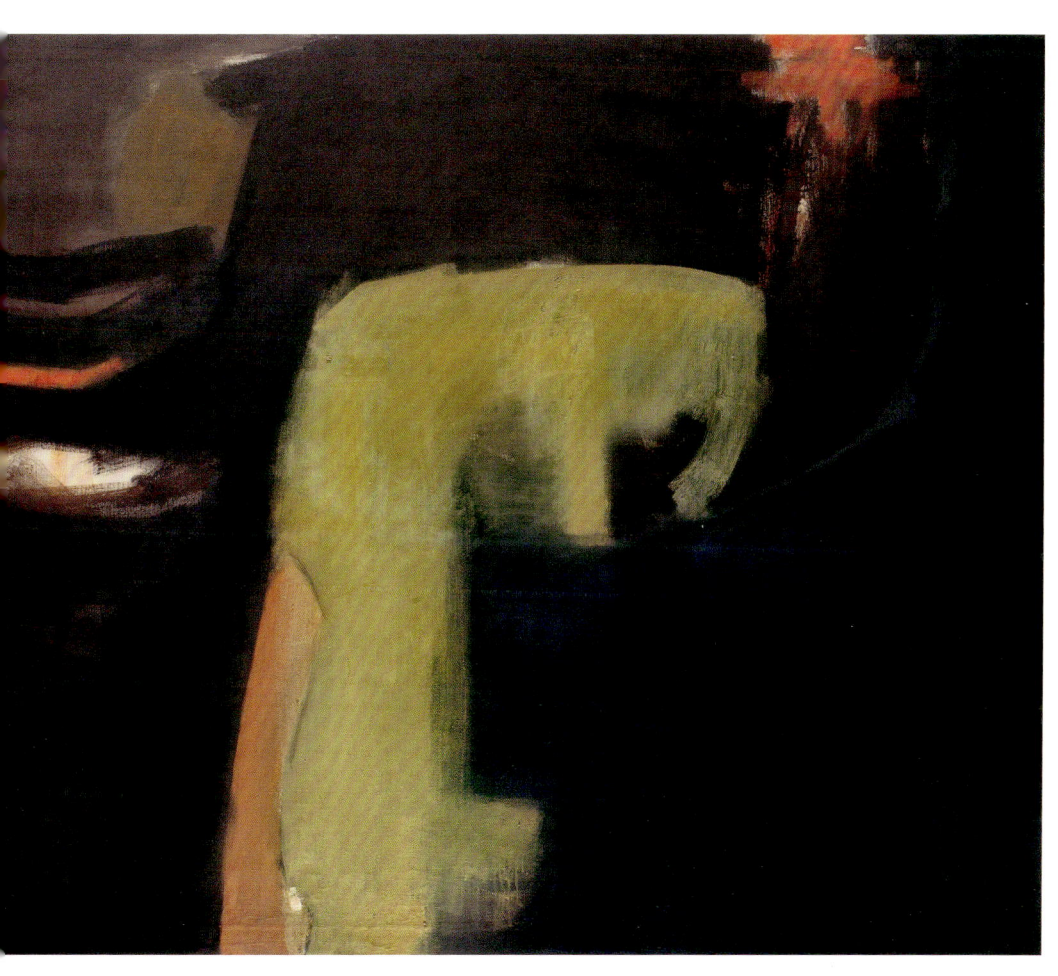

Juliette Roche
(1884–1980)

On the "ever-increasing ferment in artistic circles" in Paris in 1913:

One could feel in the atmosphere of Paris, so responsive to every slightest change, a sort of instability, a malaise, something like the restlessness displayed by animals before an earthquake. It crystallized now and again in a few words, a few sentences, then dissolved. But the unusual symptoms kept manifesting themselves in various ways.[1]

Nature morte à la carafe

c. 1918–20
Oil on cardboard
30⅜ × 20⅞ in.
(77.2 × 53 cm)

CL1390

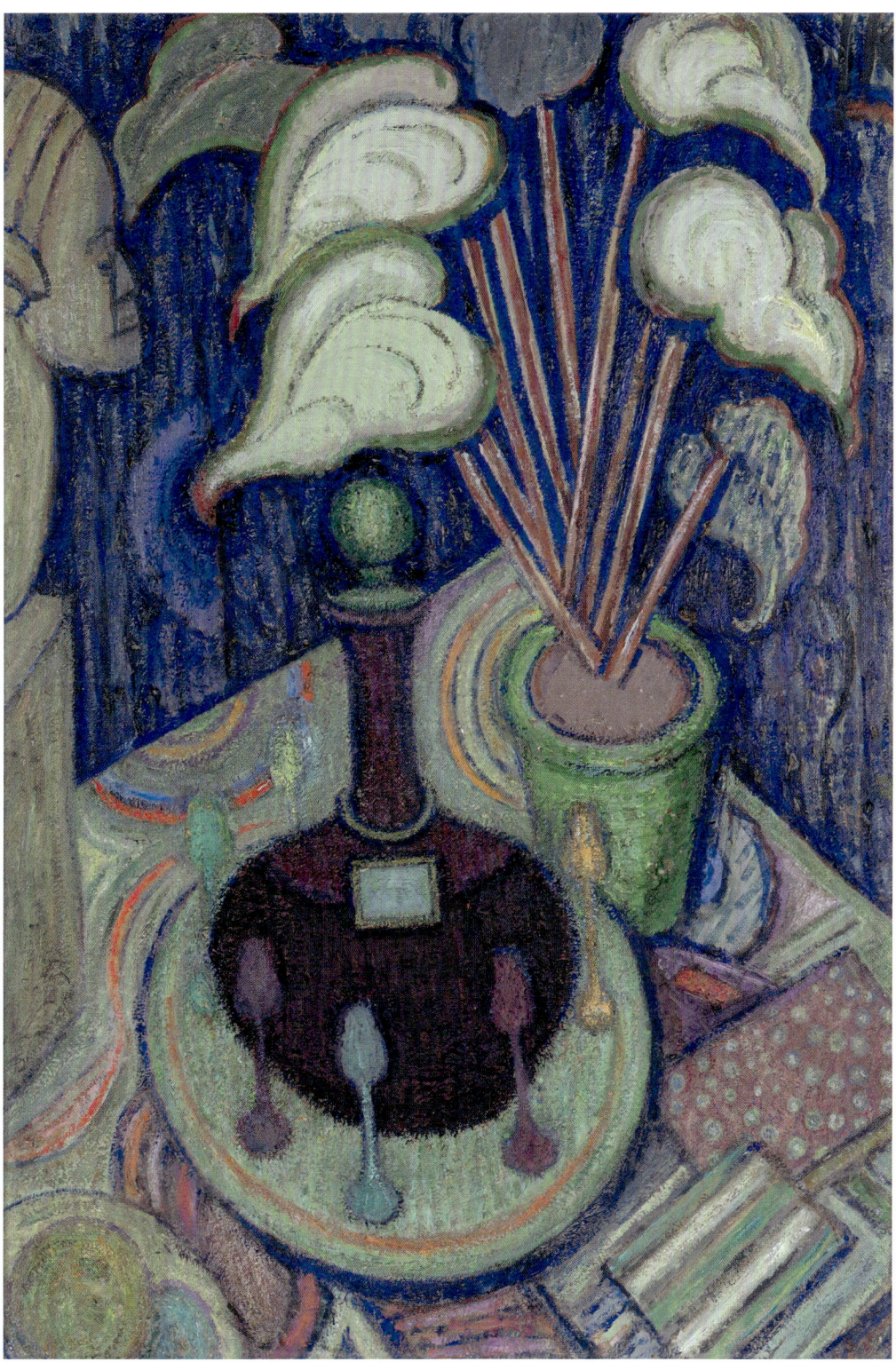

Judith Rothschild
(1921–1993)

[I] do not wish to copy nature. [I] ... do not wish to reproduce but to produce ... to produce as a plant which produces a fruit and is unable to reproduce a still life ... to produce directly, not thru an interpreter ... to reproduce is to imitate ... art, however, is reality, and the reality of all should triumph over the particular ... these works are constructed with lines, surfaces, shapes and colors, they seek to reach beyond human values and attain the infinite.[1]

Customarily, I begin a painting in a rather haphazard way, relying on past experiences to build up to an unavoidable preoccupation—not so much with a specific motif or even a specific place in mind as with a more general aura of concern ...

There is the emotional side of painting that Yeats speaks of when he writes: "Art bids us touch and taste and hear and see." At the same time, the question whether any method at all is desirable has haunted many painters who, like myself, were trained in New York during and just after the Second World War.

We learned the classical discipline of Cubism not from Gleizes but from Hans Hofmann, who was essentially a romanticist. We were also impressed by the automatism espoused by Masson and Miró, by the works of Léger, Mondrian and Calder, and by the Dadaism of Duchamp. Nevertheless, it was Hofmann who tended to dominate the student scene.

For a time the promise of the intuitive, semi-automatic approach seemed alluring to me. But many of us never totally accepted it. And perhaps because I had been trained in music before I began to paint seriously, I was soon assailed by grave doubts ...

The idea of some sort of a color–music scale correspondence occurred to me while I was an art student.[2]

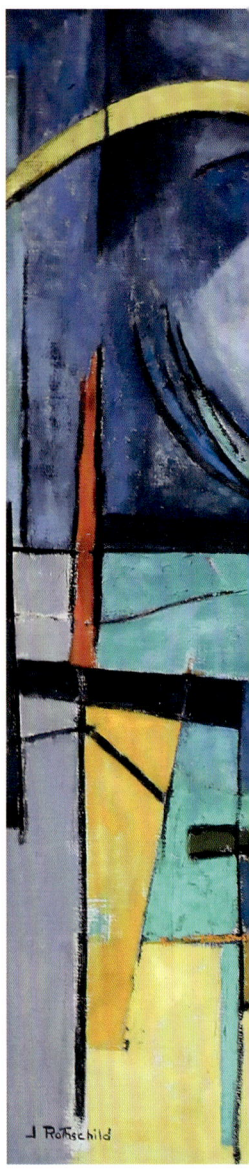

Canyon #3
1957
Oil on canvas
35⅞ × 44 in.
(91.1 × 111.8 cm)
CL1446

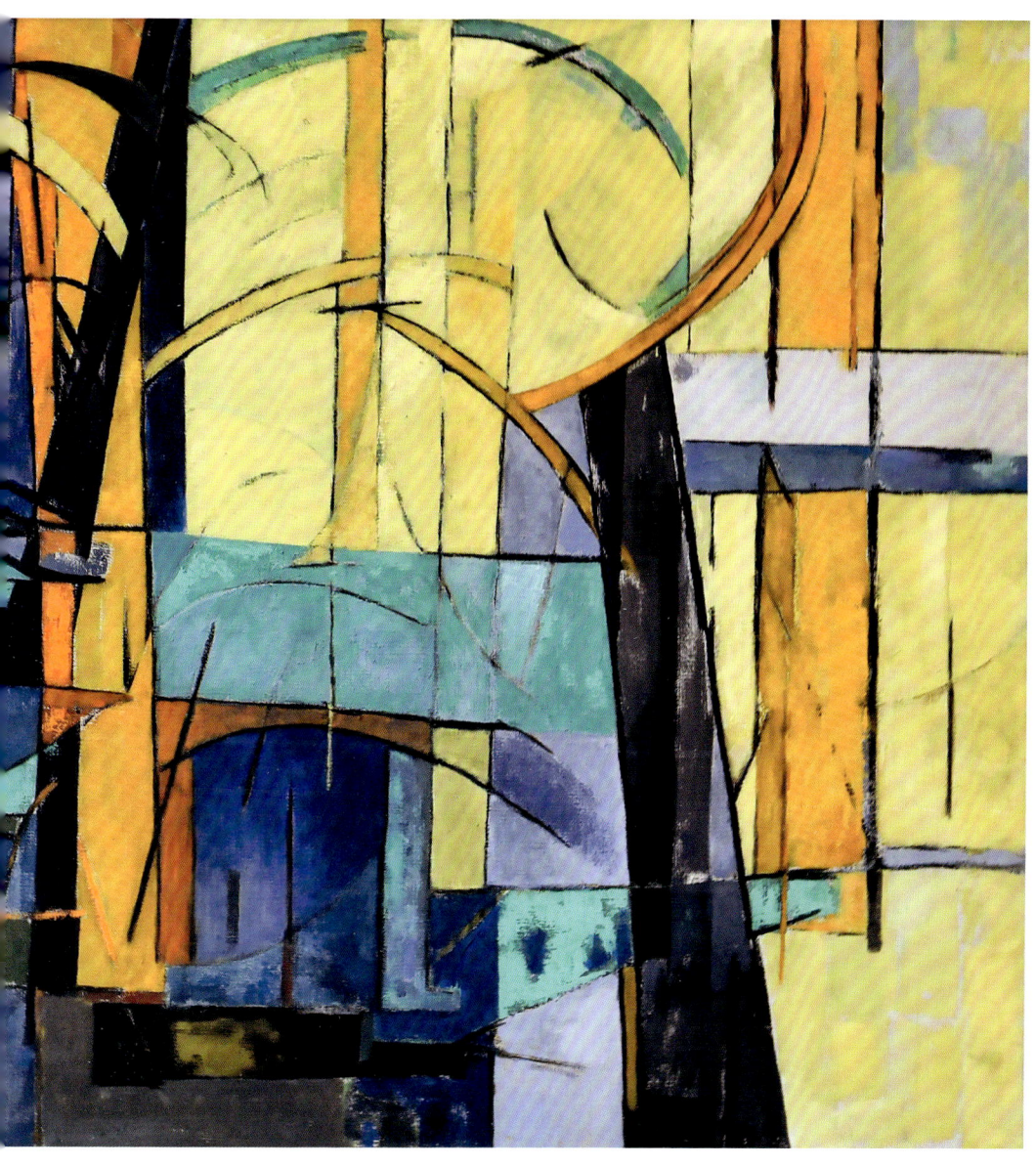

Niki de Saint Phalle
(1930–2002)

I could not identify with Mother, our grandmothers, our aunts, or Mother's friends. Their territory seemed too restrictive for my taste ... I wanted the world that belonged to men ... Very early I got the message that men had the power and I wanted it. Yes, I would steal their fire from them. I would not accept the boundaries that Mother tried to impose on my life because I was a woman.[1]

On her Tir *(shooting) paintings:*

Performance art did not yet exist, but this was a performance. Here I was, an attractive girl (if I had been ugly they would have said I had a complex and not paid any attention), screaming against men in my interviews and shooting.[2]

Art, to most people, is something terribly serious and people refuse to realize that joy is something terribly serious, too.[3]

Tir Stockholm
May 23, 1961
Paint and plaster on wooden panel
23⅝ × 20⅛ in.
(60 × 51.1 cm)
CL1250

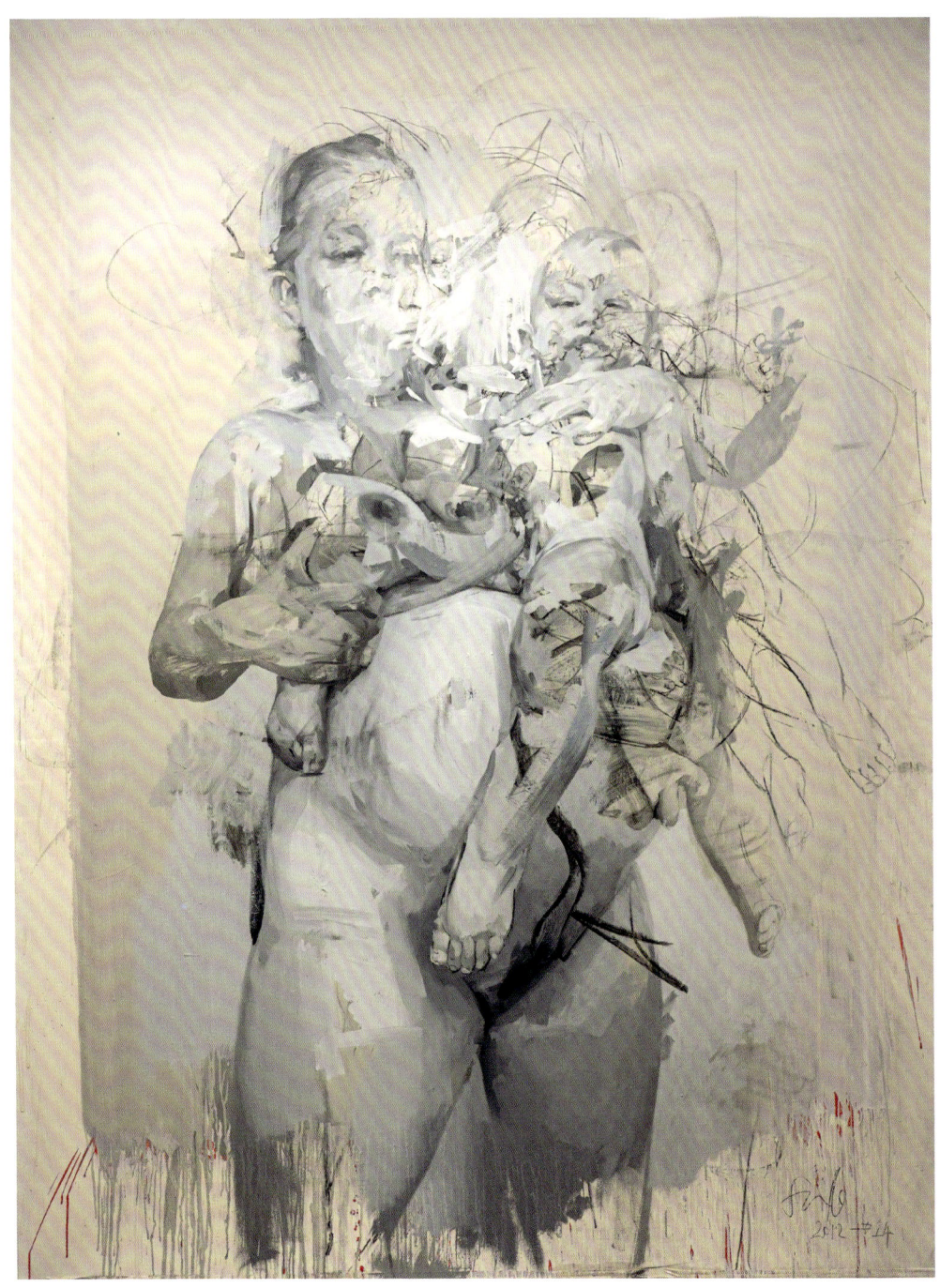

Jenny Saville
(b. 1970)

Having children had the most profound impact on the way
I make art and see the world. Making flesh in my body, and
the animalistic nature of giving birth, affected my view
of nature. The simultaneous realities I've been trying to
generate in my work over the past few years, the strata and
layering, came about through the drawings I made after
having children. It opened out a new way for me to create
space and movement. What I enjoy about my children so
much is their freedom. They move their bodies without
care or judgment, and that's a precious moment in life.[1]

Generation

2012–14
Pencil, charcoal, and
oil on paper laid on
canvas
78½ × 59¾ in.
(199.4 × 151.8 cm)

CL1396

Miriam Schapiro
(1923–2015)

A woman artist experiences a contradiction in her life. She feels herself as subject in a world that treats her as object. Her work often becomes a symbolic arena in which she can firmly establish a sense of personal identity. She asks, "Who am I?" and proceeds to depict an image, central and clear, which proclaims to an unheeding world her information about who she is. Many women have done this but their images remain unseen and the information undigested by a society that insists on only one perspective.[1]

The quality of self-analysis, probing deeply into one's historical resources—bringing to light repressed experience; learning the language of one's own unconscious—this is what leads an artist to a possible personal iconography.[2]

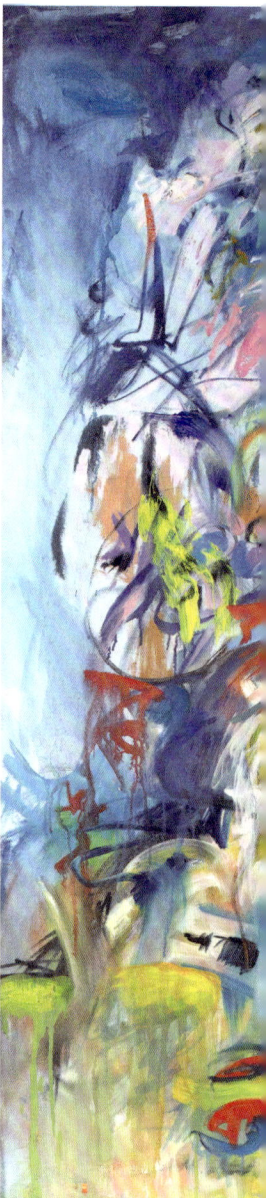

Idyll II
1956
Oil on canvas
60 × 72 in.
(152.4 × 182.9 cm)
CL870

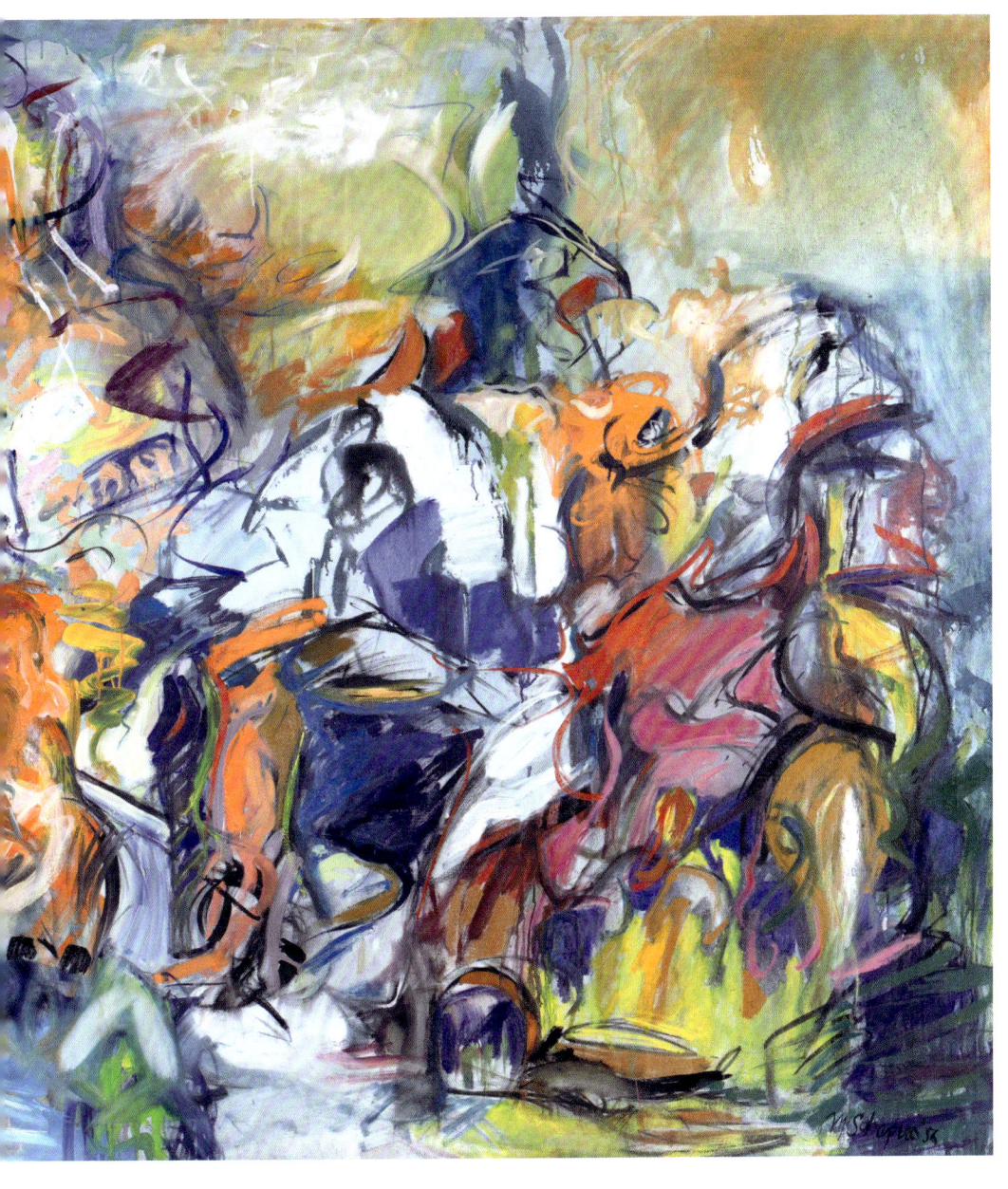

Ethel Schwabacher
(1903–1984)

My difficulty lies in the fact that I constantly see further possibilities: the calm of the sky as it extends upwards, the blazing light of the sun, the marvelous fluidity of water, the shining dewdrop on the first crocus, the icicle hanging from a winter bough flashing, immaculate. Perhaps it is unfortunate that I see these things because it fills me with longing to paint them, a longing to accomplish the impossible.[1]

I do not think there's any reason to say that this is a particularly feminine approach to art ... Beauty is everywhere. It comes to light, it lives, it vanishes, is renewed, it lives, it vanishes and is renewed again.[2]

I have sought in my work the "place where": that non-abstract element in Art which expands inward and outward: and wherein coexists the formal definition and the mystery.[3]

In painting, too, the artist must multi-relate to the size of his canvas, to the edges of it, to the individual forms which must be so thought out as to give space to other portions of the total design. I have always found it most difficult to bear in mind continually the relation of one form or ... one personality or personage to another, or if three, to have room for all three. They must coexist in this particular space, and one must find the right proportions and interrelations.[4]

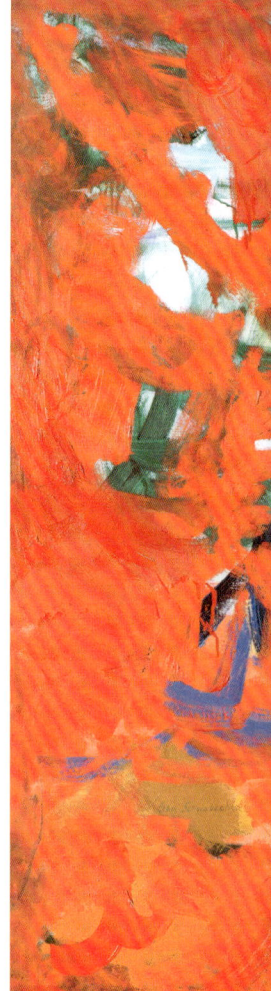

Sankaty II
1956
Oil on canvas
50 × 72 in.
(127 × 182.9 cm)
CL839

160

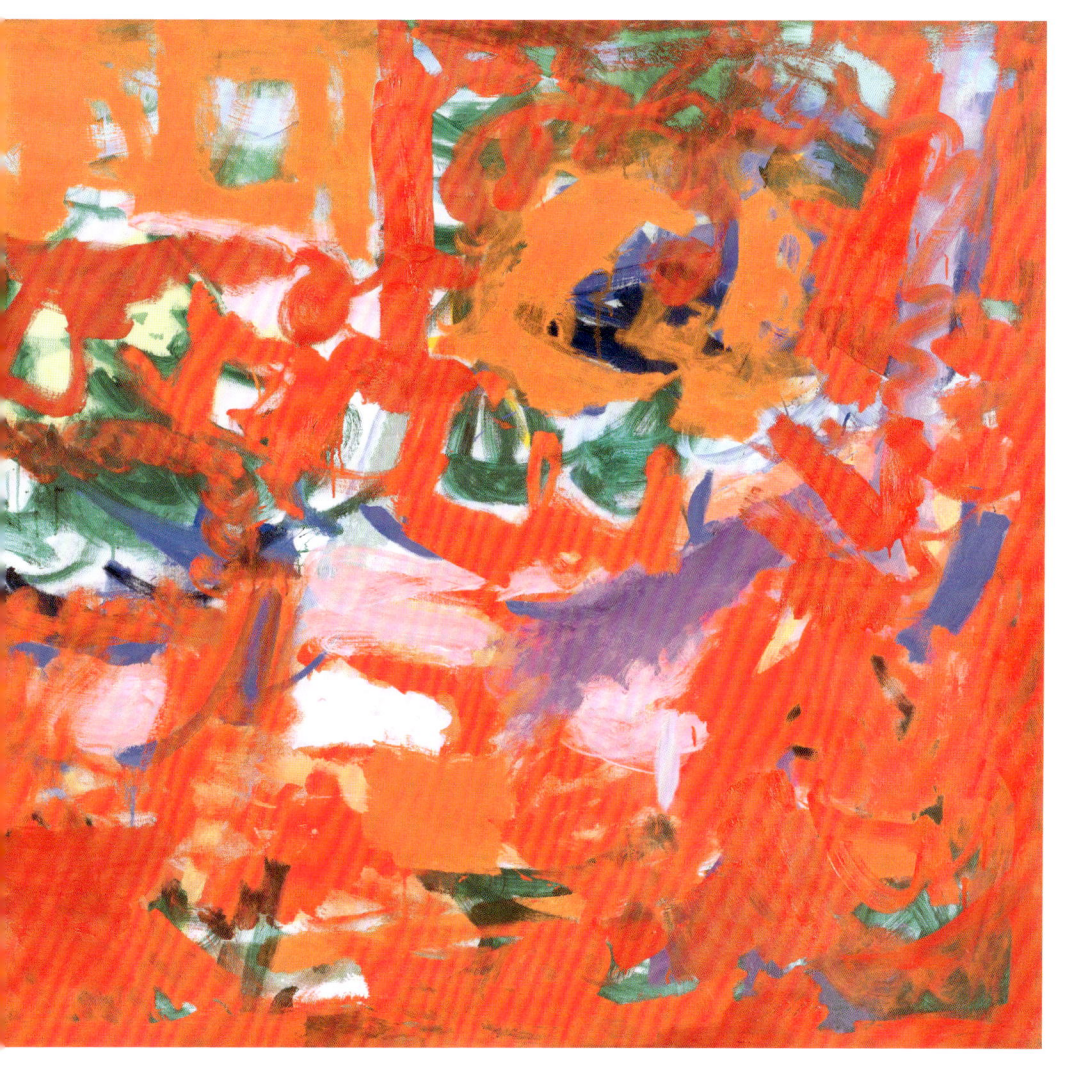

Jeanne Selmersheim-Desgrange
(1877–1958)

I do not think at all that the "subject" confers the slightest superiority on a work of art. A landscape by Cézanne or a still life by Chardin is a work of art so complete that no one thinks of regretting the absence of anything whatsoever.[1]

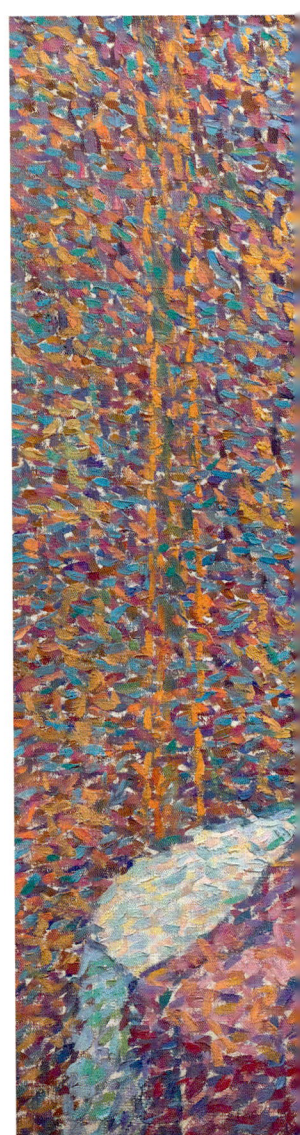

La Table aux jardin
(The Table in the Garden)

c. 1910
Oil on canvas
29⅛ × 36¼ in.
(74 × 92.1 cm)

CL1254

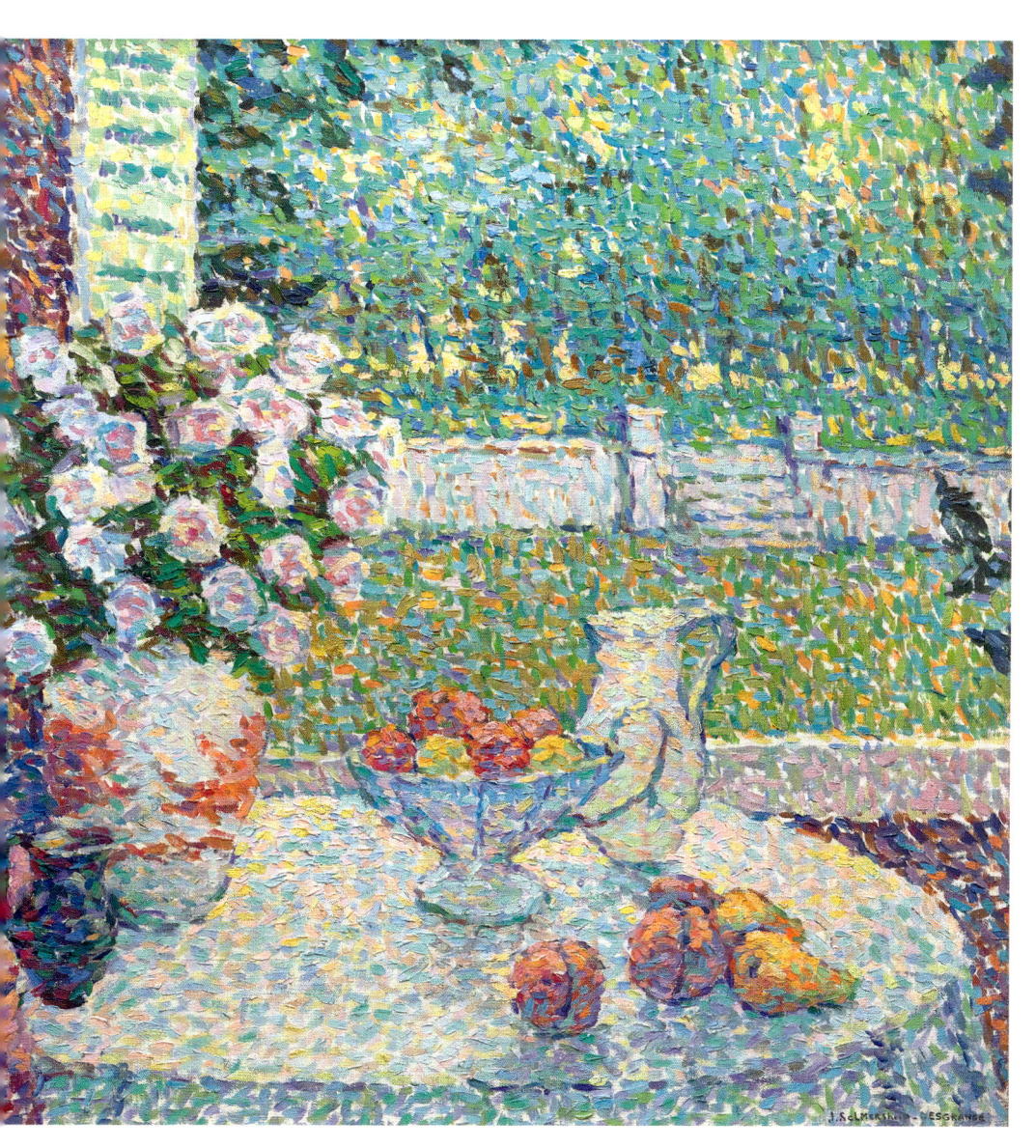

Joan Semmel
(b. 1932)

I never thought of myself as a beautiful woman displaying
her beauty. I never conceived of it that way. The reason
I used myself in this was that I wanted to make images of
women that were not fetishized. All I saw on the newsstands
were images of pin-up kind of women. I felt that it was
a false image; it was a commercialized image of selling
women's bodies. I wanted women to be seen in a way
that they really were, and with all the imperfections that
were there. I wanted to show that the kind of advertising
and movies and everything that gave women images of
themselves were false and made them always feel inferior
and not good enough.[1]

After I discovered using the camera in the painting gave it
a whole kind of almost aggressive connection to the viewer,
I decided to do a whole group of paintings that I called
With Camera ..., some of which where the camera shows
the flash, which gave me the opportunity to abstract things
somewhat to compensate for the flash, and others where
I used the mirror as a framing device, and you could see the
mirror ... so that it ... talked about how the image that we
have of ourselves is always artificial. It's always framed by
external forces.[2]

Knees Together
2003
Oil on canvas
60 × 48⅛ in.
(152.4 × 122.2 cm)

CL1036

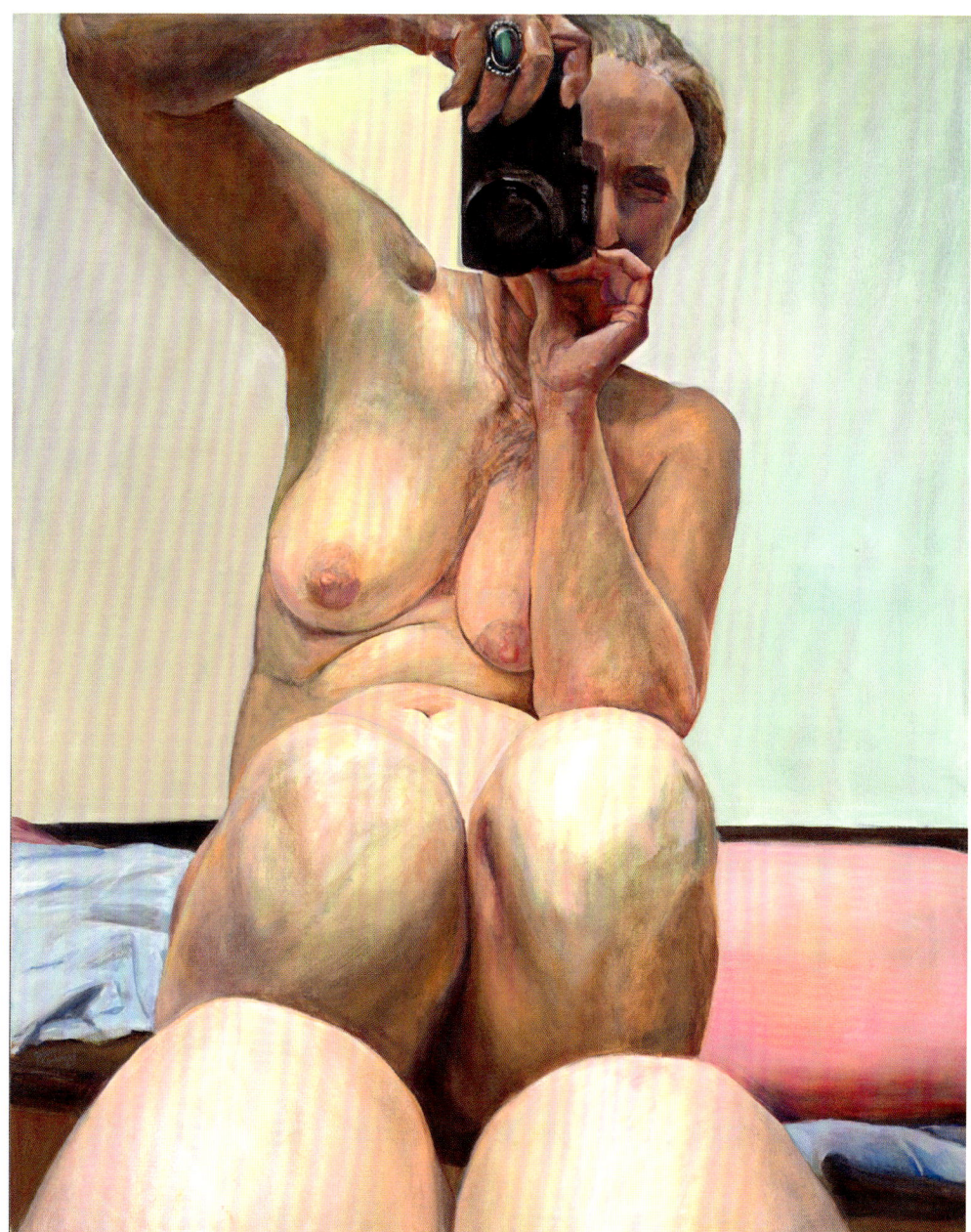

Rose Shakinovsky
(b. 1953)

This work is derived directly from an internet image of
the devastating bombing of Kharkiv. This was digitally
altered through chance procedures, until it resembled
the aesthetic and painterly qualities of traditional abstract
painting. The resulting computer image was translated
faithfully into an oil painting. The work, however,
maintains the basic underlying composition and random
colors of the original. This is part of an ongoing series
that deals with the emotional and moral challenges of
the present political, social and ecological devastation.
Importantly, the canvas, being the proportion of the
golden section, offers an underlying harmony, sense
of balance and calm.[1]

Ukraine Kharkiv
April 2022
2023
Oil on linen
14⅝ × 23⅝ in.
(37.2 × 60 cm)

CL1381

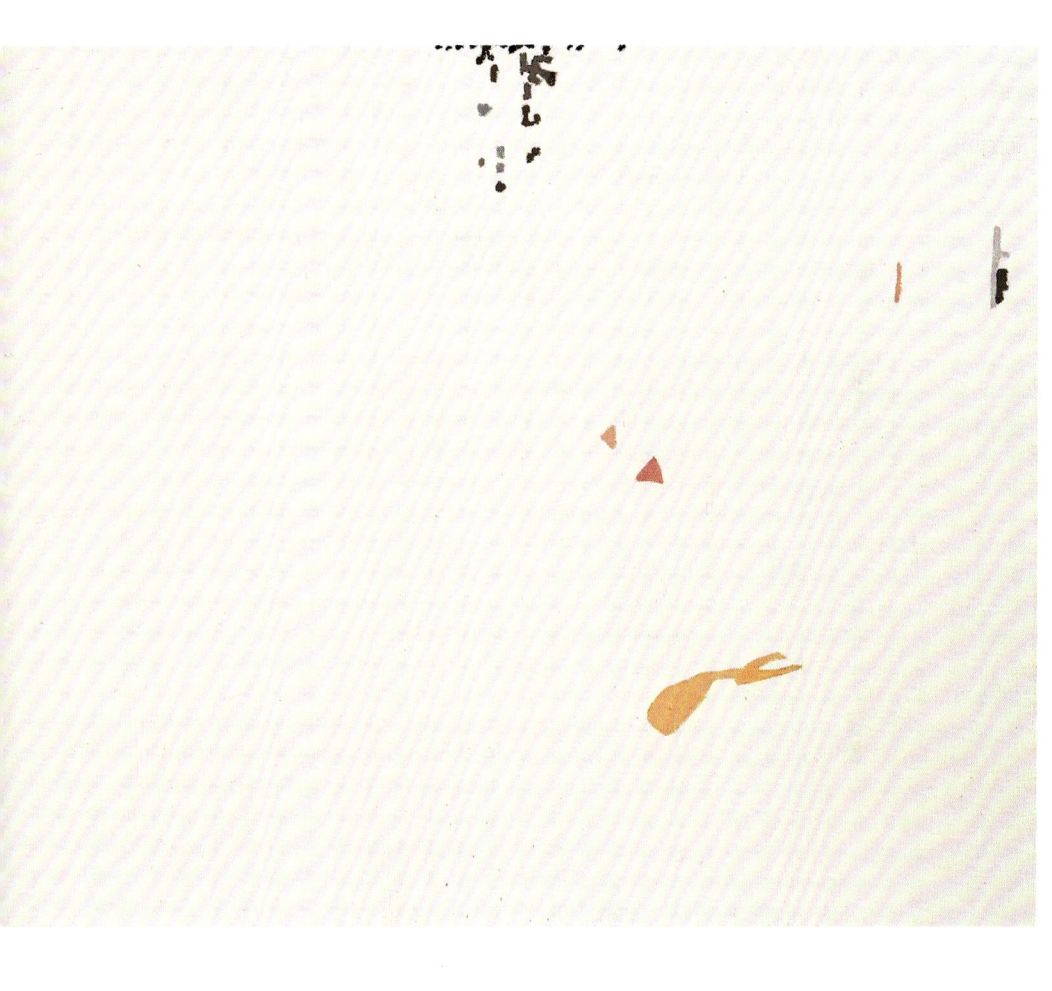

Anj Smith
(b. 1978)

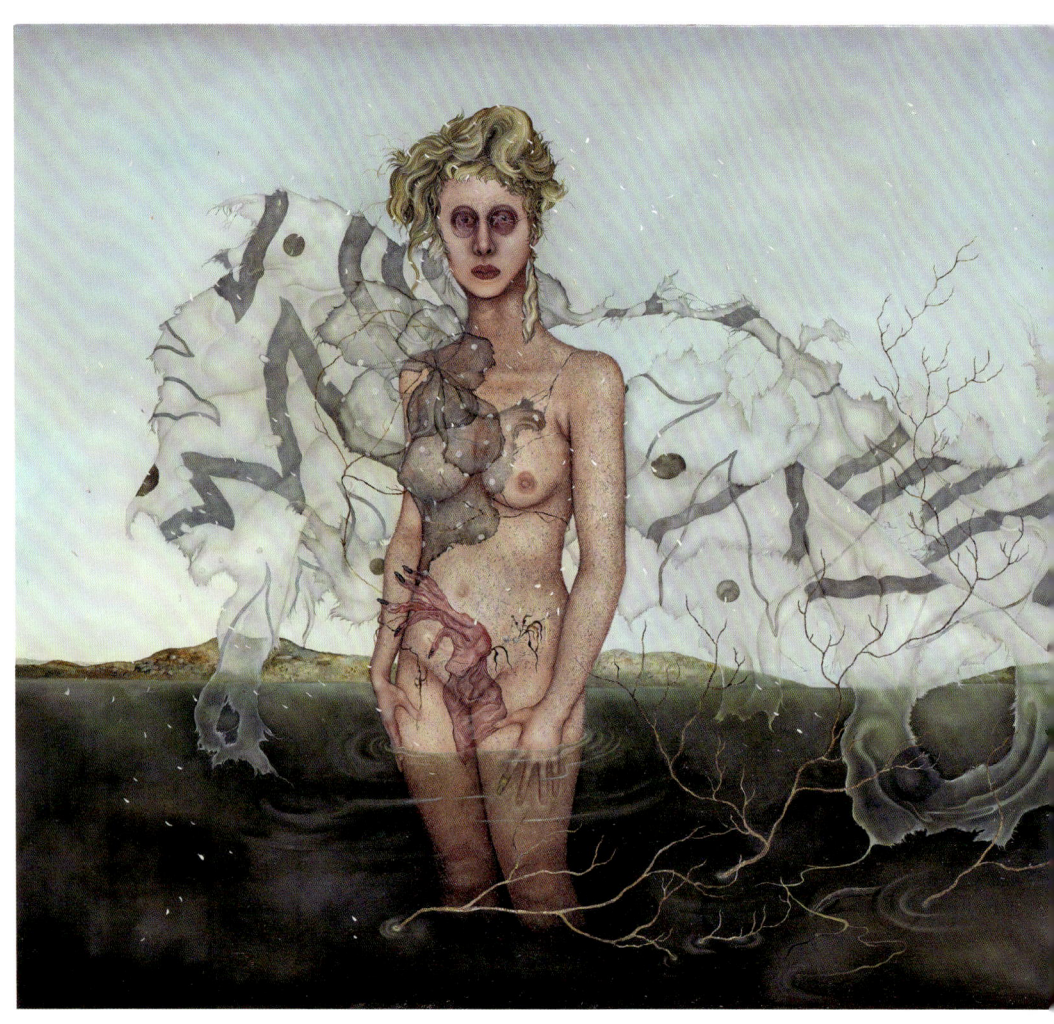

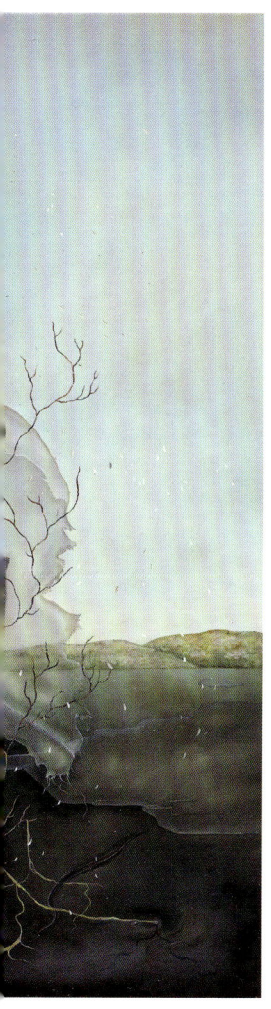

There's a particular painting, *But Tell It Slant*, where the figure is just standing in water. The element of water, being singular but something that's also very malleable and something that constantly changes shape, felt like a very apt contextualization for the figure. I think it holds connotations of rising sea levels and ecological disaster, and I was thinking about how our environment globally is shifting and morphing.

Attitudes towards the figure and conversations around gender are also similarly on the move. I started to think about a philosophical impulse of atopia, which is the idea of wandering off from a point in order to re-evaluate a lot of conventional conclusions and definitions and classifications. Roland Barthes described this atopia as "drifting habitations." All of these things were at play and could be activated by that title.[1]

But Tell It Slant
2023
Oil on linen
30¼ × 44⅛ in.
(76.8 × 112.1 cm)
CL1399

Sylvia Snowden
(b. 1942)

Michelle developed a hard shell to protect her inner feelings. I paint the inner feelings, which are soft. To reveal this softness would be painful for people who have a tendency to pluck at it, which makes survival harder. One could see the softness in her eyes and sometimes her smile—only a flash when the protection from the pain of life is no longer apparent. See the softness?[1]

Michelle Haberon
1978
Acrylic and oil pastel on Masonite
96 × 48 in.
(243.8 × 121.9 cm)
CL1306

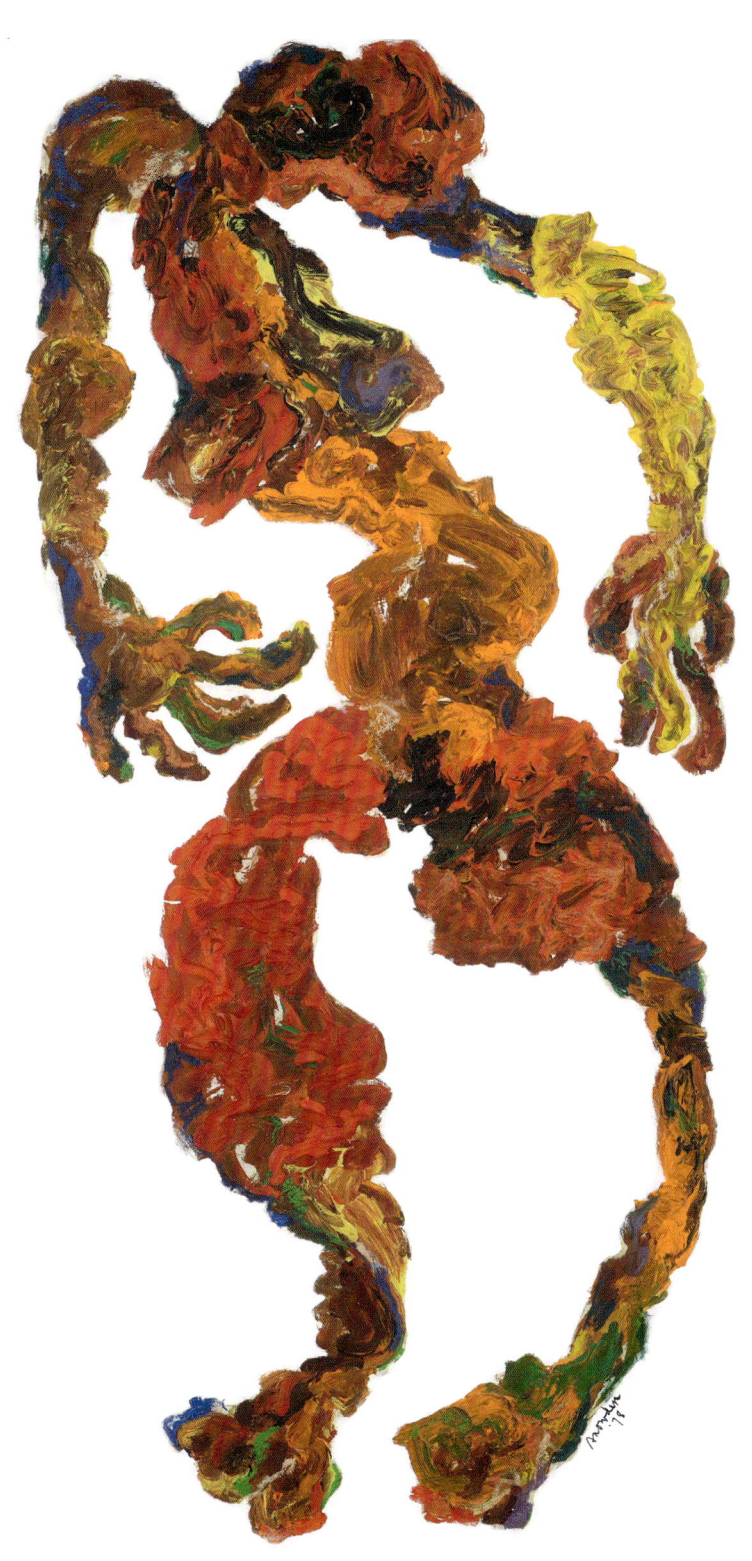

Vivian Springford
(1913–2003)

Painting is my attempt to identify with the universal whole. I want to find my own small plot or pattern of energy that will express the inner me in terms of rhythmic movement and color. The expansive center of the universe, of the stars, and of nature is my constant challenge in abstract terms.[1]

You have to be a well-ordered person to paint simply and without revising. At the same time, the discipline of working that way helps to make you well-ordered. It's very rewarding.[2]

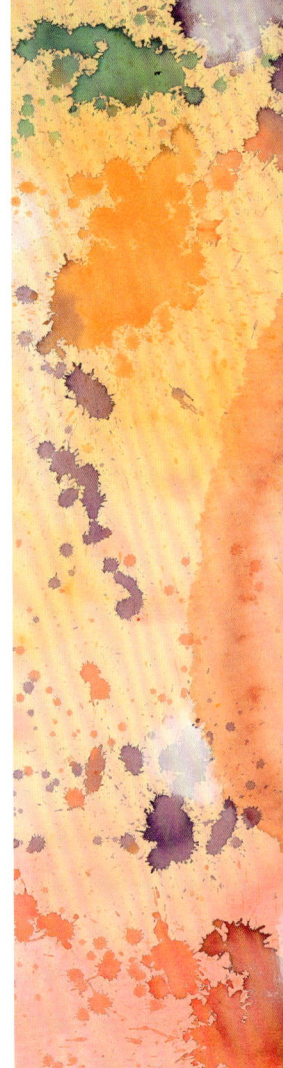

Scuba Series
Begun 1972, completed
c. 1984–85
Acrylic on canvas
56 × 70 in.
(142.2 × 177.8 cm)
CL947

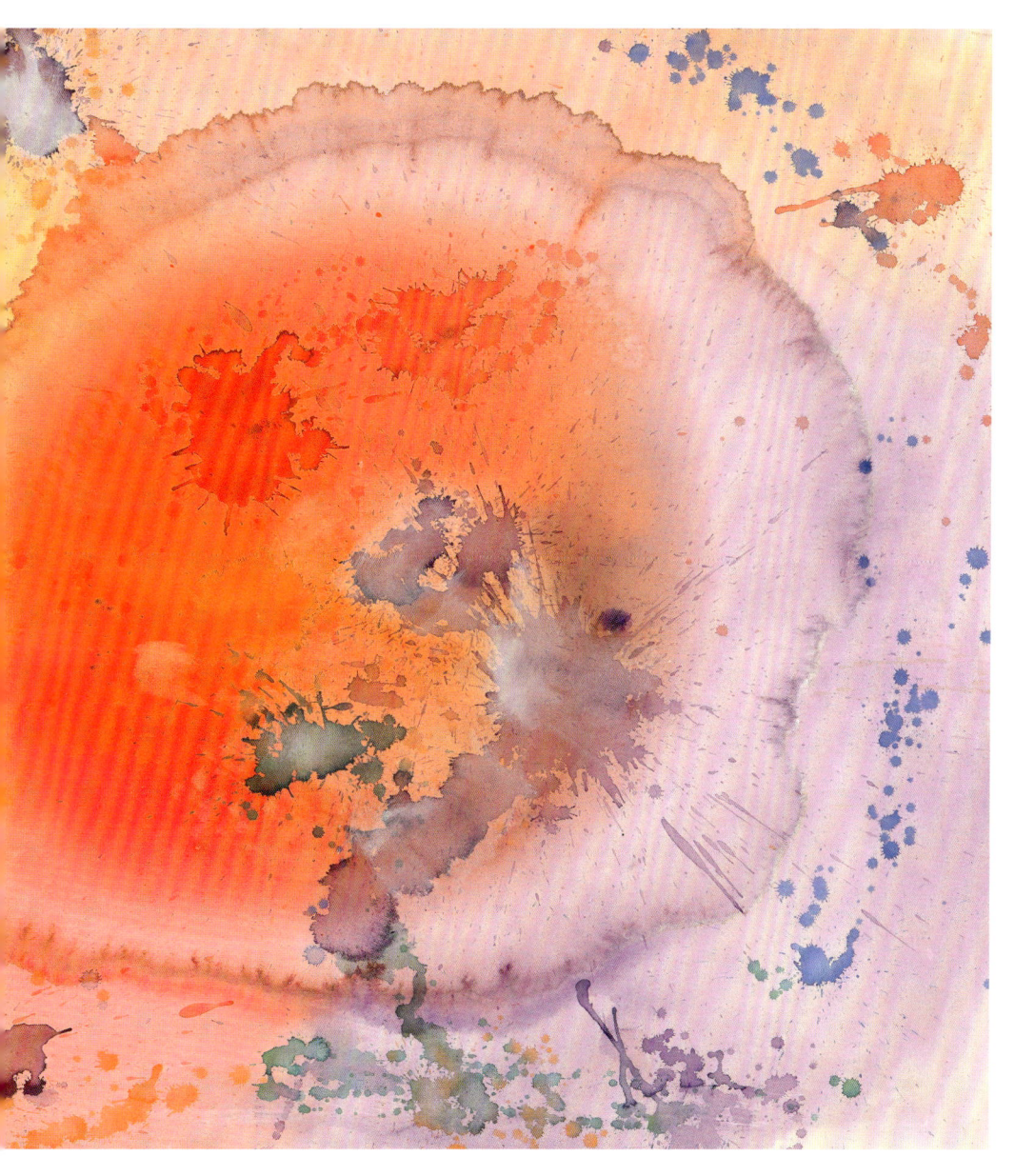

Pat Steir
(b. 1940)

I was happy with this work, the way the red, green, and yellow work together, how colors working together send a particular sensation, feeling.

When paintings really work it's not exactly how you see them, it's how you feel them.[1]

I don't think of these paintings as abstract ... these are not only drips of paint. They're paintings of drips which form waterfall images: pictures ... [Nor are] they realistic ... I haven't sat outdoors with a little brush, trying to create the illusion of a waterfall. The paint makes the picture ... Gravity makes the image.[2]

The canvases are fixed to the wall. I start by working on scaffolding, pouring and throwing paint from buckets and buckets ... I apply several coats, causing cracks and gaps to open up, through which the initial grounding shimmers. Over several sessions I just sit for ages in front of the canvas doing nothing but immersing myself in a dialogue with the painting. This process can go on for months until I finally know what to do next. Then I concentrate on the movement I am about to make, gauge the gesture, soak the brush in paint, draw back and—woosh!—in a single movement I throw the paint in a high arc across the canvas.[3]

Middle Lhamo Waterfall
1992
Oil on canvas
9 ft 7 in. × 90½ in.
(292.1 × 229.9 cm)

CL102

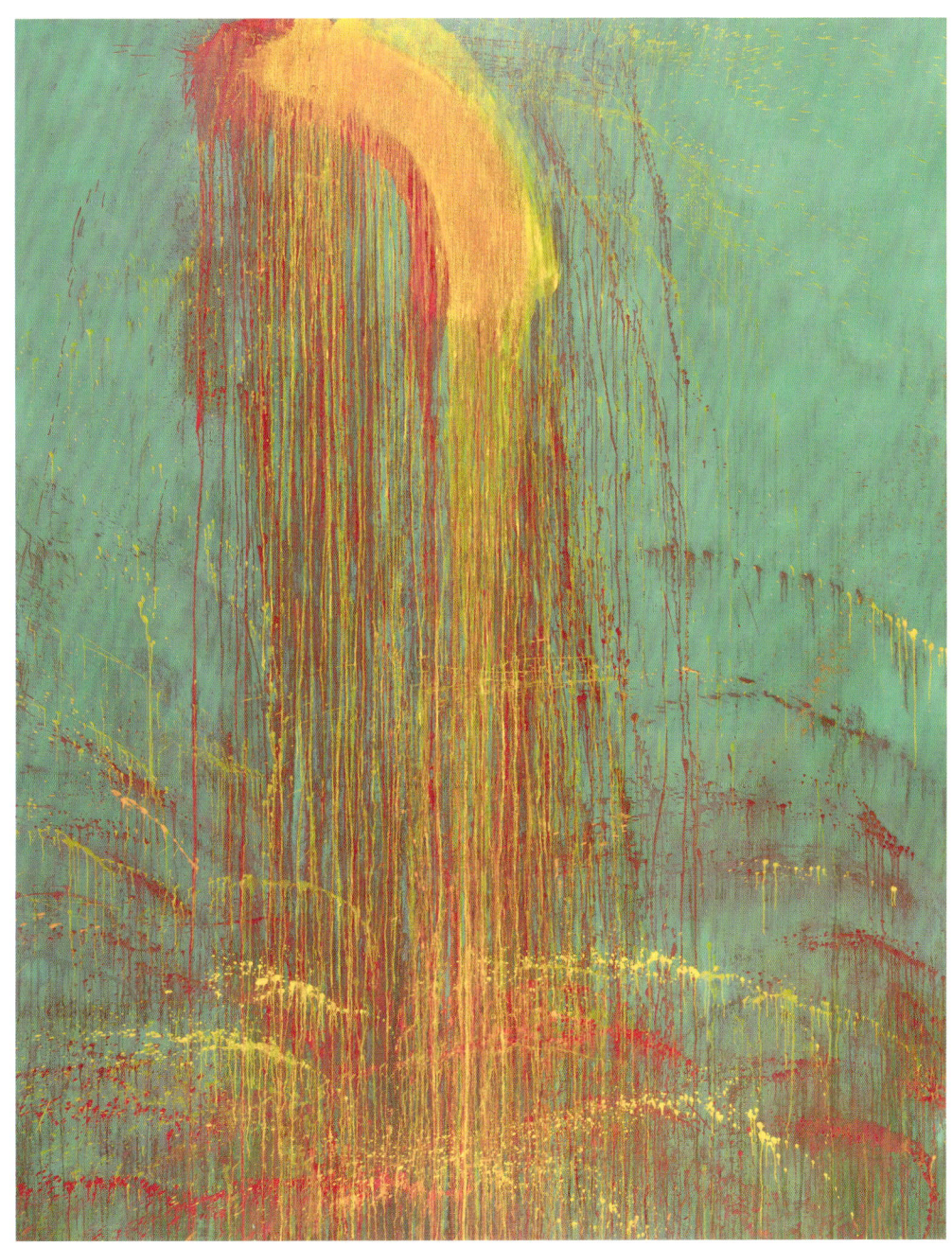

Hedda Sterne
(1910–2011)

Life is like a drawing in the sand and you only understand its meaning when it's completely finished. And I think that the work of an artist acquires its total meaning when he draws his last brushstroke. And the last brushstroke gets its meaning from the first, and the first, from the last. So it's something that never ends.[1]

For me, my painting life has been a diary. I've functioned almost like a movie camera, moving through the years from immediate nearness to medium distance to far and remote vistas and then back again.[2]

For such a long time now, painting and drawing for me have ceased to be a matter of making, but rather a way of functioning.[3]

Untitled (Lunar Halo)
c. 1950
Oil on canvas
30 × 40³/₈ in.
(76.2 × 102.6 cm)
CL843

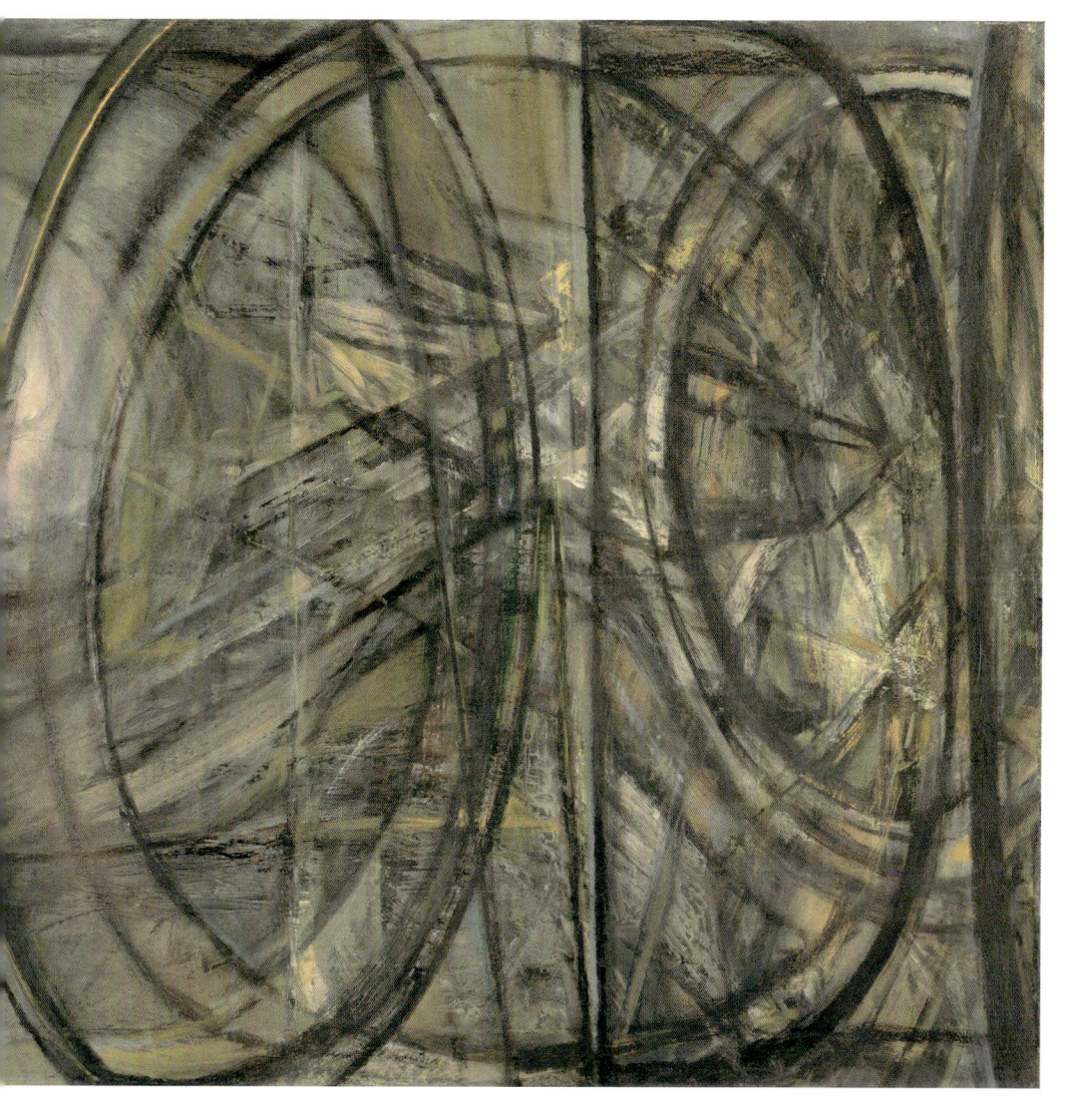

Dorothea Tanning
(1910–2012)

You see, when I paint drifting nudes, it's a statement about being human. Some people think it's a statement about being sexy. It's an obsession of the whole, not so cultural, establishment, that almost everything we do which is inexplicable must be reduced to sexuality, and that's absurd. It's certainly very strong—I would never say it wasn't—but, after all, there are other yearnings, with names like glory, incandescence, and love and knowledge. I like to think that you feel some of this when you look at my pictures.[1]

I've always been drawn towards esoteric phenomena: the illogical, the inexpressible, the impossible. Anything that is ordinary and frequent is uninteresting to me, so I have to go in a solitary and risky direction. If it strikes you as being enigmatic, well, I suppose that's what I wanted it to do.[2]

The fantastic dreams from my childhood on the great Midwestern plain had evolved into something subtle yet urgent, and necessary to me. I watched images appear on the canvas, images I had never seen. Since then my attitude has undergone some changes. I now wish to interrogate the unknown images, to impel them, to make them more real than reality.[3]

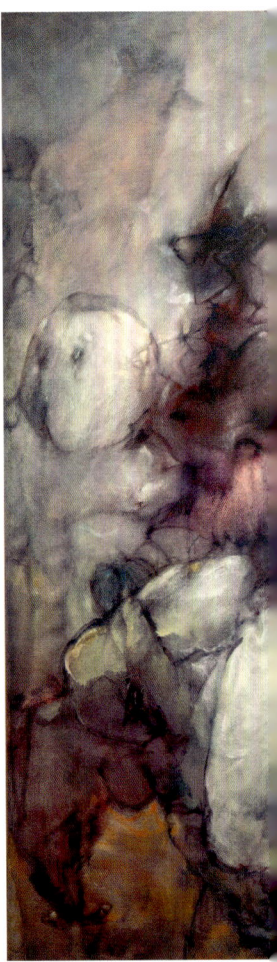

Éperdument
1962
Oil on canvas
78¾ in. × 9 ft 10⅛ in.
(200 × 300 cm)
CL1360

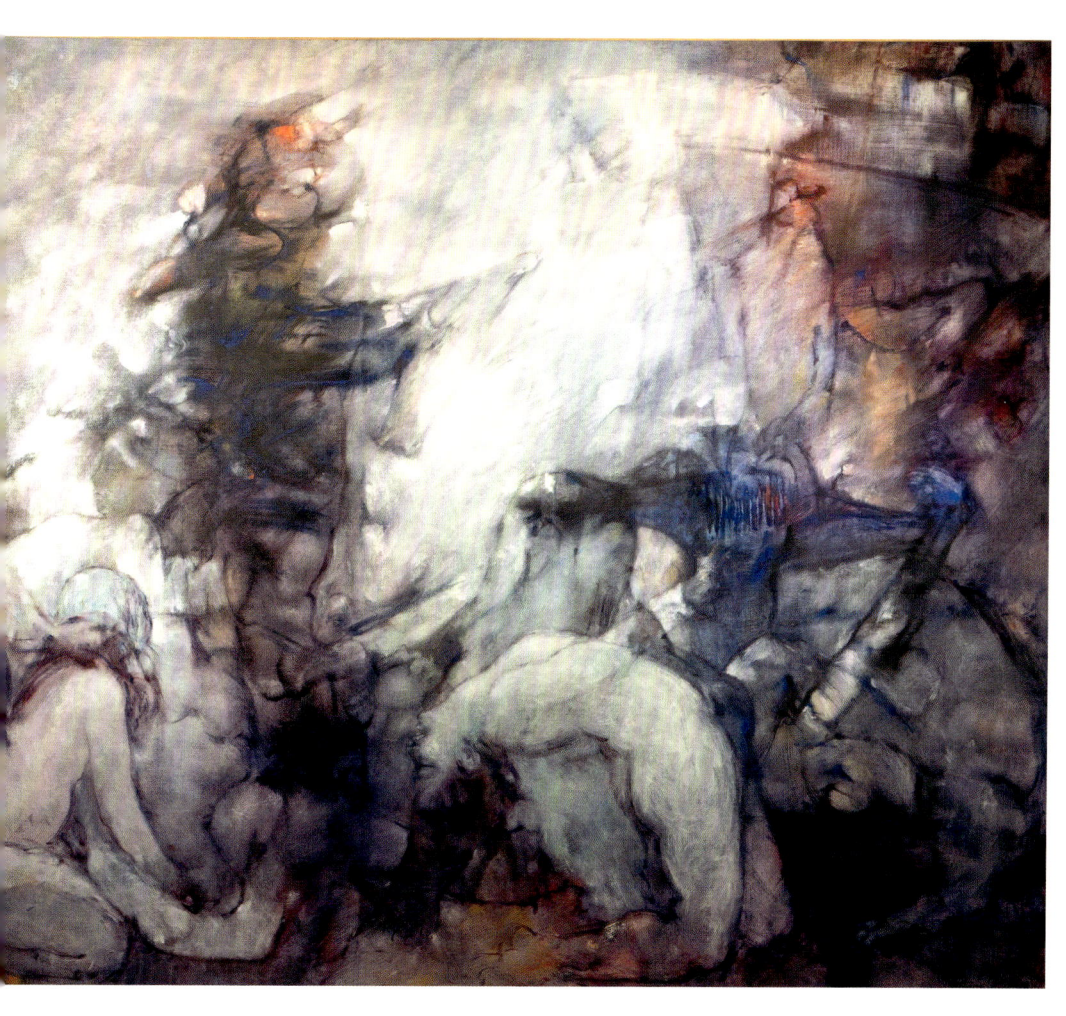

Franciszka Themerson
(1907–1988)

For a painter to discuss the meaning of paintings that he or she has painted is very difficult.

Speaking through visual means becomes a voice only when, and if, someone's eyes can hear. (Of course in the case when the painting is not representational.) My painting is decidedly not representational—even though in my paintings one can identify human faces and figures in all sorts of situations.

The paintings are an attempt to create my own language with which to express my relationship, or attitude of the world to me, or to create my own world, which I want to share with the viewer.[1]

Interest in colour is obvious for a painter. Limiting colour, like limiting another painting technique, leads to simplicity and economy of expression, which for me are enormously important.[2]

Mona Compostezza
1973
Oil on canvas
39⅜ × 29½ in.
(100 × 74.9 cm)

CL1195

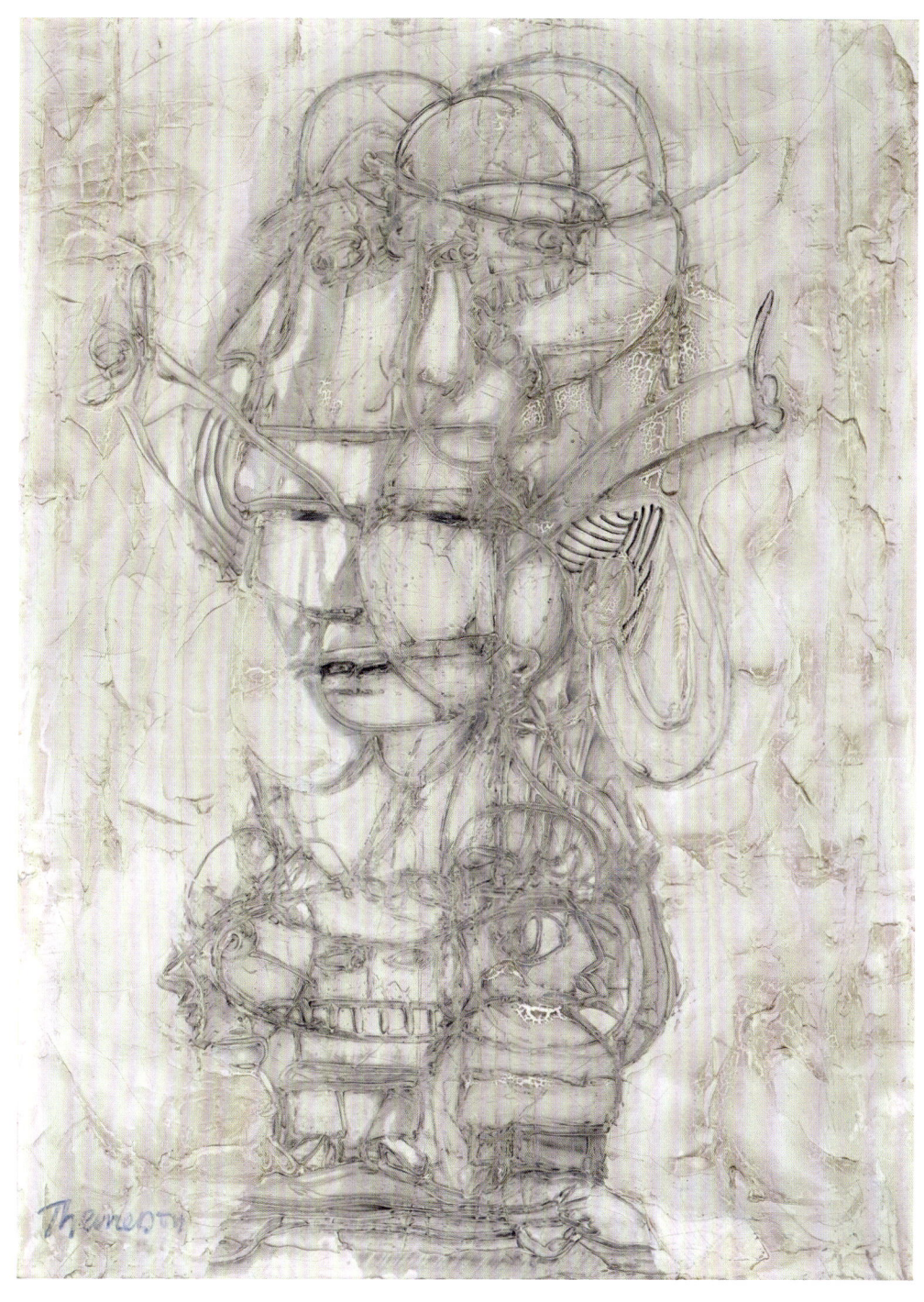

Alma Thomas
(1891–1978)

Through color, I have sought to concentrate on beauty and happiness, rather than on man's inhumanity to man.[1]

I began to think about what I would see if I were in an airplane. You look down on things. You streak through the clouds so fast you don't know whether the flower below is a violet or what. You see only streaks of color.[2]

One of the things we couldn't do was go into museums, let alone think of hanging our pictures there. My, times have changed. Just look at me now.[3]

Man's highest aspirations come from nature. A world without color would seem dead. Color is life. Light is the mother of color. Light reveals to us the spirit and living soul of the world through colors.[4]

*Etude in Brown
(Saint Cecilia at the
Organ)*

c. 1958
Oil on linen
44⅛ × 27⅞ in.
(112.1 × 70.8 cm)

CL990

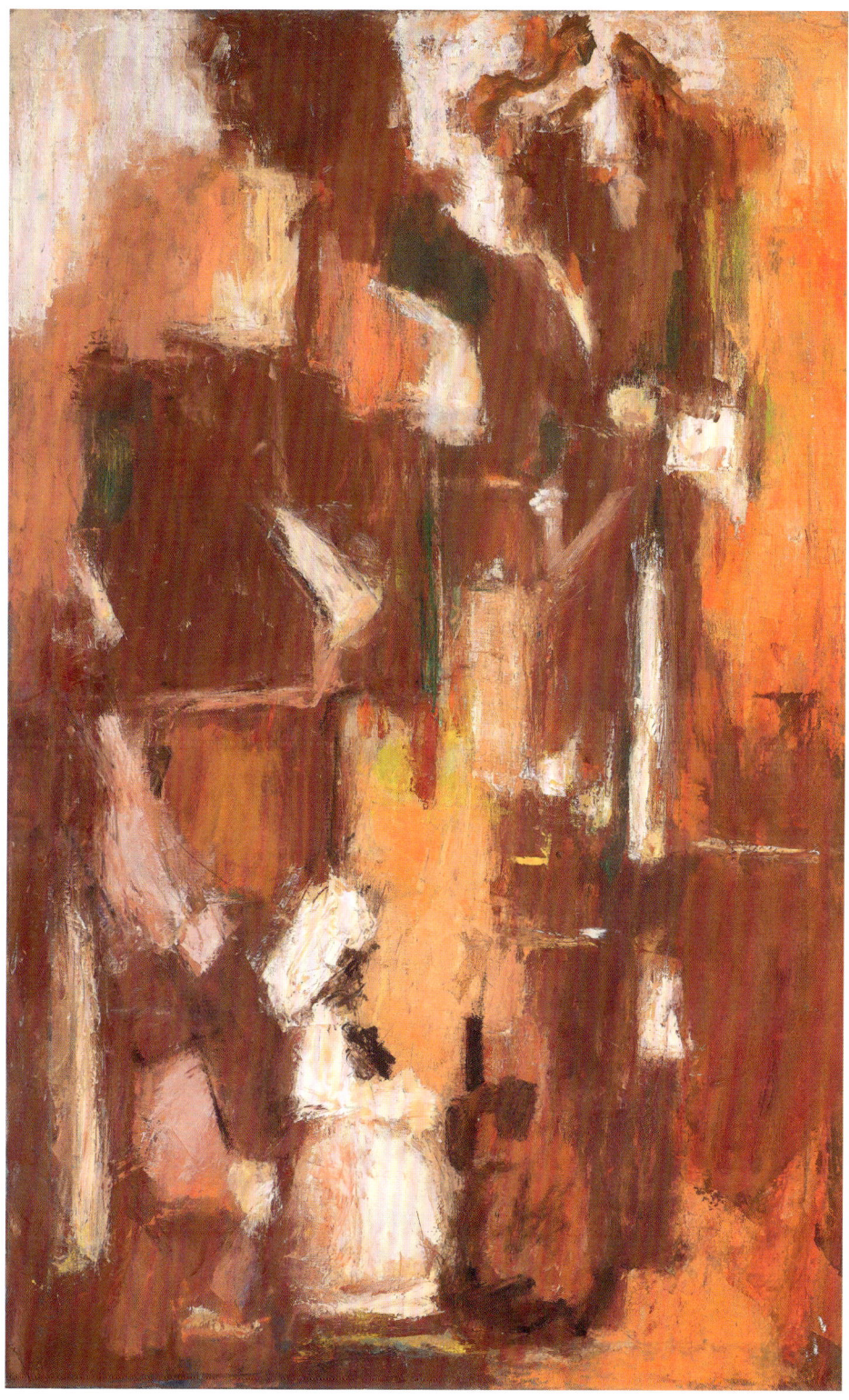

Yvonne Thomas
(1913–2009)

For me, color expresses space, structure, form, intent ...
also passion, mystery, and tension.[1]

My statement is getting simpler. I am narrowing,
simplifying. Color is turning from sober, controlled tones
to more exuberant ones. The inner symbols and ideas
are becoming the subject. I am discovering, as I go along,
interest in the periphery of the painting space rather than
in the center.[2]

I found it easier to paint large pictures than small ones.
It was the case with most of the painters, their gestural
expression took a heroic stand. Strong feeling—always
wanting to be expressed through color, form, tension,
impulse, spontaneity, and recognition of the accident—was
very much part of it. Meaning comes from many combined
elements. It is also a due ... the painting itself, at a certain
point, seems to acquire an identity of its own. When it
happens I know it's time to stop.[3]

In Abstract Expressionism the brush practically becomes a
continuation of one's nervous system; the feeling of being
one with the painting. Now a new distance is created,
having the work on the floor, so the paint will not drip ...
The accident becomes less important.[4]

Transmutation
1956
Oil on canvas
70 × 66 in.
(177.8 × 167.6 cm)
CL825

184

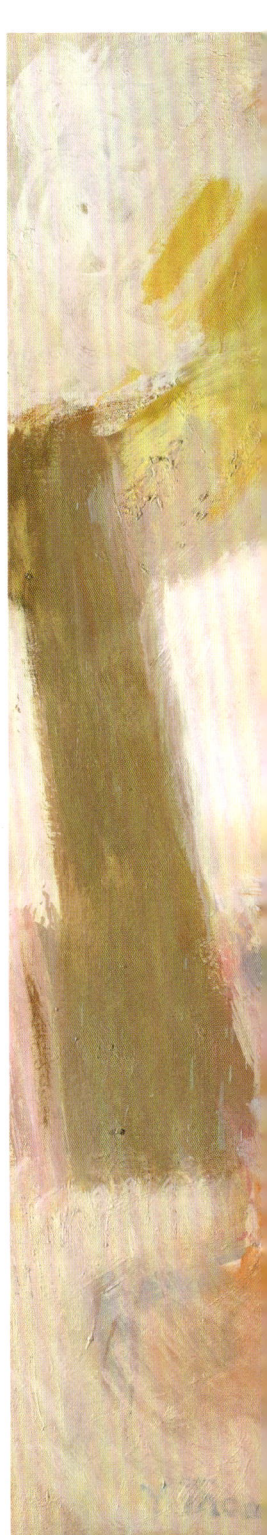

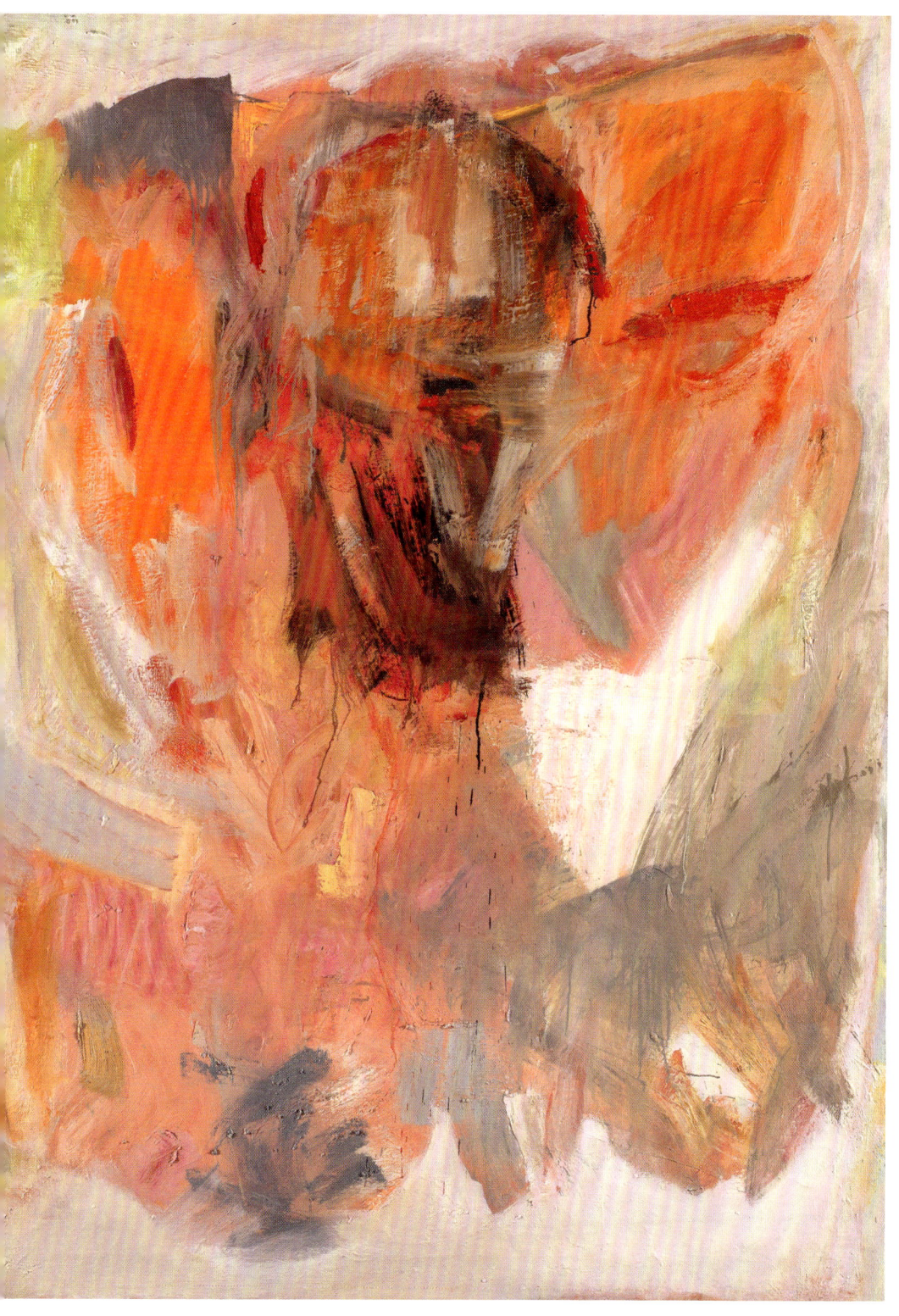

Tatiana Trouvé
(b. 1968)

This series of works, which began in 2013, bears the title *The Guardians*. By definition, a guardian is a person who exercises a legal right or responsibility to care, but a guardian is also someone who protects something. This title therefore evokes numerous guardian figures associated with exercising such care. We find this same idea in the title of the newspaper *The Guardian*, which also relates to the desire to preserve independence and the freedom to write and think, this common good that we must protect.

These sculptures were created to be present in the context of group exhibitions and to assume these same functions regarding a collective or community of works. They thus respond to a way of being together, in a world, but also warn about the importance of this world. These guardians also create viewpoints, according to their position and orientation in a space, and so draw attention in another way: to the exhibition, and to the gaze itself. I am not using the chair as an emblem of authority; on the contrary, if we were to consider these guardians in the cultural context of the exhibition, then they would refer to invisible people whose function it is to watch what the spectators are watching, and to watch over the works.

Each of these sculptures is unique and takes on a different personality, constructed from the elements that constitute it: shoes, bags, men's or women's jackets, radios or cassette players. The chair itself becomes an anthropomorphic creature, one that inhabits the space in which it has been placed.[1]

The Guardian
2023
Patinated bronze, brass, granite, and marble
26¾ × 18½ × 18½ in.
(68 × 47 × 47 cm)
CL1323

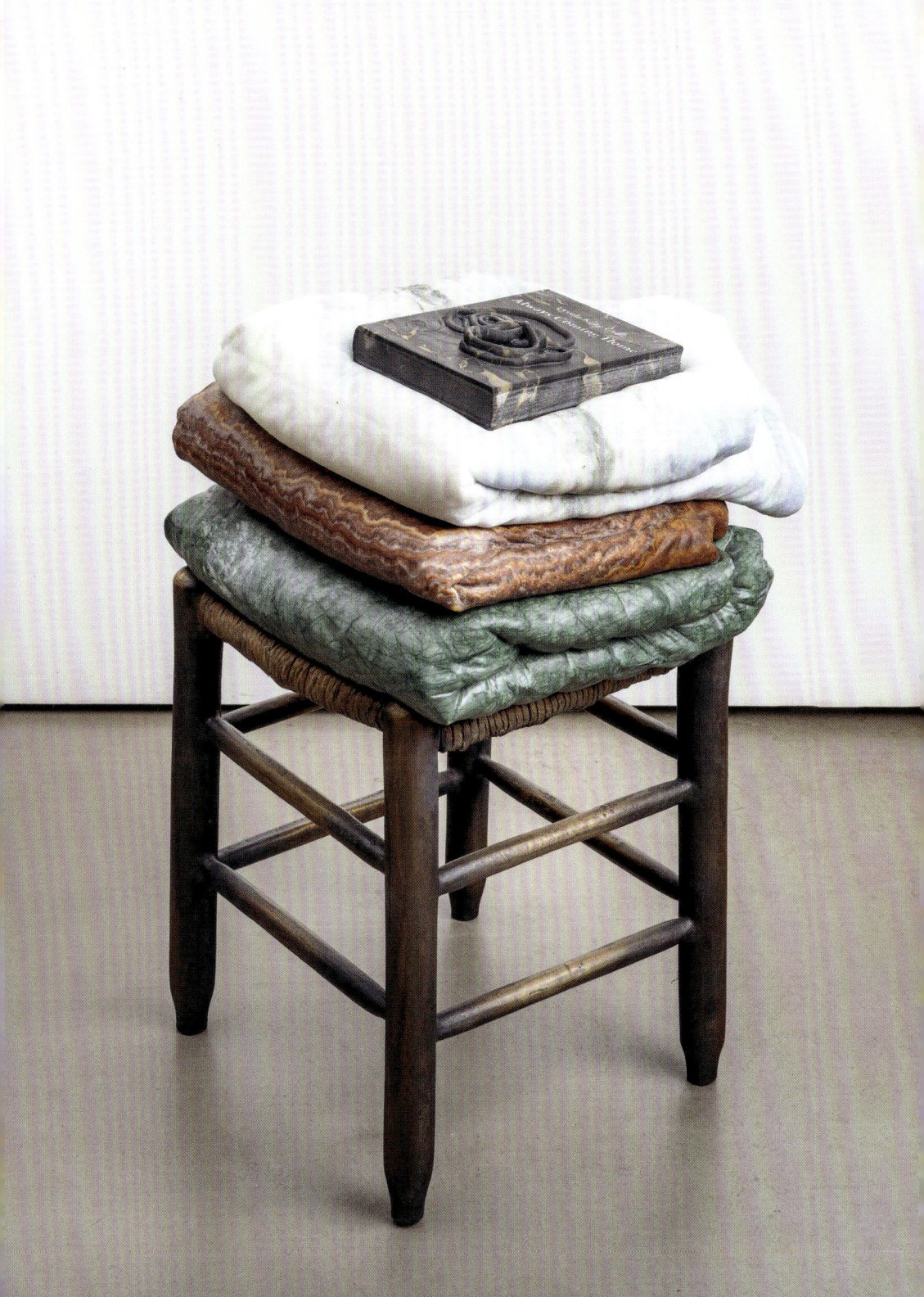

Maria Helena Vieira da Silva
(1908–1992)

When I paint a landscape or a seascape, I'm not very sure it's a landscape or a seascape. It's a thought form rather than a realistic form.[1]

I want to paint what is not there as though it existed.[2]

Everything amazes me. I paint my amazement, which at the same time is delight, fear and laughter. I do not want to exclude anything from this amazement. I want to paint pictures with many things, with all the contradictions.[3]

And then, it also happens that the painting is well constructed, with a good layout, but that I don't like. Rigour is not enough for me. I need to be able to play hooky. I need freedom, fantasy, impromptu. That is very important. I think that's the best part of me.[4]

La Demeure du matin
1960
Oil on canvas
28¾ × 45⅝ in.
(73 × 115.9 cm)
CL1247

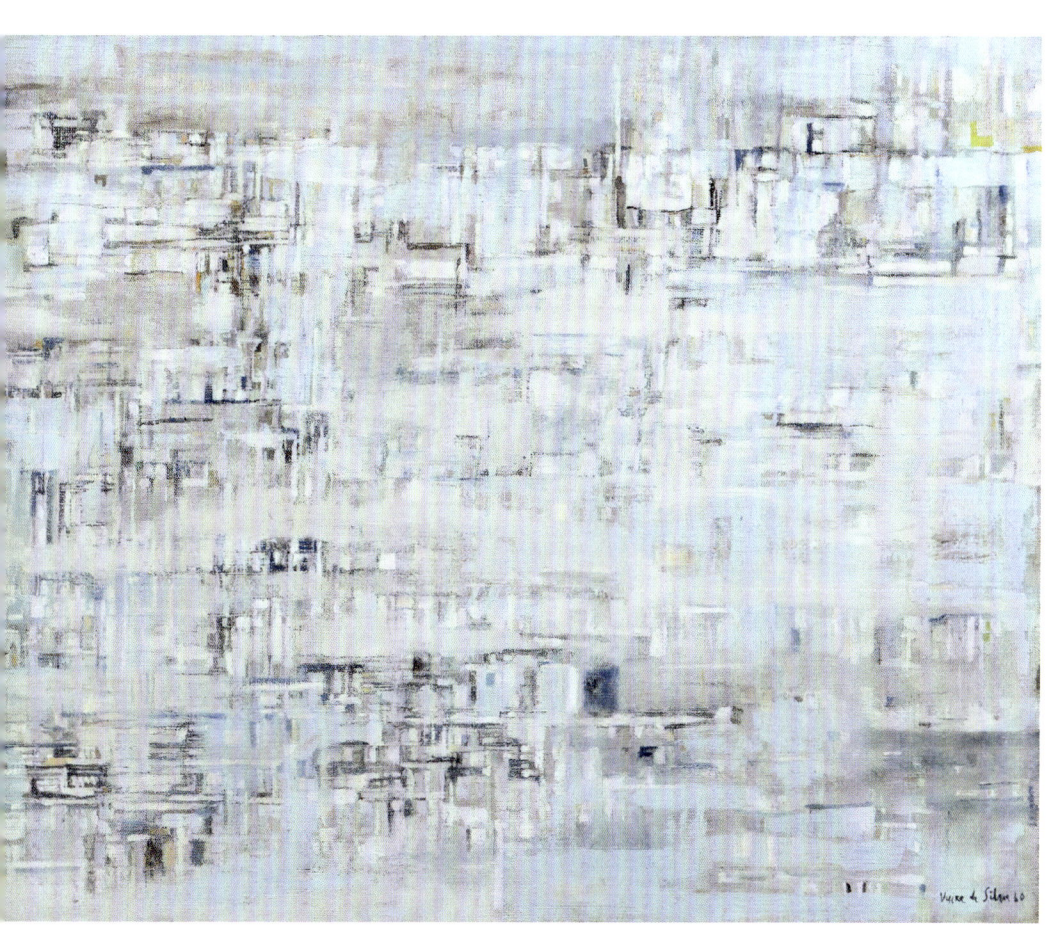

Kay WalkingStick
(b. 1935)

The painting *All Good Things, Ver. II* was made in the midst of the second Feminist Movement of the 20th century. The idea of equality for women in the workplace and also the home was discussed, written about and promulgated throughout the United States and Europe in the late 1960s and 1970s. The idea that women had the right to enjoy their bodies and their sex lives was a popular subject in books and magazines—and certainly in the films of the time. There was considerable rhetoric about women's equality in the bedroom. The content of this painting directly reflects these feminist ideas.

The painting comprises four canvas panels, each measuring 22″ square. The painting overall is therefore 44″ × 44″. It is made with acrylic paint, which was a relatively new material at the time, in a hard-edged style. The four panels can separate so that there is the possibility of space between the four canvases, and I have occasionally hung it thus.

The painting pictures a woman on her hands and knees, as seen through her own eyes. The separating panels represent the floating expansion of orgasm. The color is very cool, and quiet—in contrast to the subject.[1]

All Good Things (Version II)

1970
Acrylic on canvas
44 × 44 in.
(111.8 × 111.8 cm)

CL.972

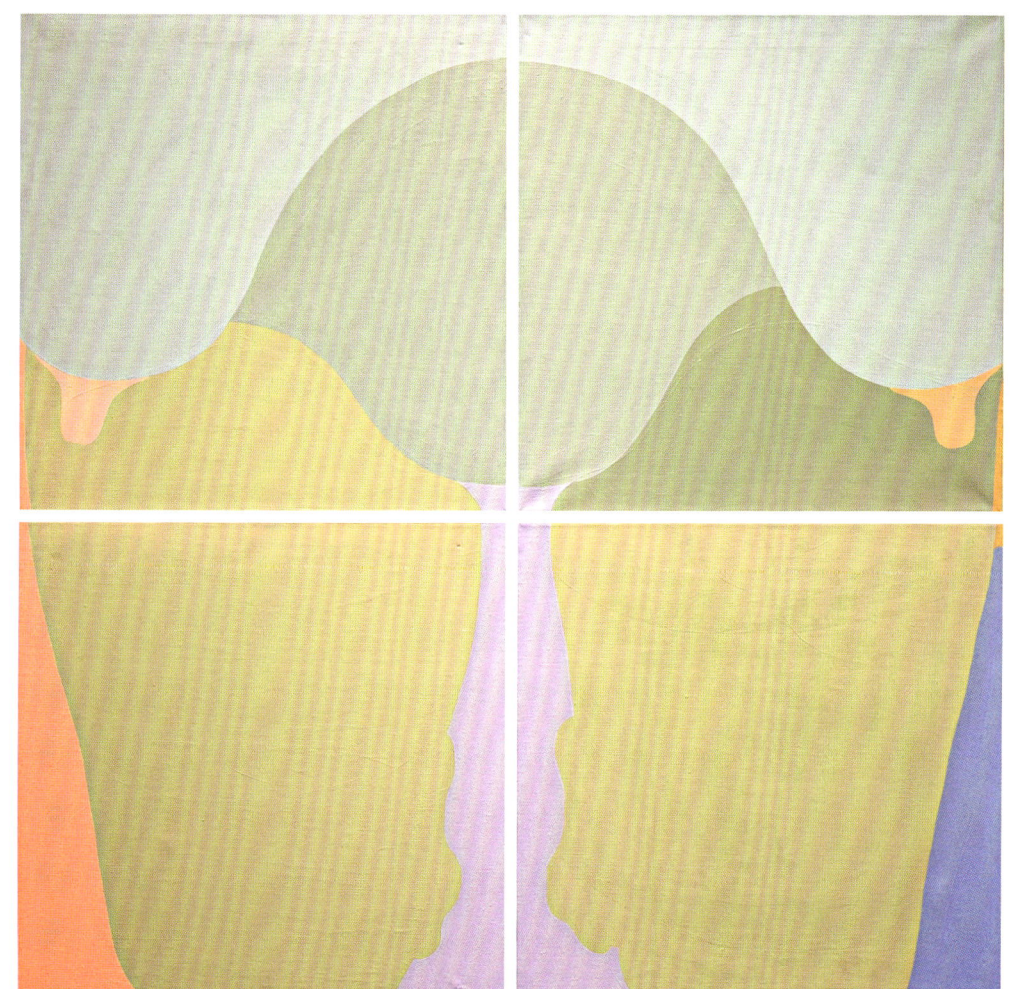

Carrie Mae Weems
(b. 1953)

Art allows us to navigate the more complicated parts of our lives in a way that is more palpable. We don't go to the movies just to see a movie; we go for the experience. I'm very interested in the experience. Art has saved my life on a regular basis. I wanted to offer that experience to children, to enlist them, to show them the possibilities that are in the arts, to persuade them to pursue it for both their own personal salvation and for changing the way we are understood.[1]

It's assumed that autobiography is key, because I so often use myself, my own experience—limited as it is at times—as the starting point. But I use myself simply as a vehicle for approaching the question of power, and following where that leads me to and through. It's never about me; it's always about something larger.[2]

It's fair to say that black folks operate under a cloud of invisibility—this too is part of the work, is indeed central to the work …

   This invisibility—this erasure out of the complex history of our life and time—is the greatest source of my longing. As you know, I'm a woman who yearns, who longs for. This is the key to me and to the work, and something which is rarely discussed in reviews or essays, which I also find remarkably disappointing. That there are so few images of African-American women circulating in popular culture or in fine art is disturbing; the pathology behind it is dangerous.[3]

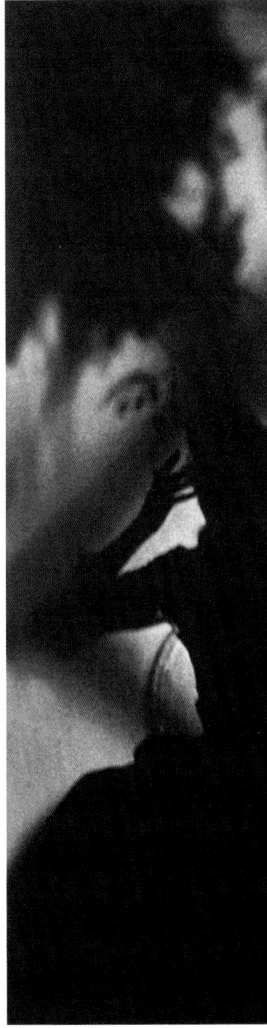

Untitled (Woman walking with candelabra), from *The Louisiana Project*
2003
Inkjet print on canvas
60⅛ × 84⅛ in.
(152.7 × 213.7 cm)
No. 1 from an edition
of 3 plus 1 artist's proof

CL1052

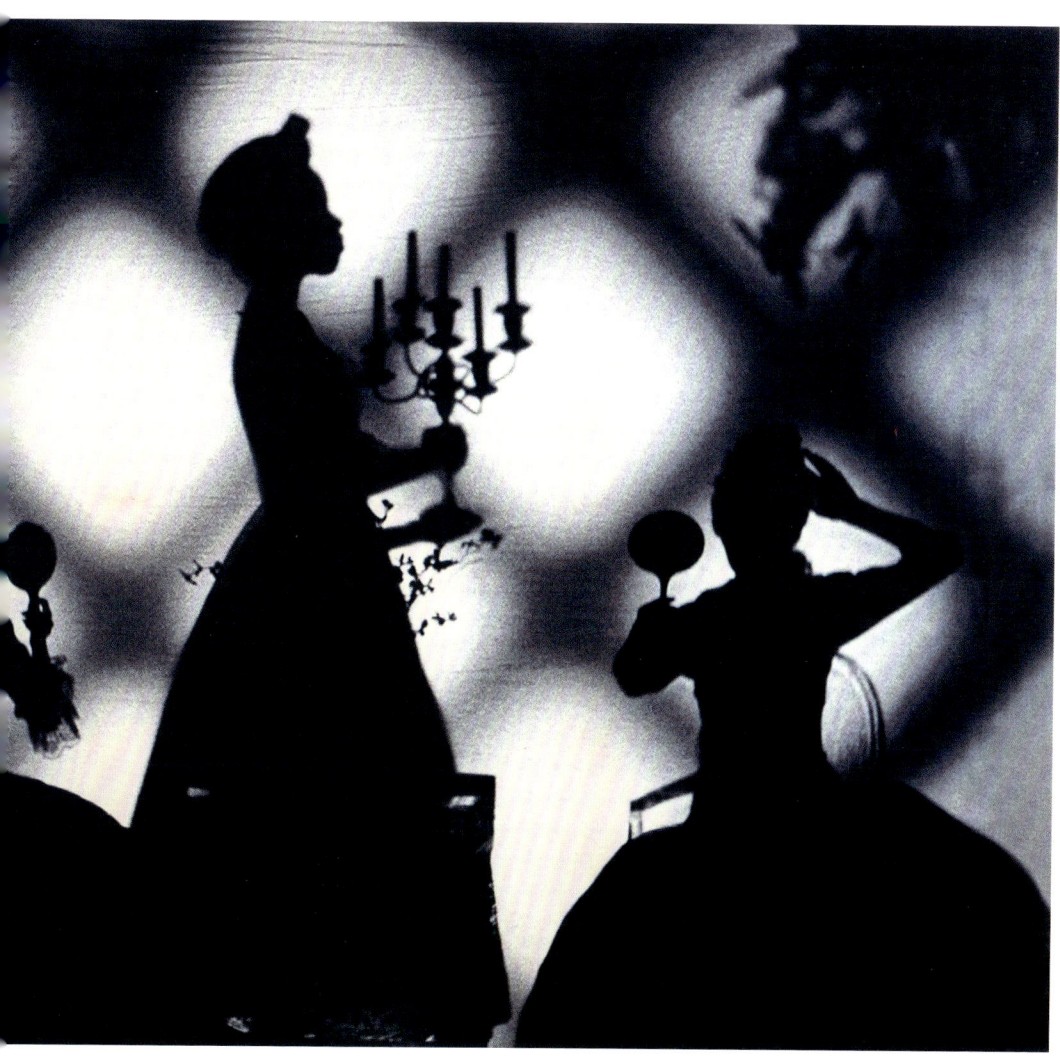

Susan Weil

(b. 1930)

I grew up in a rare and unusual landscape, human and
otherwise. My father was a writer and my mother drew
wonderfully, wrote poetry and was involved in theater.
She saw no reason to settle for one way and so diffused
her artist's energies. My parents' great creative area was
their lifestyle. They truly invented themselves. Their life
was outrageous, impractical, unreal. We spent the school
year on a farm and the summers in Connecticut, on a small
island in the Long Island Sound. The island was the farthest
island off the shore and every winter got such a battering
from the elements that each spring was completely taken
up with putting it back together, planting the trees, adding
soil, building new rock walls. Every summer all the animals
from our farm, goats, donkey, chickens, ducks, rabbits, pig,
dogs etc. would be taken to the island by truck and then
boat. When I was eleven our boat exploded, my brother
and I were burned and my brother died. My flower family's
first and permanent encounter with harsh reality. The
sources for my paintings come mostly from the time before
the fire. The beauty of the two environments in which
I grew up and my parents' responsiveness to them
increased my awareness of the natural world. The sea,
sky, rocks, the stars, the woods, the wind are some of the
threads through my work. The people with whom I shared
my world, their values and sensitivities, they are some of
the threads also. I am made of these threads too. That is
why the paintings and my rememberings are one to me.[1]

Bathers
1958
Oil on canvas
51¼ × 30⅛ in.
(130.2 × 76.5 cm)

CL1333

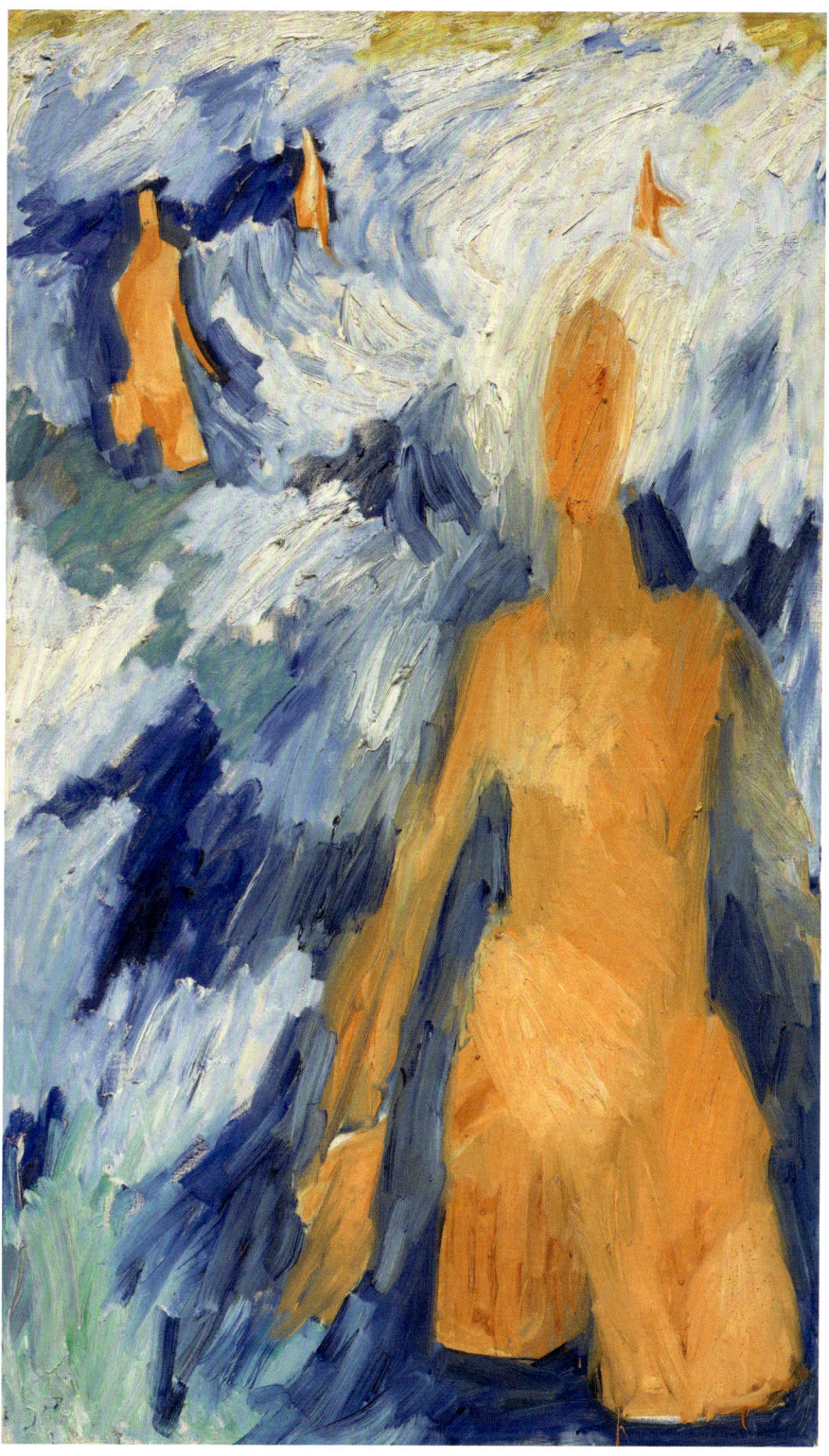

Michael (Corinne) West
(1908–1991)

Concerning "chaos" and reality—I was thinking of the
process by which reality is achieved—thru dynamic
opposites—dislocations—erosions—readjustments—
repaintings over repaintings until it would be impossible
for the viewer to experience what appears (or how it is
done) ... You can never arrive at it by copying—the inner
core is divine/spiritual—understanding.[1]

Line and space is interesting to the artist when
disassociated from objective reality—and associated with
more or less invisible reality—this speculative and analytic
approach—slows the artist up—the better to realize a
re-discovered outer space (or new space vitality).[2]

The outer world changes as our thoughts change although
our thought is usually ahead or in advance of the world
viewed materially. To disintegrate visual unity—the a
plus b—something given—to break up and change outer
appearance is necessary [so that] the individual can
penetrate the nature of our mystic universe. Everything
visual is composed of atomic matter which is composed
of ... space time movement ...[3]

Form super-imposes itself constantly creating more
space—bursting open space where none seemed formerly
to be—so that discovery or energy—finds itself to be
unlimited. This multiplication of emotion of feeling
realizes itself in forms which are the essence of painting—
painting for the sake of painting—drawing for the sake
of drawing—space movement mood emotion plastically
exposed to show creation in essence—or the nature of pure
creation which is energy and will, morality and soul.[4]

Nihilism
1949
Oil, enamel, and sand
on canvas
53⅛ × 40¼ in.
(134.9 × 102.2 cm)
CI.891

196

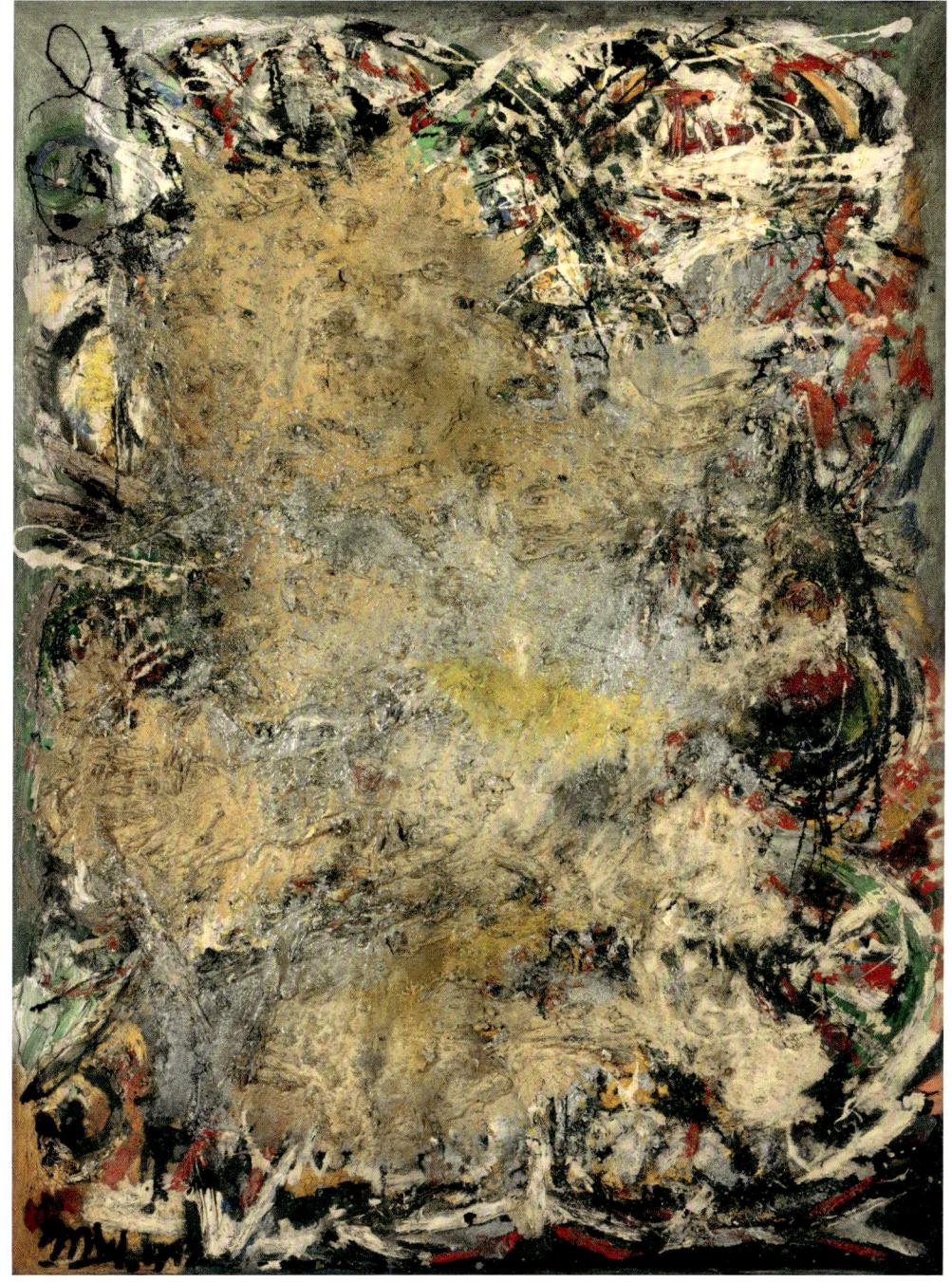

Anna Weyant
(b. 1995)

This is a painting of my mother, Char. She posed for the portrait while visiting my studio in New York. I wanted the painting to be something of a *trompe l'œil*, where she looks out the canvas as if looking out a window.[1]

I like the parts of my work that seem to have magically appeared and that I know I'll never be able to replicate. I can think of a few moments in paintings (mine and not mine) that have thrilled me and that I don't fully understand. In mine, they're usually accidents or born out of frustration and resignation. I make my best work when I'm not really thinking or when I'm tired of painting and feel like I have nothing to lose.[2]

Char

2019
Oil on panel
36 × 24 in. (91.4 × 61 cm)

CL1311

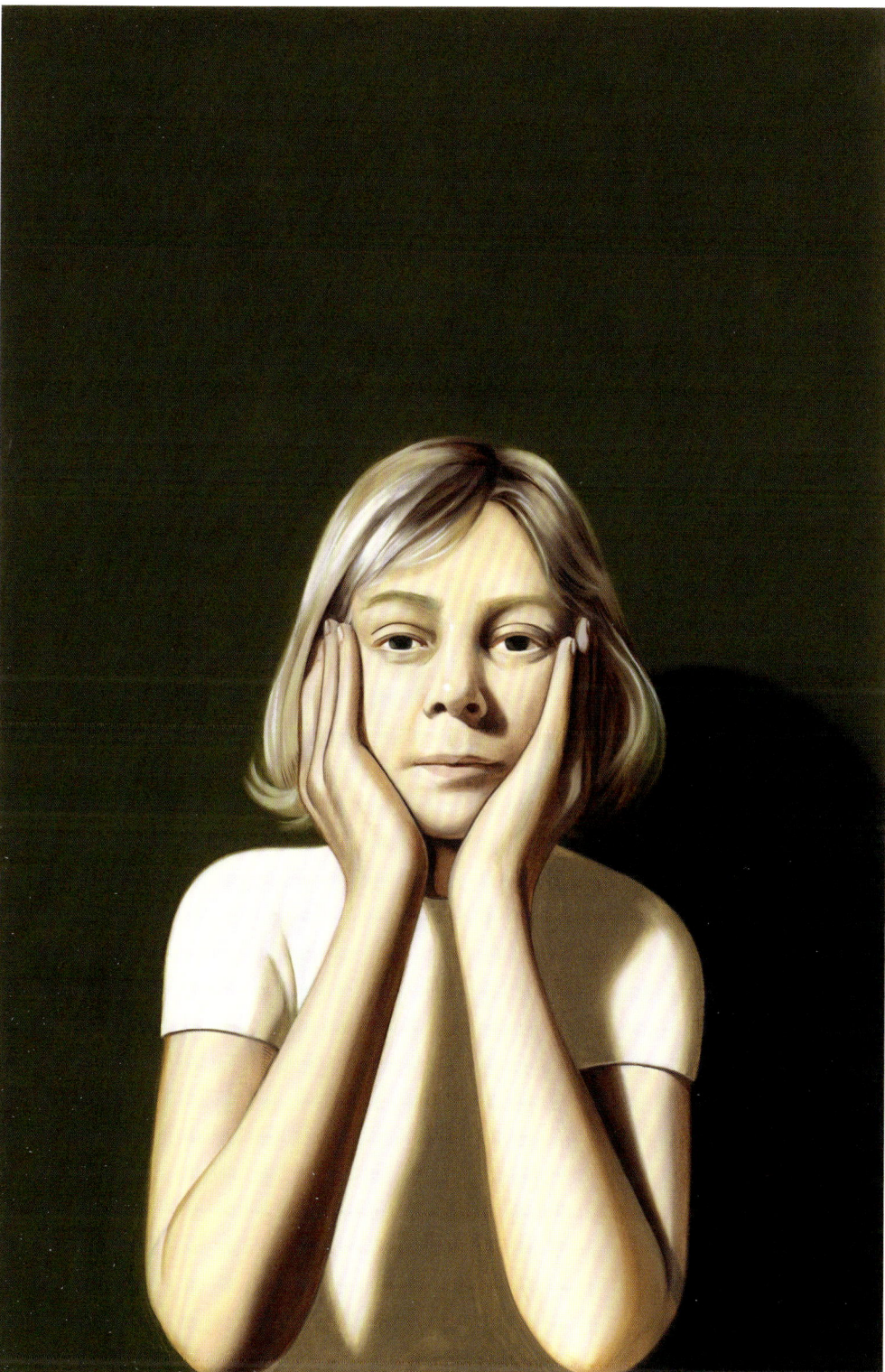

Dame Rachel Whiteread
(b. 1963)

Since the late 1980s I have made works in series.
Occasionally using a household object, e.g. a hot-water
bottle, as a mold.

   When making these pieces, I will slightly manipulate
the mold to make anthropomorphised objects have
different characteristics.

   This particular piece was made with pink dental
plaster—a material that is used when making molds for
dentistry—and, therefore, has two references to allude to
our bodies of "self."[1]

I love materials, I love playing physically with materials,
but I also love color and surface and … the things that
traditionally come with painting or printmaking …

   The process of making things has always been
something that's kind of fascinated me, and I have always
tried to use the materiality of the material for it to be the
finished form, in a way …

   One of the things that I think really makes people
connect with my work is its attachment to reality. It feels
like things that we see all the time. But they might be
slightly different. It feels like a memory that you have.
Or it feels a bit like a dream …

   I am a great believer in the fact that we make the world
a different place, a richer place actually … It's nice to know
that there are things that I have made that will always be
thought about and are part of our culture.[2]

Untitled (Pink Torso)
1991
Dental plaster
3¾ × 6¾ × 9¼ in.
(9.5 × 17.2 × 23.5 cm)
CL1376

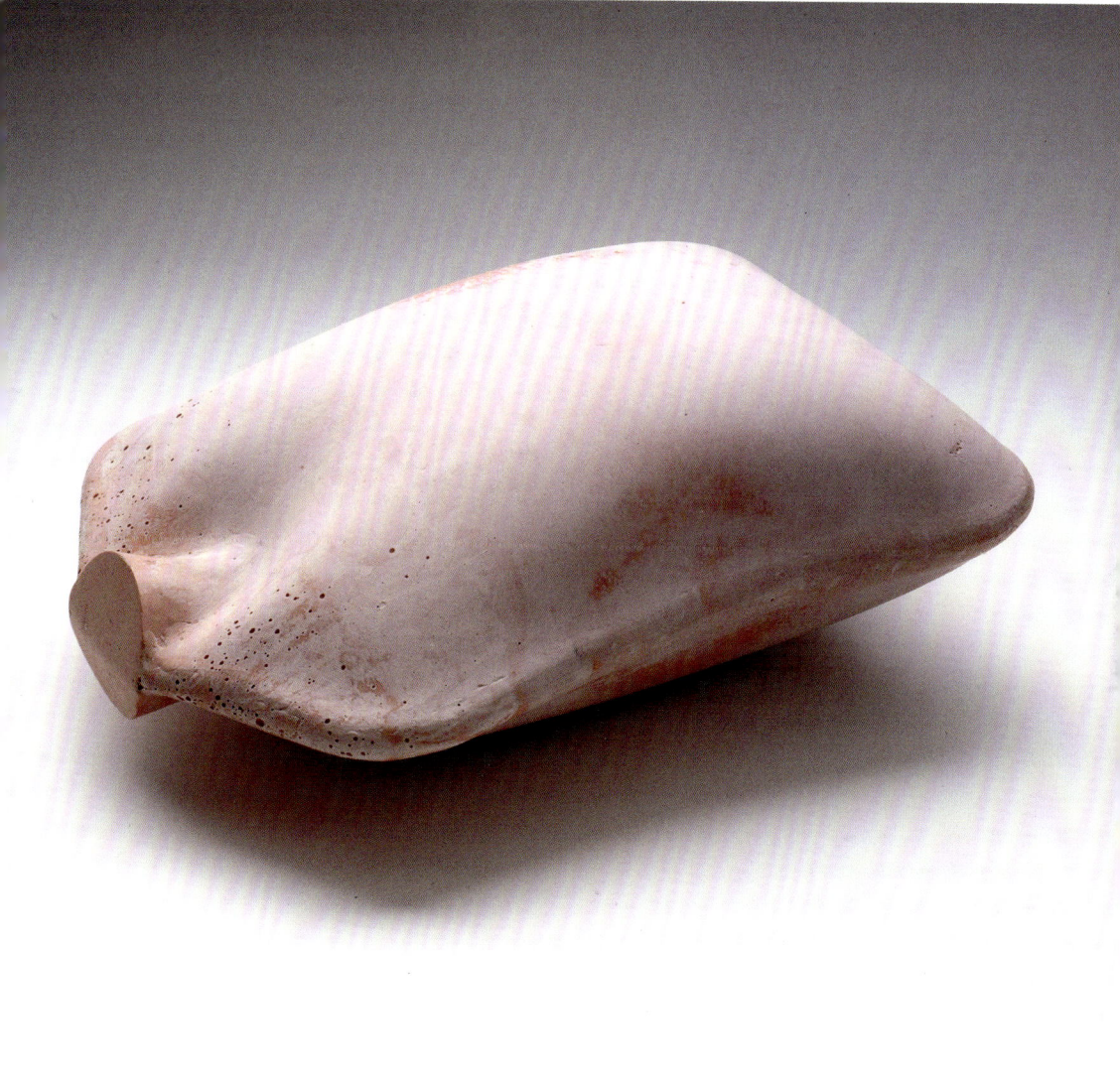

Issy Wood

(b. 1993)

When I enter my studio, I feel immense peace. I start painting primarily without thinking too much. I make maybe three or four paintings at a time, and so when one isn't abiding by my rules, I can seek refuge in the other ...

If I had to find one overarching theme [of my painting], it would probably be how terrifying desire is.[1]

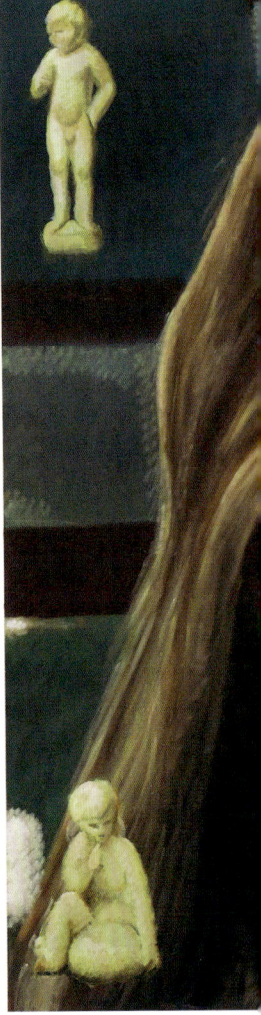

Study for the Bada Bing

2021
Oil on linen
61 × 85 in.
(154.9 × 215.9 cm)

CL1410

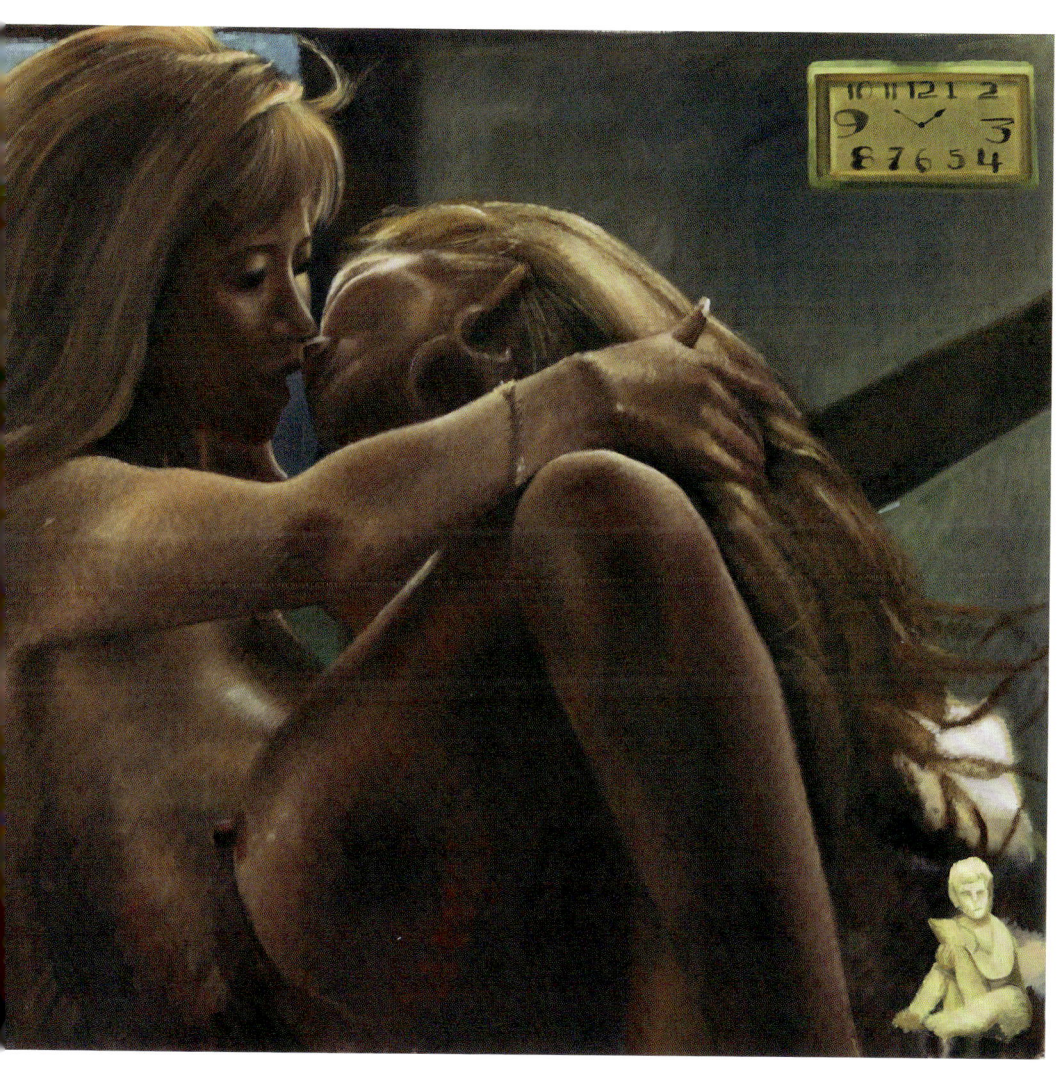

Notes

Mary Abbott

1   Abbott speaking in "*Women of Abstract Expressionism* Exhibition at the Denver Art Museum," posted March 1, 2016, by Denver Art Museum, YouTube, https://www.youtube.com/watch?v=x-1_5FGXFpE.
2   Abbott quoted in Thomas McCormick, *Mary Abbott: Works from the 1950s*, McCormick Press, 2004.
3   Abbott quoted in Diane Saxton, "Mary Abbott: Quintessential American," *HuffPost*, September 11, 2012, https://www.huffpost.com/entry/mary-abbott-quintessentia_b_1862702.

Stacey Gillian Abe

1   Abe, audio recording transcribed in email to Eleanor Walker, Levett Collection, via Unit London, March 23, 2024.
2   Abe quoted in *Stacey Gillian Abe: Shrub-let of Old Ayivu*, exhib. cat., Unit London, November 22, 2022–January 27, 2023, p. 20.

Marina Abramović

1   Abramović, email to Christian Levett, February 23, 2024.
2   Abramović interviewed in Johnny Adams, "Marina Abramović: 'I've Always Been a Soldier,'" The Talks, accessed April 2025, https://the-talks.com/interview/marina-abramovic/.
3   Abramović interviewed *ibid.*

Carla Accardi

1   Accardi quoted in "Art Quote: Carla Accardi," posted September 8, 2016, Museo del Novecento, Facebook, https://www.facebook.com/MuseodelNovecento/photos/a.153070734755323/1162744567121263/. Translated from Italian by Eleanor Walker.
2   Accardi interviewed in "Entretien entre Carla Accardi et Hans Ulrich Obrist, Studio Accardi, Rome, 2001," originally published in French in *Carla Accardi*, exhib. cat., Musée d'Art Moderne de la Ville de Paris, January 17–March 3, 2002, translated by Amina Diab in *Carla Accardi: Sicofoil*, exhib. cat., M&L Fine Art, London, February 11–May 8, 2020, pp. 39–40.
3   Accardi interviewed in Luciano Marucci, "Incontro con Carla Accardi. Seconda conversazione," originally published in Italian in *Hortus: Rivista di poesia e di arte*, November 1997, translated *ibid.*, p. 70.

Evelyne Axell

1   Axell, 1970, quoted in Francesca Gavin, "Evelyne Axell: Pop Art's Forgotten Star Takes the Limelight," *Financial Times*, August 6, 2020, https://www.ft.com/content/2734fc86-297b-429e-ba70-21b88acd748e.
2   Axell interviewed 1969, quoted in Kate Brown, "The Belgian Pop Artist Evelyne Axell's Career Was Cut Tragically Short. Now, Her Work Is Getting New Life in a Show at a Swiss Monastery," *Artnet News*, August 20, 2020, https://news.artnet.com/art-world/evelyn-axell-museum-susch-1901394.

Gillian Ayres

1   Ayres quoted in Fiammetta Rocco, "It's Colour She Loves," *The Independent*, September 23, 1995, https://www.independent.co.uk/arts-entertainment/it-s-colour-she-loves-1602676.html.
2   Ayres quoted *ibid.*
3   Ayres quoted *ibid.*
4   Ayres quoted in John Wallace, "Gillian Ayres, Camberwell Alumna and Celebrated Abstract Painter Dies Aged 88," UAL: Camberwell College of Arts, April 16, 2018, https://www.arts.ac.uk/colleges/camberwell-college-of-arts/stories/gillian-ayres-camberwell-alumna-and-celebrated-abstract-painter-dies-aged-88.

Anna-Eva Bergman

1   Bergman, September 22, 1949, quoted in Thomas Schlesser, *Luminous Lives: A Biography of Anna-Eva Bergman*, trans. Charles Penwarden, Eris, 2023, pp. 199–200.
2   Bergman, April 21, 1978, quoted *ibid.*, p. 374.

Bernice Bing

1   Bing interviewed in "Interview with Artist," August 13 and 24, 1991, in *Bernice Bing*, exhib. cat., ed. Moira Roth and Diane Tani, SOMAR Gallery, San Francisco, September 12–October 12, 1991, pp. 12–15.
2   Bing quoted in Valerie Soe, "Introduction," in *Bernice Bing*, exhib. cat., p. 4.

3   Bernice Bing, "Artist's Statement," in *Completing the Circle: Six Artists*, exhib. cat., ed. Florence Wong and George Rivera, Southern Exposure, San Francisco, October 10–November 8, 1990, online at https://queerculturalcenter.org/artists-statement/.

Han Bing

1   Bing, email to Eleanor Walker, Levett Collection, via Thaddaeus Ropac, February 14, 2025.
2   Bing quoted in "Han Bing," Thaddaeus Ropac, accessed April 2025, https://ropac.net/artists/233-han-bing/.

Louise Bonnet

1   Bonnet, email to Eleanor Walker, Levett Collection, via Gagosian, April 3, 2024.

Louise Bourgeois

1   Bourgeois quoted in *Louise Bourgeois. Structures of Existence: The Cells*, exhib. cat., ed. Julienne Lorz, Haus der Kunst, Munich, February 27–August 2, 2015, and traveling, p. 107.
2   Bourgeois quoted in *Louise Bourgeois*, exhib. cat., Tate Modern, London, October 10, 2007–January 20, 2008, and traveling, p. 186.
3   Bourgeois quoted in Robert Storr, *Intimate Geometries: The Art and Life of Louise Bourgeois*, Thames & Hudson, 2016, p. 34.

Carol Bove

1   Bove speaking in "Art + Perception: Carol Bove," *Art+*, posted June 30, 2023, by David Zwirner, YouTube, https://www.youtube.com/watch?v=2slkXe07lkM.
2   Bove interviewed in Erik Wysocan, "Carol Bove on Exhibiting: An Interview with Carol Bove," *Metropolis M Magazine*, December 2011/January 2012, online at http://erikwysocan.com/bove-interview.pdf, p. 1.
3   Bove interviewed *ibid.*, p. 4.

Marie Bracquemond

1   Bracquemond quoted in Jean-Paul Bouillon and Elizabeth Kane, "Marie Bracquemond," *Woman's Art Journal*, vol. 5, no. 2, Autumn 1984/Winter 1985, p. 22.

Cecily Brown

1   Brown speaking in "Meet the Artist—Cecily Brown: *Death and the Maid*," *Met Exhibitions*, posted March 19, 2023, by The Met, YouTube, https://www.youtube.com/watch?v=wmPGBlxOUbo.
2   Brown speaking *ibid.*
3   Brown quoted in *Cecily Brown: Where, When, How Often and With Whom*, exhib. cat., ed. Lærke Rydal

Jørgensen and Anders Kold, Louisiana Museum of Modern Art, Humlebæk, Denmark, November 8, 2018–March 10, 2019, p. 101.
4   Brown speaking in "The Artist Project: Cecily Brown," *The Artist Project*, posted June 6, 2016, by The Met, YouTube, https://www.youtube.com/watch?v=iYq_8afLtT0.

Leonora Carrington

1   From Carrington's response to André Breton's *L'Art magique*, originally published in 1957, reproduced in Leonora Carrington, "On Magic Art: A Conversation, 1996," in *Surrealist Women: An International Anthology*, ed. Penelope Rosemont, University of Texas Press, 1998, p. 273.
2   Leonora Carrington, "The Cabbage Is a Rose," in Rosemont, *Surrealist Women*, pp. 375–76.
3   Carrington quoted in Katy Hessel, *The Story of Art Without Men*, Hutchinson Heinemann, 2022, p. 171.

Mary Cassatt

1   Cassatt to Bertha Palmer, 1892, quoted in Griselda Pollock, *Mary Cassatt: Painter of Modern Women*, Thames & Hudson, 2022, p. 65.

Joana Choumali

1   Choumali interviewed in Lydia Caston, "Joana Choumali in Conversation," *V&A Blog*, April 29, 2022, https://www.vam.ac.uk/blog/museum-life/joana-choumali-in-conversation.
2   Choumali interviewed *ibid.*

Elizabeth Colomba

1   Colomba, audio recording transcribed in email to Leisa Paoli, FAMM, March 13, 2024.

Dadamaino

1   Dadamaino interviewed in Jole de Sanna, "Intervista con Dadamaino," in *Zero Italien: Azimut/Azimuth 1959/60 in Mailand und heute. Castellani, Dadamaino, Fontana, Manzoni und italienische Künstler im Umkreis / Zero Italia: Azimut–Azimuth 1959–60 a Milano e oggi. Castellani, Dadamaino, Fontana, Manzoni e artisti italiani nell'ambito*, exhib. cat., Villa Merkel, Galerie der Stadt Esslingen, December 3, 1995–February 25, 1996, online at https://archiviodadamaino.it/interviste/. Translated from Italian by Eleanor Walker.
2   Dadamaino quoted in "*Carla Accardi and Dadamaino: Between Sign and Transparency*, 20 May–18 September 2021," Tornabuoni Art, https://www.tornabuoniart.com/en/exhibitions/carla-accardi-and-dadamaino-between-sign-and-transparency/.

Elaine de Kooning

1   De Kooning quoted by Lee Hall in *Elaine de Kooning: Portraits*, exhib. cat. by Maria Catalano Rand, The Art Gallery, Brooklyn College, February 28–April 19, 1991, p. 21.
2   Elaine de Kooning in conversation with Bruce Duff Hooton, "My First Exhibit—To Now—Elaine de Kooning," *Art/World*, no. 7, October 1982, p. 12.
3   De Kooning interviewed October 3, 1987, in Ann Eden Gibson, *Abstract Expressionism: Other Politics*, Yale University Press, 1997, p. 135.
4   De Kooning, "My First Exhibit—To Now," p. 12.

Dorothy Dehner

1   Dehner Writings, Reel 796 (Scan 11855), *c.* 1966, Dorothy Dehner Papers, 1920–1987, bulk 1951–1987, Archives of American Art, Smithsonian Institution, Washington, DC.
2   Extract from a lecture given by Dehner, January 16, 1966, Dorothy Dehner Foundation, http://www.dorothydehnerfoundation.org/writings.html.

Sonia Delaunay

1   Sonia Delaunay, "The Influence of Painting on Fashion Design," lecture given at the Sorbonne, 1926, translated in *The New Art of Color: The Writings of Robert and Sonia Delaunay*, ed. Arthur A. Cohen, Viking Press, 1978, p. 207.
2   Sonia Delaunay, "Collages of Sonia and Robert Delaunay," *XXième Siècle*, no. 6, January 1956, translated and reprinted *ibid.*, p. 210.

Marlene Dumas

1   Marlene Dumas, "Framing and Naming," in *Marlene Dumas: Measuring Your Own Grave*, exhib. cat., The Museum of Contemporary Art, Los Angeles, June 22–September 22, 2008; The Museum of Modern Art, New York, December 14, 2008–February 16, 2009; The Menil Collection, Houston, TX, March 26–June 21, 2009, p. 261.
2   Marlene Dumas, "Accepting Painting for What It Is," in *A Fruitful Incoherence: Dialogues with Artists on Internationalism*, ed. Gavin Jantjes, Iniva, 1998, p. 50.

Amaranth Ehrenhalt

1   Ehrenhalt quoted in Molly Petrilla, "Hidden Treasure," *Pennsylvania Gazette*, vol. 111, no. 5, May–June 2013, https://thepenngazette.com/hidden-treasure/.
2   Ehrenhalt interviewed in Denise Carvalho, "An Interview with Ninety Year Old Artist Amaranth Ehrenhalt: Gesture Unhinged," December 2018, *Whitehot Magazine*, https://whitehotmagazine.com/articles/artist-amaranth=ehrenhalt-gesture-unhinged/4120.

Aube Elléouët

1   Elléouët quoted in "Surréalisme. L'héritière d'André Breton," *Le Télégramme*, July 16, 2013, https://www.letelegramme.fr/toute-l-information-de-la-bretagne/spansurrealismespan-lheritiere-dandre-breton-1897366.php. Translated from French by Eleanor Walker.

Dame Tracey Emin

1   Emin interviewed in Dr. Vikas Shah, "A Conversation with Tracey Emin CBE RA, Artist," *Thought Economics*, October 19, 2023, https://thoughteconomics.com/tracey-emin/.
2   Emin quoted in Jennifer Higgie, "The Wound and the Healing: The Evolution of Tracey Emin's Paintings," in *Tracey Emin: Paintings*, by David Dawson and Jennifer Higgie, Phaidon, 2024, p. 7.
3   Emin quoted *ibid.*, p. 11.

Jadé Fadojutimi

1   Fadojutimi quoted in "Jadé Fadojutimi: Overview," Pippy Houldsworth Gallery, accessed April 2025, https://www.houldsworth.co.uk/artists/39-jade-fadojutimi/overview/.
2   Fadojutimi quoted in Rebecca Mead, "The Intensely Colorful Work of a Painter Obsessed with Anime," *New Yorker*, November 11, 2024, https://www.newyorker.com/magazine/2024/11/18/the-intensely-colorful-work-of-a-painter-obsessed-with-anime.
3   Fadojutimi quoted *ibid*.

Claire Falkenstein

1   Falkenstein, oral history interview by Paul Karlstrom, March 2, 1995, Archives of American Art, Smithsonian Institution, Washington, DC.
2   Falkenstein quoted in *Structures en devenir*, exhib. cat., Galerie Stadler, Paris, October 16–November 15, 1956, n.p., translated in *Claire Falkenstein*, essays by Susan M. Anderson, Michael Duncan, and Maren Henderson, Falkenstein Foundation, 2012, p. 157.

Perle Fine

1   Perle Fine, "Statement," *It Is: A Magazine for Abstract Art*, no. 2, Autumn 1958, reprinted in *Sparkling Amazons: Abstract Expressionist Women of the 9th St. Show*, exhib. cat., ed. Michele Wije, Katonah Museum of Art, NY, October 6, 2019–January 26, 2020, p. 95.
2   Fine quoted in *American Abstract Expressionism of the 1950s: An Illustrated Survey with Artists' Statements, Artwork, and Biographies*, ed. Marika Herskovic, New York School Press, 2003, p. 126.

Leonor Fini

1 Fini quoted in Richard Overstreet and Neil Zukerman, eds., *Leonor Fini: Catalogue Raisonné of the Oil Paintings*, Scheidegger & Speiss, 2021, vol. 1, p. 56.
2 Fini quoted *ibid.*, p. 49.
3 Fini quoted *ibid.*, p. 32.
4 Fini quoted in "Leonor Fini, Argentinian, 1907–1996," Weinstein Gallery, accessed April 2025, https://www.weinstein.com/artists/31-leonor-fini/.

Giosetta Fioroni

1 Fioroni quoted in *Giosetta Fioroni: The 60s in Rome*, exhib. cat., ed. Marco Meneguzzo and Piero Mascitti, Moscow Museum of Modern Art, September 6–October 22, 2017, p. 30.
2 Fioroni quoted *ibid.*, p. 31.

Helen Frankenthaler

1 Frankenthaler, oral history interview by Barbara Rose, 1968, Archives of American Art, Smithsonian Institution, Washington, DC.
2 Frankenthaler quoted in Elizabeth A.T. Smith, "Redefining a Practice: Helen Frankenthaler and Painting in the Early 1960s," in *Helen Frankenthaler—Composing with Color: Paintings 1962–1963*, exhib. cat., Gagosian, New York, September 11–October 18, 2014, p. 26.
3 Frankenthaler quoted *ibid.*, p. 13.

Dame Elisabeth Frink

1 Frink quoted in Stephen Gardiner, *Frink: The Official Biography of Elisabeth Frink*, HarperCollins, 1998, pp. 148–49.

Claire Gavronsky

1 Gavronsky, email to Eleanor Walker, Levett Collection, April 13, 2024.

Sonia Gechtoff

1 Gechtoff interviewed in Marshall N. Price, "Interview with Sonia Gechtoff, 2006," in *Sonia Gechtoff: The Ferus Years*, exhib. cat., Nyehaus, New York, October 29–December 17, 2011, p. 4.
2 Gechtoff interviewed *ibid.*, p. 11.

Françoise Gilot

1 Gilot quoted in Malte Herwig, *The Woman Who Says No: Françoise Gilot on Her Life With and Without Picasso*, trans. Jane Billinghurst, Greystone Books, 2016, p. 15.
2 Françoise Gilot, *Interface: The Painter and the Mask*, 1983, quoted *ibid.*, p. 21.
3 Gilot, *Interface*, quoted *ibid.*, p. 74.

Nan Goldin

1 Goldin quoted in *Nan Goldin: I'll Be Your Mirror*, exhib. cat., Whitney Museum of American Art, New York, October 3, 1996–January 5, 1997, p. 452.
2 Goldin speaking in "TateShots: Nan Goldin," *TateShots*, posted May 1, 2014, by Tate, YouTube, https://www.youtube.com/watch?v=r_rVyt-ojpY.
3 Goldin speaking in "Nan Goldin in Conversation with Nicholas Cullinan," 2019, video posted in "Nan Goldin," Marian Goodman Gallery, https://www.mariangoodman.com/artists/44-nan-goldin.
4 Goldin speaking in "The Artist Project: Nan Goldin," *The Artist Project*, posted June 6, 2016, by The Met, YouTube, https://www.youtube.com/watch?v=3MgS8U1YoUY.

Catherine Goodman

1 Goodman, email to Victoria Delgado, FAMM, May 6, 2024.

Jane Graverol

1 Graverol quoted by FAMM (@famm_mougins), "Jane Graverol, *Untitled*, 1959," Instagram, April 11, 2024, https://www.instagram.com/famm_mougins/p/C50PixtJXIY/?img_index=1.
2 Graverol quoted in "Jane Graverol, *La Chute de Babylone*, 1967," lot 25, Bonhams Cornette de Saint Cyr, Brussels, Art Belge et Contemporain auction, June 12, 2023, https://www.bonhams.com/auction/29022/lot/25/jane-graverol-1905-1984-la-chute-de-babylone/. Translated from French by Eleanor Walker.
3 Graverol quoted *ibid.*
4 Graverol interviewed by José Vovelle in René de Solier, *Jane Graverol*, André de Rache, 1974. Translated from French by Google Translate.

Jenna Gribbon

1 Gribbon, email to Eleanor Walker, Levett Collection, via Lévy Gorvy Dayan, April 12, 2024.

Wenhui Hao

1 Hao, email to Eleanor Walker, Levett Collection, via Vermillon Partners, February 14, 2025.

Grace Hartigan

1 Hartigan interviewed in Cindy Nemser, *Art Talk: Conversations with 15 Women Artists*, rev. edn, IconEditions, 1995, p. 148.
2 *The Journals of Grace Hartigan, 1951–1955*, ed. William T. LaMoy and Joseph P. McCaffrey, Syracuse University Press, 2009, November 6, 1951, p. 16.

3 Hartigan quoted in William Grimes, "Grace
   Hartigan, 86, Abstract Painter, Dies," *New York
   Times*, November 18, 2008, https://www.nytimes.
   com/2008/11/18/arts/design/18hartigan.html.

Dame Barbara Hepworth

1 Barbara Hepworth, "Sculpture," in *Circle:
   International Survey of Constructive Art* [1937],
   ed. J.L. Martin, Ben Nicholson, and N. Gabo,
   Praeger, 1971, p. 115.
2 Barbara Hepworth, "Notes by the Artist," in
   Barbara Hepworth: Carvings and Drawings, 1937–1954,
   exhib. cat., Walker Art Center, Minneapolis,
   April 15–May 29, 1955, and traveling, n.p.
3 Hepworth interviewed in "Alan Bowness:
   Conversations with Barbara Hepworth," in
   *The Complete Sculpture of Barbara Hepworth,
   1960–69*, ed. Alan Bowness, Lund Humphries,
   1971, p. 14.
4 Hepworth interviewed *ibid.*, p. 12.

Martha Jungwirth

1 Jungwirth quoted in "Martha Jungwirth,"
   Thaddaeus Ropac, accessed April 2025,
   https://ropac.net/artists/213-martha-jungwirth/.
2 Jungwirth quoted *ibid.*

Frida Kahlo

1 Kahlo, diary entry from 1951, quoted in Alexxa
   Gotthardt, "How Frida Kahlo's Love Affair with
   a Communist Revolutionary Impacted Her Art,"
   Artsy, April 30, 2019, https://www.artsy.net/
   article/artsy-editorial-frida-kahlos-love-affair-
   communist-revolutionary-impacted-art.
2 Frida Kahlo, "I Paint My Own Reality," in *Surrealist
   Women: An International Anthology*, ed. Penelope
   Rosemont, University of Texas Press, 1998, p. 145.
3 Kahlo quoted in Arianna Richetti, "Frida Kahlo:
   The Suffering Behind Her Paintings," *Daily Art
   Magazine*, December 9, 2024, https://www.
   dailyartmagazine.com/frida-kahlo-suffering-
   paintings/.

Lee Krasner

1 Krasner quoted in *Lee Krasner: Living Colour*, exhib.
   cat., ed. Eleanor Nairne, Barbican Art Gallery,
   London, May 30–September 1, 2019, and traveling,
   p. 111.
2 Krasner interviewed in Richard Howard,
   "A Conversation with Lee Krasner," in *Lee Krasner:
   Paintings 1959–1962*, exhib. cat., Pace Gallery, New
   York, February 3–March 10, 1979, n.p.
3 Krasner interviewed in Cindy Nemser, *Art Talk:
   Conversations with 15 Women Artists*, rev. edn,
   IconEditions, 1995, pp. 83–84.
4 Krasner, 1960, quoted in Katy Hessel, *The Story of Art
   Without Men*, Hutchinson Heinemann, 2022, p. 235.

Lalan

1 Lalan quoted in *Extended Figure: The Art and
   Inspiration of Lalan*, exhib. cat., Asia Society Hong
   Kong Center, April 27–October 24, 2021.
2 Lalan quoted *ibid.*
3 Lalan quoted *ibid.*

Marie Laurencin

1 Laurencin quoted in Renee Sandell, "Marie
   Laurencin: Cubist Muse or More?" *Woman's Art
   Journal*, vol. 1, no. 1, Spring/Summer 1980, p. 26.

Lifang

1 Lifang quoted by FAMM (@famm_mougins),
   "Li Fang, *Untitled*, 1969," Instagram, April 16, 2024,
   https://www.instagram.com/p/C50XccLtbBK/.
2 Lifang quoted in *Artist Magazine*, no. 37, 1977.
   Translated from Chinese and German by the
   artist's son, Theobald Brun.
3 Lifang quoted *ibid.*
4 Lifang quoted *ibid.*

Sahara Longe

1 Longe interviewed in "Sahara Longe: Interview,"
   2021, She Curates, https://www.she-curates.com/
   interviews/artists/sahara-long.
2 Longe interviewed in Lydia Figes, "Seven
   Questions with Sahara Longe," Art UK, October 28,
   2021, https://artuk.org/discover/stories/
   seven-questions-with-sahara-longe.

Sarah Lucas

1 Lucas, email to Eleanor Walker, Levett Collection,
   via Sadie Coles Gallery, April 2, 2024. Description
   of work from Sadie Coles Gallery.
2 Lucas quoted in *Sarah Lucas: Au Naturel*, exhib. cat.,
   ed. Massimiliano Gioni and Margot Norton, New
   Museum, New York, September 26, 2018–January
   20, 2019, p. 20.
3 Lucas interviewed in *The Guardian*, quoted *ibid.*,
   p. 94.

Dora Maar

1 Maar quoted in James Lord, *Picasso and Dora: A
   Personal Memoir*, Farrar Straus Giroux, 1993, p. 124.
2 Maar quoted *ibid.*, p. 123.

Jacqueline Marval

1 Marval quoted in Y. Sarlès, "Comment ils
   peignent," *Le Siècle*, November 15, 1927, p. 2/6.
   Translated from French by Eleanor Walker.

Joan Mitchell

1   Mitchell to Michael Goldberg, July 27, 1965, Michael Goldberg Papers, 1942–1981, Archives of American Art, Smithsonian Institution, Washington, DC.
2   Mitchell to Sally Perry, quoted in Patricia Albers, *Joan Mitchell: Lady Painter—A Life*, Alfred A. Knopf, 2011, p. xix.
3   Mitchell quoted in Judith E. Bernstock, *Joan Mitchell*, Hudson Hills Press in association with Herbert F. Johnson Museum of Art, Cornell University, 1988, p. 67.
4   Mitchell quoted in Yves Michaud, "Conversations with Joan Mitchell, January 12, 1986," in *Joan Mitchell: New Paintings*, exhib. cat., Xavier Fourcade, New York, April 3–May 10, 1986, n.p.

Jesse Mockrin

1   Mockrin, email to Eleanor Walker, Levett Collection, via James Cohan Gallery, May 18, 2024.
2   Mockrin speaking in "Jesse Mockrin on Re-framing Art History," posted September 26, 2023, by New York Studio School, YouTube, https://www.youtube.com/watch?v=NK1BNvnlN9s.

Berthe Morisot

1   Berthe Morisot, *Carnet vert A*, 1885–86, translated in *Berthe Morisot: Shaping Impressionism*, exhib. cat., ed. Marianne Mathieu, Dulwich Picture Gallery, London, March 31–September 10, 2023, p. 30.
2   Morisot, 1890, quoted in Janet Whitmore, "Berthe Morisot: Woman Impressionist," *Nineteenth-Century Art Worldwide*, vol. 18, no. 1, Spring 2019, p. 182.

Sabine Moritz

1   Moritz, email to Eleanor Walker, Levett Collection, via Gagosian, April 11, 2024. Translated from German by Google Translate.

Alice Neel

1   Neel quoted in Patricia Hills, *Alice Neel*, Harry N. Abrams, 1983, p. 141.
2   Neel quoted in *Alice Neel: Hot Off the Griddle*, exhib. cat., ed. Eleanor Nairne, Barbican Art Gallery, London, February 16–May 21, 2023, p. 80.
3   Neel speaking in "Alice Neel: They Are Their Own Gifts," 1978, *From the Vaults*, posted December 18, 2020, by The Met, YouTube, https://www.youtube.com/watch?v=MQtSDLOg05c.
4   Neel quoted in "The Art of Portraiture, in the Words of Four New York Artists," *New York Times*, October 31, 1976, p. D29.

Shirin Neshat

1   Shirin Neshat, "Artist Statement," in "Visibility and Visuality: Reframing Gender in the Middle East, North Africa, and Their Diasporas," ed. Andrew Mazzaschi, special virtual issue, *Signs: Journal of Women in Culture and Society*, 2012, http://signsjournal.org/shirin-neshat/.

Louise Nevelson

1   Louise Nevelson, *Dawns + Dusks: Taped Conversations with Diana MacKown*, Charles Scribner's Sons, 1976, pp. 59–64.
2   Nevelson speaking in "Nevelson in Process," 1977, *From the Vaults*, posted March 27, 2020, by The Met, YouTube, https://www.youtube.com/watch?v=nnfEmNRzoCs.
3   Nevelson speaking *ibid*.
4   Nevelson quoted in Aldo Iori, "Louise Nevelson: A Life of Adventure," in *Louise Nevelson*, exhib. cat., ed. Bruno Corà, Fondazione Roma Museo, Palazzo Sciarra, Rome, April 16–July 21, 2013, p. 188.

Pat Passlof

1   Passlof quoted in *Pat Passlof: The Brush Is the Finger of the Brain—Paintings 1949–2011*, exhib. cat. by Karen Wilkin, The Milton Resnick and Pat Passlof Foundation, New York, October 11, 2019–April 11, 2020, p. 10.
2   Passlof quoted *ibid*., p. 12.
3   Passlof quoted *ibid*., p. 14.
4   Pat Passlof, *To Whom the Shoe Fits: Letters to Young Painters*, ed. David Jacobsen Loncle, The Milton Resnick and Pat Passlof Foundation, 2018, p. 9.

Celia Paul

1   Paul, email to Eleanor Walker, Levett Collection, via Victoria Miro Gallery, March 12, 2024.

Lilla Cabot Perry

1   Perry interviewed in the *Boston Herald*, 1921, quoted in Susan Sipple Elliott, "Images of Gentility: Lilla Cabot Perry's Portraits of Women," master's thesis, University of Alabama, 1993, p. 41, https://ir-api.ua.edu/api/core/bitstreams/00c8d716-de5c-42fb-b380-084f4ddf6af8/content.

Howardena Pindell

1   Pindell interviewed in "Howardena Pindell on Colour Theory and the Politics of the Circle," Something Curated, June 21, 2023, https://somethingcurated.com/2023/06/21/interview-howardena-pindell-on-colour-theory-the-politics-of-the-circle/.

2 Pindell interviewed in Hans Ulrich Obrist, "Why I'm Not a Hard-Edge Painter: A Conversation with Howardena Pindell," in *Howardena Pindell: Rope/Fire/Water*, exhib. cat., ed. Adeze Wilford, The Shed, New York, October 16, 2020–April 11, 2021, p. 26.

Alice Rahon

1 Rahon, Willard Gallery exhibition catalogue, 1951, quoted in Karli Wurzelbacher and Emily A. Finan, "Collection Spotlight: Alice Rahon's *La Conjuration des Antilopes*," The Heckscher Museum of Art, accessed April 2025, https://www.heckscher.org/collection-spotlight-alice-rahons-la-conjuration-des-antilopes/.
2 Rahon quoted in "Alice Rahon," *The Art Story*, accessed April 2025, https://www.theartstory.org/artist/rahon-alice.

Marie Raymond

1 Marie Raymond, "Créer pour voir," in *Témoignages pour l'art abstrait*, Art d'Aujourd'hui, 1952, pp. 241–42, translated from French by Archives Marie Raymond, accessed April 2025, https://marieraymond.com/documents/.
2 Marie Raymond, undated writing, "Meeting the Real," translated from French by Archives Marie Raymond, accessed April 2025, https://marieraymond.com/documents/.

Judit Reigl

1 Reigl speaking (Hungarian with English subtitles) in "Judit Reigl: The Artist Talks About Her Paintings, 2005, Műcsarnok," posted April 5, 2012, by Kálmán Makláry Fine Arts, YouTube, https://www.youtube.com/watch?v=gjMlRp6hS4I.
2 Reigl quoted in "*Judit Reigl: Dance of Death*, 26 May–24 September, 2023," Museum of Fine Arts, Budapest, https://www.mfab.hu/exhibitions/judit-reigl-dance-of-death/.

Deborah Remington

1 Remington interviewed by Arlene Raven in Betty Ann Brown and Arlene Raven, *Exposures: Women and Their Art*, NewSage Press, 1989, p. 66.
2 Remington quoted in Sabine Marchand, "Exhibition at Galerie Darthea Speyer, Paris," *Le Figaro*, September 30, 1971.
3 Remington quoted in *Drawing Now: 10 Artists*, exhib. cat. by Corinne Robins, Soho Center for Visual Arts, New York, June 3–26, 1976, n.p.
4 Remington quoted in Alexandra Anderson, "A Singular Painter Sees Double," *Village Voice*, September 6, 1976, p. 80.

Juliette Roche

1 Roche quoted in Carolyn Burke, "Recollecting Dada: Juliette Roche," in *Women in Dada: Essays on Sex, Gender, and Identity*, ed. Naomi Sawelson-Gorse, MIT Press, 1998, p. 551.

Judith Rothschild

1 Rothschild, 1945, based on diary notes by Jean Arp, quoted in Jack Flam, *Judith Rothschild: An Artist's Search*, Hudson Hills Press, 1998, p. 19.
2 Judith Rothschild, "On the Use of a Color–Music Analogy and on Chance in Paintings," *Leonardo*, vol. 3, no. 3, July 1970, pp. 275–77.

Niki de Saint Phalle

1 Niki de Saint Phalle, *Traces: An Autobiography Remembering 1930–1949*, Acatos, 1999, quoted in "The Evolution of a Woman Artist," Niki de Saint Phalle, October 16, 2017, https://nikidesaintphalle.org/evolution-woman-artist/.
2 Saint Phalle quoted *ibid.*
3 Saint Phalle speaking in "Niki de Saint Phalle: Rebel with a Cause," posted July 13, 2021, by Art Basel, YouTube, https://www.youtube.com/watch?v=lxkJ2TFsiaI.

Jenny Saville

1 Saville interviewed in "Jenny Saville and Sally Mann in Conversation," in *Jenny Saville*, Gagosian in association with Rizzoli, 2018, p. 30.

Miriam Schapiro

1 Schapiro, 1970 statement from unpublished journals, notes, correspondence, and interviews, quoted in *Miriam Schapiro: Shaping the Fragments of Art and Life*, exhib. cat. by Thalia Gouma-Peterson, Polk Museum of Art, Lakeland, FL, December 11, 1999–March 5, 2000; Miami University Art Museum, Oxford, OH, March 17–June 2, 2000; Lowe Art Museum, University of Miami, FL, February 22–April 8, 2001, p. 28.
2 Schapiro, 1975 statement, quoted *ibid.*, p. 29.

Ethel Schwabacher

1 *Hungry for Light: The Journal of Ethel Schwabacher*, ed. Brenda S. Webster and Judith Emlyn Johnson, Indiana University Press, 1993, pp. 111–12.
2 *Ibid.*, p. 233.
3 *Ibid.*, p. 55.
4 *Ibid.*, p. 107.

Jeanne Selmersheim-Desgrange

1   Selmersheim-Desgrange quoted in "L'Oeuvre d'art exige-t-elle un 'sujet'?," *Le Bulletin de la vie artistique*, vol. 5, no. 14, July 15, 1924, pp. 311–12. Translated from French by Eleanor Walker.

Joan Semmel

1   Semmel interviewed in Marta Gnyp, "'I Wanted a Real Person to Be Seen': Joan Semmel on Her 60-Year Career Painting the Female Form—for the Female Gaze," *Artnet News*, December 27, 2021, https://news.artnet.com/art-world/joan-semmel-new-waves-marta-gnyp-2052947.

2   Semmel speaking in "Virtual Tour of *Joan Semmel: Skin in the Game*," posted March 23, 2022, by Pennsylvania Academy of the Fine Arts, YouTube, https://www.youtube.com/watch?v=RqOk1Gx5Ll0.

Rose Shakinovsky

1   Shakinovsky, email to Eleanor Walker, Levett Collection, April 13, 2024.

Anj Smith

1   Smith speaking in "Anj Smith: In the Studio," posted October 19, 2023, by Hauser & Wirth, YouTube, https://www.youtube.com/watch?v=7oqPu2abfms.

Sylvia Snowden

1   Snowden, email to Eleanor Walker, Levett Collection, January 20, 2025.

Vivian Springford

1   Springford quoted in *Vivian Springford*, exhib. cat. by Alexandra Schwartz and Arlene Shechet, Almine Rech, New York, September 12–October 20, 2018, p. 37.

2   Springford quoted in press materials for her first solo show, Great Jones Gallery, New York, September 26–October 16, 1960.

Pat Steir

1   Steir, email to Eleanor Walker, Levett Collection, February 12, 2025.

2   Steir quoted in Thomas McEvilley, *Pat Steir*, Harry N. Abrams, 1995, p. 68.

3   Steir quoted in Doris von Drathen, "Rhythm of Silence: Some Observations on the Oeuvre of Pat Steir," in *Pat Steir: The Rhythm of Silence*, exhib. cat., Locks Gallery, Philadelphia, October 22–November 29, 2003, p. 13.

Hedda Sterne

1   Sterne interviewed by Ruth Bowman, April 23, 1970, quoted in Cosmin Nasui, *Hedda Sterne: The Discovery of Early Years, 1910–1941*, PostModernism Museum, 2015, p. 5.

2   Sterne quoted in "The Artist," The Hedda Sterne Foundation, accessed April 2025, https://heddasternefoundation.org/artist.

3   Sterne quoted *ibid.*

Dorothea Tanning

1   Tanning interviewed in Carlo McCormick, "Dorothea Tanning," *BOMB*, October 1, 1990, https://bombmagazine.org/articles/1990/10/01/dorothea-tanning/.

2   Tanning interviewed *ibid.*

3   Tanning quoted in Alexander Watt, "Paris Commentary," *The Studio*, vol. 158, no. 798, October 1959, p. 92.

Franciszka Themerson

1   Themerson, notes prepared for an interview, 1963, quoted in Nick Wadley, *Franciszka Themerson*, Themerson Estate, 2019, p. 110.

2   Themerson, notes prepared for an interview, 1963, quoted *ibid.*, p. 111.

Alma Thomas

1   Thomas, 1970 statement, quoted in *Alma Thomas*, exhib. cat., ed. Ian Berry and Lauren Hayes, The Frances Young Tang Teaching Museum and Art Gallery at Skidmore College, Saratoga Springs, NY, February 6–June 5, 2016; The Studio Museum in Harlem, New York, July 14–October 30, 2016, p. 18.

2   Thomas, 1978 statement, quoted *ibid.*, p. 106.

3   Thomas, 1972 statement, quoted *ibid.*, p. 154.

4   Thomas, 1972 statement, quoted *ibid.*, p. 203.

Yvonne Thomas

1   Thomas quoted in Jane Wilson, "Yvonne Thomas Exhibits at TBFA," *Aspen Times*, August 1, 1991, quoted in Vittorio Colaizzi, "Yvonne Thomas: The 'Singleness of the Poetry,'" *Woman's Art Journal*, vol. 41, no. 1, Spring/Summer 2020, p. 8.

2   Thomas quoted in J.B., "Art Impressions," *Aspen Times*, August 10, 1962, quoted *ibid.*, p. 9.

3   Thomas quoted in *American Abstract Expressionism of the 1950s: An Illustrated Survey with Artists' Statements, Artwork, and Biographies*, ed. Marika Herskovic, New York School Press, 2003, p. 330.

4   "Yvonne Thomas: Chronological Biography," unpublished typescript, courtesy Berry Campbell, New York, quoted in Colaizzi, "Yvonne Thomas," p. 5.

Tatiana Trouvé

1   Trouvé, email to Eleanor Walker, Levett Collection, via Gagosian, February 29, 2024. Translated from French by Google Translate.

Maria Helena Vieira da Silva

1   Vieira da Silva quoted in "Artist Spotlight: Maria Helena Vieira da Silva," National Museum of Women in the Arts, November 19, 2010, https://nmwa.org/blog/artist-spotlight/artist-spotlight-maria-elena-vieira-da-silva/.
2   Vieira da Silva quoted in "Maria Helena Vieira da Silva: *The Town*," National Museum of Women in the Arts, accessed April 2025, https://nmwa.org/art/collection/town/.
3   Vieira da Silva quoted in "Maria Helena Vieira da Silva," Art Institute of Chicago, accessed April 2025, https://www.artic.edu/artists/37156/maria-helena-vieira-da-silva.
4   Vieira da Silva quoted in "Maria Helena Vieira da Silva," Galeria Mayoral, accessed April 2025, https://galeriamayoral.com/artists/39-maria-helena-vieira-da-silva/.

Kay WalkingStick

1   WalkingStick, email to Eleanor Walker, Levett Collection, March 11, 2024.

Carrie Mae Weems

1   Weems interviewed in "Artist Carrie Mae Weems on 30 Years of Genius," *Ebony*, February 5, 2014, https://www.ebony.com/artist-carrie-mae-weems-on-30-years-of-genius-999/#axzz2senYEk9L.
2   Weems interviewed in "Carrie Mae Weems by Dawoud Bey," *BOMB*, July 1, 2009, https://bombmagazine.org/articles/2009/07/01/carrie-mae-weems/.
3   Weems interviewed *ibid.*

Susan Weil

1   Susan Weil and Sylvia Whitman, *Two Notebooks*, Untitled Press, 1976. Sent by Weil in email to Eleanor Walker, Levett Collection, April 24, 2024.

Michael (Corinne) West

1   Michael West, draft of an undated message addressed to "Gloria," last name not identified, included in West's unpublished "Notes on Art," Michael West Archives, Hollis Taggart, New York.
2   West, "Notes on Art," marked only as having been written in "June," with no day or year specified.
3   Michael West, "The New Mysticism in Painting," *c.* 1946, published for the first time in *Space Poetry: The Action Paintings of Michael West*, exhib. cat.

by Ellen G. Landau, Hollis Taggart, New York, November 7, 2019–January 4, 2020, p. 88.
4   West, "The New Mysticism," p. 89.

Anna Weyant

1   Weyant, email to Eleanor Walker, Levett Collection, via Gagosian, February 29, 2024.
2   Weyant interviewed in "Anna Weyant in Conversation with Edward Steed," in *Anna Weyant*, by John Elderfield, Naomi Fry, Yvonne Owens, Edward Steed, and Anna Weyant, Gagosian, 2023, p. 131.

Dame Rachel Whiteread

1   Whiteread, email to Eleanor Walker, Levett Collection, via Gagosian, May 14, 2024.
2   Whiteread speaking, June 2022, in "Artist Rachel Whiteread: 'Artists Reflect upon What Is Happening,'" posted October 19, 2023, by Louisiana Channel, YouTube, https://www.youtube.com/watch?v=9436JCNqsmk.

Issy Wood

1   Wood speaking in "Meet the Artists: Issy Wood," *Meet the Artists*, posted October 9, 2023, by Art Basel, YouTube, https://www.youtube.com/watch?v=6nDcN1oPkSg.

Picture Credits

White Cube. Photo: © 2025 Christie's Images Limited; 143: Photo: Bonhams; 144–45: © ADAGP, Paris and DACS, London 2025. Photo: Jérôme Kelagopian/The Levett Collection; 146–47: © ADAGP, Paris and DACS, London 2025. Photo: Jérôme Kelagopian/The Levett Collection; 148–49: © ARS, NY and DACS, London 2025. Photo: Fraser Marr/The Levett Collection; 151: © ADAGP, Paris and DACS, London 2025. Photo: Jérôme Kelagopian/The Levett Collection; 152–53: © Judith Rothschild. Courtesy GRAY Chicago/New York. Photo: Courtesy of Jody Klotz Fine Art; 155: © Niki de Saint Phalle Charitable Art Foundation/ADAGP, Paris and DACS, London 2025. Photo by Tadzio. Private collection, courtesy Galerie GP & N Vallois; 156: © Jenny Saville. All rights reserved, DACS 2025. Photo: Jérôme Kelagopian/The Levett Collection; 158–59: © Estate of Miriam Schapiro/ARS, NY and DACS, London 2025. Photo: Fraser Marr/The Levett Collection; 160–61: © Estate of Ethel Schwabacher. Courtesy Berry Campbell Gallery, New York. Photo: Fraser Marr/The Levett Collection; 162–63: Photo: Courtesy of M.S. Rau, New Orleans; 165: © ARS, NY and DACS, London 2025. Photo: Courtesy Alexander Gray Associates, New York; 166–67: © Rose Shakinovsky. Courtesy Goodman Gallery; 168–69: © Anj Smith. Courtesy the artist and Hauser & Wirth. Photo: Alex Delfanne; 171: © Sylvia Snowden. Photo: Edel Assanti; 172–73: © The Vivian Springford Administration/Courtesy of Almine Rech. Photo: Fraser Marr/The Levett Collection; 175: © Pat Steir. Courtesy the artist and Hauser & Wirth. Photo: Fraser Marr/The Levett Collection; 176–77: © ARS, NY and DACS, London 2025. Photo: Fraser Marr/The Levett Collection; 178–79: © ADAGP, Paris and DACS, London 2025. Photo: Jérôme Kelagopian/The Levett Collection; 181: © Franciszka Themerson Estate; 183: © 2025 Estate of Alma Thomas/ARS, New York and DACS, London. Photo: Fraser Marr/The Levett Collection; 184–85: © Estate of Yvonne Thomas. Courtesy Berry Campbell Gallery, New York. Photo: Fraser Marr/The Levett Collection; 187: © ADAGP, Paris and DACS, London 2025. Photo: Florian Kleinefenn. Courtesy the artist and Gagosian; 188–89: © ADAGP, Paris and DACS, London 2025. Photo: Jérôme Kelagopian/The Levett Collection; 191: © Kay WalkingStick. Courtesy the artist and Hales, London and New York. Photo: Michele Kipplen Photography; 192–93: © Carrie Mae Weems. Courtesy of the artist and Gladstone Gallery, New York, Fraenkel Gallery, San Francisco, and Galerie Barbara Thumm, Berlin. Photo: Jérôme Kelagopian/The Levett Collection; 195: © Susan Weil. Photo: © Phillips Auctioneers LLC; 197: © Michael (Corinne) West Estate. Courtesy of Hollis Taggart, New York. Photo: Fraser Marr/The Levett Collection; 199: © Anna Weyant. Photo: Rob McKeever. Courtesy Gagosian; 201: © Rachel Whiteread. Courtesy the artist and Gagosian; 202–203: © Issy Wood, courtesy the artist, Carlos/Ishikawa, London, and Michael Werner Gallery. Photo: © Phillips Auctioneers LLC

The publishers have made every effort to trace and contact copyright holders of the illustrations reproduced in this book; they will be happy to correct in subsequent editions any errors or omissions that are brought to their attention.

First published 2025 by Merrell Publishers,
London and New York

Merrell Publishers Limited
70 Cowcross Street
London EC1M 6EJ
merrellpublishers.com

in association with

Femmes Artistes du Musée de Mougins/
Female Artists of the Mougins Museum
32, rue du Commandeur
06250 Mougins
France
famm.com

ISBN 978-1-8589-4723-5

Produced by Merrell Publishers Limited
Designed by Nicola Bailey
Project-managed by Claire Chandler
Picture research by Nick Wheldon
Proofread by Barbara Roby

Printed and bound in Italy by Graphicom

Note on text:
*The dimensions in the captions indicate height followed by
width followed by depth. The letters "CL" in an accession
number indicate that the artwork is in the Levett Collection;
the abbreviation "MMoCA" indicates the collection of the
former Musée d'Art Classique de Mougins/Mougins Museum
of Classical Art.*

Jennifer Samet is Senior Director of Eric Firestone
Gallery and a faculty member of the New York
Studio School. She has interviewed over 100 artists
for her "Beer with a Painter" column for the online
arts magazine *Hyperallergic*, and has contributed
to monographs and authored dozens of catalogue
essays. She wrote the chapter on contemporary art
in *FAMM: Female Artists of the Mougins Museum, France*,
published by Merrell in 2025.

Eleanor Walker is Collection Manager for the Levett
Collection. She studied at the Courtauld Institute of
Art, and previously worked at Sotheby's in London
and at the Stanford University Study Abroad Centre,
Florence, where she helped teach the classes on
Renaissance art and Italian culture. She continues
to lecture on fifteenth- and twentieth-century art,
with a focus on female artists.